The "Liberated" Woman
of 1914

Studies in
American History and Culture, No. 6

Other Titles in This Series

The "Liberated" Woman of 1914

of 1914

Prominent Women in the Progressive Era

by
Barbara Kuhn Campbell

RESEARCH PRESS

Library of Congress Cataloging in Publication Data

Campbell, Barbara Kuhn, 1946-
  The "liberated" woman of 1914.

    (Studies in American history and culture ; no. 6)
    Bibliography: p.
    Includes index.
    1. Women—United States—Social conditions.
  2. Feminists—United States—Biography. I. Title. II. Series.

HQ1412.C35 1978   301.41'2'0973   78-27703
ISBN 0-8357-0980-9
ISBN 0-8357-0981-7 pbk.

CONTENTS

CONTENTS

TABLES

FIGURES

CONTENTS

INTRODUCTION

The concept of prominence for women changed over the course of the nineteenth century. In early and mid-century, prominence for all but a handful of women remained a local matter dependent upon the social standing of the woman's husband and father. This essentially reflected woman's restricted role in society. By the later decades of the nineteenth century general social changes had also altered the status of American women. Increasing educational and career opportunities, together with the growth of national women's organizations, prompted large numbers of women for the first time to take an active interest in professional fields and in public affairs. A woman could now more easily achieve distinction on a regional or national level. Such notability rested upon her own accomplishments rather than those of the men in her life. Thus, by 1914, some 9000 American women were considered eminent enough, by an editor familiar with standards of prominence for men, to warrant inclusion in a *Who's Who* of American women.

These women who were so vital in the Progressive reform movement and who achieved victory in the suffrage cause have been misrepresented in historiography by the towering image of Jane Addams and other settlement house workers, who remained unmarried and dedicated their lives to reform-related careers. Allen Davis's work has led people to assume that women such as Jane Addams, Grace Abbott, and Julia Lathrop were typical of women reformers.[1] Besides biographies, historians have confined themselves to political and ideological analyses of the suffrage movement, as in the studies by Eleanor Flexner and Aileen Kraditor,[2] or to far-reaching and often dubious investigations of feminism and the woman's movement in general, as in the books by William O'Neill, Andrew Sinclair, and Page Smith.[3] But we know little about the characteristics of women who became involved in suffrage or reform work at the turn of the century. Nor do we know what the life histories of these women were like.

Recent historical discussions have shed greater light upon specific aspects of women's lives in the nineteenth century. Barbara Welter's essay on the "cult of true womanhood" described the ideological consensus about womanhood in the early to mid-nineteenth century. That seminal article has been refined, expanded, and questioned in newer works.[4] Carroll Smith-Rosenberg has offered other insights in "The Female World of Love and Ritual." She has claimed that men and women were polarized into two cultures from at least the late eighteenth to the mid-nineteenth centuries.[5] Kirk Jeffrey has suggested a different kind of bifurcation in mid-century American families--that between the "home" and the "world."[6]

While such works illumine the environment into which the notable women of 1914 were born, more pertinent are studies that address themselves to central aspects of the women's lives. Jill Conway and Roberta Wein have reassessed the development of women's higher education and the ways in which various kinds of institutions affected their graduates.[7] Daniel Scott Smith and Peter Uhlenberg have examined questions concerning sexuality, fertility, and mortality. Of special importance is Smith's emphasis on the declining birth rate and its ramifications for the role of women in the family. His concept of "domestic feminism"--women's increasing autonomy within the family--is particularly applicable to the notable women in this study.[8]

Investigations of Victorian sexuality have been proliferating, but Carl Degler's discovery of the Clelia Mosher questionnaires has provided the first insights into actual behavior.[9] Still, few historians have explored marriage relationships between particular husbands and wives. Two of the few works that treat this subject are the study by Blanche Hersh of the early feminist-abolitionists, and the article by Kirk Jeffrey on the marriage of Lydia Maria Child. Hersh's collective biography of women reformers is especially apropos as a comparison with eminent Progressive women.[10]

But except for Hersh and Anne Firor Scott,[11] historians have failed to tell us what women's lives, from beginning to end, have been like. Nor has anyone assessed a large number of women from any era to discern patterns in their lives. Another void has been data on women's associations and activities, although the recent re-examination of woman's separate sphere has demonstrated the importance of supportive female networks.

To confront such questions and to challenge the assumption that Jane Addams was typical of prominent women of the Progressive Era, we need information about a large number of women. The data must be relatively uniform, and the sample sufficiently large to reduce the margin for statistical error to acceptable levels. The source that most fully meets these criteria is the *Woman's Who's Who of America, 1914-1915*, edited by John William Leonard and published by the American Commonwealth Company in New York, 1914.

John William Leonard was born in England in 1849 and emigrated to the United States in 1868 at the age of 19. After a brief career as a lawyer and newspaper editor in Texas and Arizona, Leonard married and settled in Illinois in the 1880's. He was twice nominated for Congress on the Democratic ticket in the Eighth Illinois District, and was director of the Wheaton, Illinois, Board of Education for a number of years. About 1907, he and his family moved to New York City.[12]

Professionally, Leonard had already established himself as an author and editor by the 1880's. He originated the "who's who" idea in the United States, and was the sole editor of the first four biennial volumes of *Who's Who in America* from 1897 to 1906. Leonard also edited a *Who's Who in New York* (1907) and *Men of America* (1908). Concurrently, Leonard became convinced of the desirability of a "who's who" for American women. Leonard had noted that in the national volume, data on a few hundred women was mixed in with entries for about seventeen thousand men. Yet women's activities had increased in all social dimensions. Women had become visible to their peers in a wide variety of occupations as well as in women's clubs and reform work. Leonard stated in his preface to the 1914 volume:

> These activities and these movements, interesting in the mass, are the composite results of individual expression. The personalities behind them become objects of increasing interest, and it is the demand for information as to the careers of those who are leading in or contributing to woman's larger participation in the good causes and higher endeavors of our time, which this volume is intended to supply.

Although Leonard had to abandon his first efforts, he renewed the project in 1912 and collected data for two years before publishing the *Woman's Who's Who* in 1914.[13]

Leonard's volume focused on the prominent woman of 1914, one who was socially visible either in the nation, in her region, or in her particular locale. It included biographical data on over 9000 American and Canadian women. Exactly how women were selected for the volume is difficult to ascertain. It is likely that they were suggested by the local officers of women's clubs, since national officers of the clubs were on the general editorial board. Many prominent women were *not* included in the book. Florence Kelley, head of the National Consumer's League, is a good example. Leonard admitted that there were others he wanted to include, but about whom he could get no information. For a group statistical study it makes little difference, however, whether any given individual is or is not included. Unless one can prove a bias in the source against a particular group of women, the large numbers in the book balance out idiosyncrasies of selection. A sample of 9000--or even 900--is more than an adequate statistical basis for determining general patterns of behavior with only minor margins of error.

The *Woman's Who's Who* did ignore two groups of active women prominent in their own locales--Roman Catholic nuns who were school administrators, and black club women. The small number of Catholics and Jews in the volume (3% of the whole) qualified on the basis of their participation with white Protestant women in women's clubs and suffrage and reform work. Only one black woman, Josephine St. Pierre Ruffin, appeared in the book. She belonged to white women's groups, such as the Woman's Press Association of New England and the Equal Suffrage League, besides being a leader of black women's associations. But the volume did not include other black club women, presumably because they were not sufficiently visible to the white Protestant women who dominated women's activities in the United States--of whom the book is representative.

The autobiographical statements presented in the *Woman's Who's Who* generally contained information on the woman's place of birth and present place of residence; her education and career; her activities and interests; and her attitudes on woman suffrage. A random sample of 879 women was taken from the work. Every American woman in the left column of every fifth page was coded according to forty variables. The variables fell into five general categories: life cycle, environment, career development, values and beliefs, and activities and interests. (See "How to Handle a Liberated Woman" in the appendix on the coding of the variables.) When the coding was completed, a packaged computer program, the Statistical Package for the Social Sciences, was used to generate multivariate contingency tables.

The least exhaustive information was that on the families of the women. The *Woman's Who's Who* contained such information as their marital status and the number of their children, but it did not inform the reader about the professions of their fathers and husbands, the number of siblings, or their socio-economic status while they were growing to maturity. For that information one must turn to individual biographies and autobiographies, of which there are a considerable number, and to the other two major biographical sources on women, *Notable American Women* and *Woman of the Century*.

The modern *Notable American Women*[14] is an excellent source for detailed biographical information on women about whom little has been published. Researchers combed archives to provide comprehensive biographical entries. Such information proved invaluable for this study. The entries also provided bibliographical data useful for locating biographies and autobiographies, and the introduction, by Janet Wilson James, afforded a perceptive overview of women's experience in America. On occasion, the writers left out such basic facts as the age of a husband. The most serious fault of the source, however, is its cut-off date. Women had to have died by 1950 to be included in the volumes. Thus, such eminent Progressive women as Edith Abbott, Mary Beard, Vida Scudder, Mary Simkovitch, and Alice Paul did not qualify for *Notable American Women*.

Of the 1,359 women highlighted in the three volumes, 366 were also in the *Woman's Who's Who*, or 4% of the total in Leonard's work. The biographical essays on these women common to both sources provided valuable information on all aspects of the women's lives. The marital data was especially profitable. By using the 192 married women common to the two works, statistics could be generated on separation, divorce, widowhood, remarriage, and child mortality.

Woman of the Century[15] is another useful biographical source quite different from the above. Edited by Frances Willard and Mary Livermore in the late nineteenth century, the book affords glimpses of women deemed of not sufficient historical importance to appear in *Notable American Women*. The individual entries in the volume are concise, comprehensive, and reasonably accurate.

The Clelia Mosher questionnaires[16] in the Stanford University Archives provided very specialized biographical data for this study. The forty-seven questionnaires, gathered by Mosher at the end of the nineteenth century and the beginning of the twentieth, offer a unique look at sexual behavior and attitudes of middle class women who married in the nineteenth century. This data formed the basis of a section on sexual relationships in marriage.

The purpose of the study is to analyze the lives of the women who were prominent in the early twentieth century and to establish a typology for them. It is easy to think of notable women as a unit, a homogeneous group--women of substantial means who attended the same schools, belonged to the same clubs, worked for the same charities, and held the same opinions. In fact, socially visible women were very diverse. Annie Smith Peck made a career of mountain climbing, and in 1911, at the age of 61, planted a "Votes for Women" pennant on the top of a 21,000 foot mountain in Peru. At the same time Hetty Howland

INTRODUCTION

Robinson Green was multiplying her wealth by lending money on Wall Street, while she lived in broken down boarding houses and sought medical treatment at charity clinics. A millionaire in her own right, Green had refused to underwrite the debts of her millionaire husband when he had gone bankrupt, thus causing a separation. But just as the differences among prominent women should not be ignored, neither should the idiosyncrasies of individual women be generalized into norms.

In order to establish a typology, one must discover if there was one, two or even more distinctive patterns into which the lives of most women fell. Was it a woman's marital status that determined other aspects of her life history? Or was career type or the region of her birth more important? How much variation was there among notable women in the Progressive Era and what forms did it take? What kind of woman was likely to be interested in reform work? Who was likely to be a suffragist or an anti-suffragist? What kind of inter-relations existed among the various women's groups? What kind of women were likely to become leaders of women's clubs? What roles did husbands play in their wives' careers and interests? How did vocations and avocations affect the marriages of the women? The interweaving of statistical analyses and literary sources constitutes the fundamental approach of this attempt to answer such questions and to develop a typology for socially visible American women in the early twentieth century.

NOTES

[1] Allen F. Davis, *American Heroine: The Life and Legend of Jane Addams* (New York: Oxford University Press, 1973) and *Spearheads for Reform* (New York: Oxford University Press, 1967).

[2] Eleanor Flexner, *Century of Struggle* (Cambridge: Harvard University Press, 1959). Aileen S. Kraditor, *The Ideas of the Woman Suffrage Movement* (New York: Columbia University Press, 1965).

[3] William L. O'Neill, *Everyone Was Brave* (Chicago: Quadrangle Books, 1969). Andrew Sinclair, *The Better Half* (New York: Harper & Row, 1965). Page Smith, *Daughters of the Promised Land* (Boston: Little, Brown and Company, 1970).

[4] Barbara Welter, "The Cult of True Womanhood: 1820-1860," *American Quarterly*, 18 (Summer 1966), pp. 151-74. See also Mary Patricia Ryan, "American Society and the Cult of Domesticity, 1830-1860" (Ph.D. diss., University of California, Santa Barbara, 1971) and the historiographical essay by Barbara Sicherman, "Review Essay: American History," *Signs*, 1 (Winter 1975), p. 470.

[5] Carroll Smith-Rosenberg, "The Female World of Love and Ritual: Relations between Women in Nineteenth-Century America," *Signs*, 1 (Autumn 1975), pp. 1-29.

[6] Kirk Jeffrey, "Family History: The Middle-Class American Family in the Urban Context, 1830-1870" (Ph.D. diss., Stanford University, 1972).

[7] Jill K. Conway, "Perspectives on the History of Women's Education in the United States," *History of Education Quarterly*, 14 (Spring 1974), pp. 1-12. Robert Wein, "Women's Colleges and Domesticity, 1875-1918," *History of Education Quarterly*, 14 (Spring 1974), pp. 31-47.

[8] Daniel Scott Smith, "Family Limitation, Sexual Control, and Domestic Feminism in Victorian America," *Clio's Consciousness Raised: New Perspectives on the History of Women*, ed. Mary S. Hartman and Lois W. Banner (New York: Harper & Row, 1974), pp. 119-36. Peter R. Uhlenberg, "A Study of Cohort Life Cycles: Coherts of Native Born Massachusetts Women, 1830-1920," *Population Studies*, 23 (November 1969), pp. 407-20.

[9] Carl N. Degler, "What Ought to Be and What Was: Women's Sexuality in the Nineteenth Century," *American Historical Review*, 79 (December 1974), pp. 1467-90.

[10] Blanche Glassman Hersh, "'The Slavery of Sex:' Feminist-Abolitionists in Nineteenth Century America" (Ph.d. diss., University of Illinois, Chicago, 1975). Kirk Jeffrey,

"Marriage, Career, and Feminine Ideology in Nineteenth-Century America: Reconstructing the Marital Experience of Lydia Maria Child, 1828-1874." *Feminist Studies,* 2 (1975), pp. 113-30.

[11]Anne Firor Scott, *The Southern Lady: From Pedestal to Politics 1830-1930* (Chicago: University of Chicago Press, 1970).

[12]"John William Leonard,"*Who's Who in America,* 1901-1902, ed. John William Leonard (Chicago: A. M. Marquis & Company, 1901), pp. 676-77. "John William Leonard," *Men of America,* ed. John William Leonard (New York: L.R. Hamersly & Company, 1908), p. 1463.

[13]John William Leonard, "Preface," *Woman's Who's Who of America, 1914-1915,* ed. John William Leonard (New York: American Commonwealth Company, 1914), pp. 21, 22. Hereafter the *Woman's Who's Who* will be cited as *WWW.*

[14]Edward T. James, Janet Wilson James, and Paul S. Boyer, eds. *Notable American Women, 1607-1950: A Biographical Dictionary,* 3 vols. (Cambridge: Harvard University, Belknap Press, 1971). Hereafter cited as *NAW.*

[15]Frances E. Willard and Mary A. Livermore, eds., *A Woman of the Century* (Buffalo: Charles Wells Moulton, 1893). Hereafter cited as *WOC.*

[16]Clelia Mosher, "Statistical Study of the Marriage of Forty Seven Women," found in volume 10 of Mosher's unpublished work, "Hygiene and Physiology of Women," Mosher Papers, Stanford University Archives.

CHAPTER I

FAMILY ENVIRONMENT

Americans of the nineteenth century had definite ideals about the family and woman's relation to it. The young women who were reared in the decades following the Civil War were influenced in a variety of ways by those ideals. As important as the ideology which surrounded their upbringing were the realities of family life as they knew them. This chapter proposes to examine the family environment of the prominent women of the Progressive Era by looking at both the prevalent ideology regarding women and the family, and at the realities of family life in the mid-nineteenth century.

A.   Family Ideals

A central concept for the nineteenth century idea of the family was the role of the woman as the hub, the constant, about which family life revolved.[1] To gain that position, the woman must become a mother; and more than that, she must *glory* in her motherhood. That motherhood was the supreme *raison d'etre* of woman was a universal tenet. This idea was reiterated over and over in everything from novels and articles in women's magazines to medical and scientific literature. In a very feminist novel published in 1867, Caroline Fairfield Corbin supported innovations, such as woman's suffrage and a widening of woman's opportunities to earn a living; yet motherhood remained as the highest calling of woman. In a book of short stories published almost forty years later, Abby Meguire Roach said of a young woman, "Motherhood brought her the woman's ecstatic vision of the divinity of life that makes a Madonna. . .even of the peasant new initiated." Science and theology reinforced the biology--equals--destiny consensus. After reviewing all the medical and biological literature on the differences between males and females and on the advisability of educating women, G. Stanley Hall, a noted educator and psychologist, stated in his major work *Adolescence:*

> As Augustine said, the soul is made for God and is not happy till it finds rest in him, so woman's body and soul are made for maternity and she can never find true repose for either without it. The more we know of the contents of the young woman's mind the more clearly we see that everything conscious and unconscious in it points to this as the true goal of the way of life. Even if she does not realize it, her whole nature demands first of all children to

love. . . .This alone can complete her being, and without it her sphere, however she shape it, is but a hemisphere; she is a little détraqué, and her destiny is more or less disarticulated from her inmost and deepest nature.[2]

As a mother, the woman must dutifully offer herself to the needs of her family. She must be a good household manager so that her husband's economic support may be efficiently transformed into food, clothing, and other familial necessities. In sickness, she must be a competent nurse. She must sacrifice individual whims and desires so that the family as a whole may flourish. And more than mere material well-being, she must provide a wholesome, cheerful, and peaceful atmosphere to which the family members could retire from the active outside world. As one woman stated, "a good wife is the immovable shore to her husband's restless life."[3]

The woman was not only to submit in general to the needs of the family, but specifically to the husband as the head of the household. His position was ordained by biology and theology. He had the superior brain and the superior brawn. Woman was unfortunately handicapped in both regards by her reproductive capacities. Her physical and mental helplessness necessitated dependence upon male members of her family-- from father, to husband, to son. This dependence was not just economic in nature, but extended to decision-making outside the home. The woman was even dependent upon her husband for the authority she exercised over her children, as she had no legal rights over them. One male writer even stated that man's right to decide what women should be like is "inalienable and eternal."[4]

The true woman was also to be wholly innocent in both knowledge and feelings. She was to know nothing of sex before she married. The abolitionist and author, Lydia Maria Child, in giving advice to mothers in 1831, suggested that a mother tell her daughter a few facts when she was about twelve years old to "set her mind at rest." The child's modesty was then to keep her from thinking about the information until she was called upon to use it. Even a physiology book for children published in 1902 superficially discussed the growth of babies in their mother's womb but never hinted at how they got there. Innocence about such an essential element of marriage could handicap a girl in making her marital choice. But, as one male author stated, "Far better is it that women should make infinite errors through innocence and inexperience, than that they should attain to a knowledge of good and evil by perverting all that is noblest in their natures."[5]

Although women had been midwives from time immemorial, the nineteenth century woman, paradoxically, was not to increase her knowledge of bodily functions much even after marriage and motherhood. The profession of treating woman's ills had been co-opted by male gynecologists. Lucretia Blankenburg recorded in her autobiography that she was persecuted as a child in Philadelphia in the 1850's because her mother was a doctor. ". . .at school one of the teachers advised the children not to play with me because my mother was an improper person. . .it was considered improper and vulgar for a woman to study anatomy and physiology, in fact to know anything about the human body and its ailments. . . ."[6] Nor were women to know anything of the vice, such as prostitution and venereal disease, which flourished in the world outside of their homes.

Although there was not complete consensus on the nature of woman's sexuality, a vocal segment of writers, both popular and medical, contended that women did not and should not feel sexual impulses.[7] Although the one aim in life of a young girl was to marry a man and have children by him, those ends were to be entirely free of any erotic implications. In fact, that was but the nature of woman. As the author Prestonia Mann Martin declared in a diatribe against feminism, "Normally man desires a wife for the sake of having the woman; woman desires a husband for the sake of having the child. . . ." She also stated, ". . .With men nature has avoided the danger of race extinction by implanting a strong sexual craving; with women nature has supplied no such safeguard." A male author in writing of ideal young womanhood wrote," Yet the thoughts and day-dreams of the normal girl are wholly innocent. They are free from even the faintest tinge of eroticism." Later, in speaking of the wedding night he queries, "How do women pass through the first crisis of their marriage when they definitely come to know that they are cold where others would be ardent, that they are full of strange reserves when love would have overwhelmed them with the indescribable joy of self-abandonment?"[8]

Such wholehearted denials of women's sexual nature reinforced the notion that women were spiritually and morally superior to men. They had an affinity for religious precepts which men in general lacked. Mrs. Theodore Birney, president of the Mother's Congress in 1900, wrote of the ideal girl: "She is not perplexed over philosophies or isms, since her conduct from her earliest recollections has been regulated by the pure teachings of Christ, and she has neither read nor heard anything since which seemed to her soul-satisfying and so logical."[9]

That women were morally superior to men was a feature of novel after novel by women authors, especially those written to attack the double standard of morality prevalent in the nineteenth century. One good example is Lillie Devereux Blake's *Fettered for Life*, published in 1874. The title alone is indicative of the author's feelings about most marriages. While all of the wives in the novel are sensitive and intelligent, most of the husbands are tyrannical brutes. The plot revolves around a young woman who must support herself in New York City. Throughout the book she is pursued by a profligate young judge who is determined to make her his mistress and probably force her into prostitution. True to form, the heroine marries a nice colorless young man at the end, but the most sympathetic male figure in the novel, the one who rescues the heroine countless times from the clutches of the judge, turns out to be a woman in disguise. This woman had found that she could not succeed in her chosen field of journalism as a female, so she adopted male dress and a male name. Throughout the novel several "ruined" girls appear. Though innocent, they had been seduced by prominent men, and were forced to earn a living through prostitution when those men left them. The lives of the men, of course, were unaffected by such gross immorality; the men were still accepted by the best people in society. Other novels which illustrate the nineteenth century belief that women were morally better than men included Caroline Fairfield Corbin's *A Woman's Secret* (1867), interesting for its explicit hints about Victorian sexual matters and Ursula N. Gestefeld's *The Woman Who Dares* (1892), which also contains some fairly frank discussions on sexual topics by its characters.[10]

Single women proved to be an anomaly in the overall ideal of womanhood. While they could follow strict religious precepts, maintain their purity, and even be submissive to the menfolk in their families, they could not fulfill the criteria of motherhood, with all its responsibilities to society. In novels, single women either eventually married or they took over the care of orphaned children.[11] A single woman who was not caring for someone's family by definition could not be really happy or fulfilled no matter what her profession. As one lady stated, "[A woman] must realize, also, that she is incomplete without motherhood. . .It is, indeed, the very exceptional single woman who does not exhibit some abnormality, some lack of completeness, some one-sideness. Woman needs contact with man to complete her nature." In talking of a spinster librarian, another female author said that her smile ". . .means that women, deprived of the real woman's life, can yet hypnotically convince themselves and one another that they are happy." Even when writing of a successful president of Wellesley, the popular writer Lavinia Hart said, "That Miss [Caroline] Hazard will some day marry is ardently hoped. The sons and daughters of such a woman would be leaders among men. . ."[12]

The supreme function and importance of woman was thus again to be found in her motherhood, to which she must add the other ideal qualities to perfect that function. In an article against the suffrage movement, Katrina Trask summed up the essence of the womanly ideal:

"And above all let the ideal of true womanhood be held high before the world's daughters. Woman must compass in herself a trinity: physical well-being, because she is the mother of the race; mental well-being, because she has its youth to teach; spiritual well-being, because to her keeping have been given souls to save."[13]

If women were the important but passive element in the world, men were the active. They were expected to be strong in physique and spirit and to devote their energies to economic, political, intellectual, and religious pursuits. The whole world was open to them, was their "sphere" in fact. As one woman stated, "[woman] is *par excellence* the lover, and man the doer."[14]

At the same time, ideal husbands had certain familial obligations. Chief among these were economic support and the direction of all important family affairs. It was the man's sole prerogative to decide where the family would live and how the family's economic resources would be invested or allocated, and it was up to the wife to make the best of the repercussions of his decisions. Although the wife may have held the actual purchasing power for the family, the husband still was to have final authority in financial matters and was to disburse funds to her.[15]

Men were also expected to be morally pure according to Christian principles, but there was the lurking suspicion reinforced by the double standard, that they could not or would not be. In a sensational broadside against the double standard called *Is This Your Son, My Lord?*, Helen Hamilton Gardener compared the lives of three young men. One fellow was led into a life of debauchery by his father and eventually took his life because he could not stand living a lie to those he loved, specifically his mother and sister. The second young man was perfectly at peace in living a lie. In fact, the sole arbiter of morality to him was social convention. So a life of secret immorality would in no way prevent him from becoming a "broad Church" minister in Boston. The third man led an openly moral life, and by so doing was deemed worthy of the heroine's love. So according to Gardener's view of prevalent male morality in 1892, many men engaged in sexual license.[16]

In another interesting novel published the same year, Ursula N. Gestefeld tackled the same topic in relation to marriage. In *The Woman Who Dares* a doctor, one of the male protagonists, says that a man has greater sexual needs than a woman, and hints that it is understandable for husbands to fulfill those needs secretly outside of marriage. The doctor's friend is bolder in advocating extra marital relations or "freedom" for men. The doctor marries Kate, the secondary heroine, who unfortunately is injured the day of the wedding in a carriage accident. She recovers but is left an invalid for life. Murva, the heroine, after nursing Kate, married the doctor's friend. After some seven years of marriage, Kate confesses to Murva that her accident has prevented her from ever being a wife to her husband. Her knowledge of man's physical needs leads Kate to conclude that her husband must be satisfying his needs outside of their marriage. This conclusion has caused Kate to pine away to death's very door. Murva reassures her friend by saying that physical union has nothing to do with the essence of marriage. She states, "It [sex] is of the lower order which has the least place in true marriage, for that is unity of two beings on a plane far above the physical."[17] Finally, Kate's mind is relieved and she recovers when her husband assures her that he has always been true to their wedding vows. At the same time Murva wins a battle in her own marriage. Though she is happily married, she is repulsed by the idea that her husband owns her body. She separates from him, opening a home for "fallen women," until he can see her moral superiority and is willing to request rather than demand her sexual favors. The author clearly reveals her views on man's sexual nature in such a plot. While the doctor did remain true to Kate despite her invalidism, his highly moral response to his dilemma is regarded as a gross exception in a world where men failed to keep their marital vows even when their wives were not invalids.

Man's sexual predilictions aside, bachelors seem to have been regarded rather better than were spinsters. Men could still contribute to society through business and the professions without being husbands and fathers; women without a family were denying their chief function in life.[18]

B.   Family Realities

Many realities of family life failed to measure up to the ideals. Although motherhood was placed on a pedestal as the supreme function of a woman's life, women often failed to glory in that function. Harriot Stanton Blatch recorded that her famous mother, Elizabeth Cady Stanton, welcomed her, the sixth child, as a girl, but not as another baby. Women not as self-consciously feminist as Stanton often felt the same sense of dismay in the face of bearing yet another child. In a sensational article in favor of birth control published in 1903, an anonymous man, "Paterfamilias," described the lot of his mother:

> I do not say that she regretted having a large family. She would not willingly have spared one of her loved ones; but I do know that some of them were not wanted at the time they came, and that twelve years of constant child-bearing reduced her to the physical

wreck which she has remained for thirty years. Yet she was looked upon in her younger days as the typical wife and mother."

Writing in 1932 of her youth in the post-Civil War Middle West, the author Mary Hunter Austin stated that she could "remember and still be moved by the recollection of the anguish of over-burdened mothers of eight or ten, for whom the very necessities of life lacked, in the face of the never-to-be-evaded expectation--the time poor little Mrs. Rogers, when she knew there was to be a tenth, climbed up and jumped off the buggy shed. . ."[19]

While women did not always revel in their supreme function, they did often sacrifice themselves to the needs of their families as the ideal required of them. That caring for a family in the nineteenth century entailed hard physical work cannot be denied. The amount and kind of work demanded of the mother of the household depended upon the station of her husband. For a life of sheer physical exertion, none could compare with that of the pioneer farm wife. The suffragist Abigail Scott Duniway succinctly described her burdens as a pioneer farm wife in Oregon in the 1850's, while showing distinct resentment toward the physical work she was required to do:

> To bear two children in two and a half years from my marriage day, to make thousands of pounds of butter every year for market, not including what was used in our free hotel at home [the bachelors of the neighborhood congregated there at mealtimes]; to sew and cook, and wash and iron; to bake and clean and stew and fry; to be, in short, a general pioneer drudge, with never a penny of my own, was not pleasant business for an erstwhile school teacher. . .
>
> . . .As I look back over those weary years, the most lingering of my many regrets is the fact that I was often compelled to neglect my little children, while spending my time in the kitchen, or at the churn or wash tub, doing heavy work for hale and hearty men [the hired hands]--work for which I was poorly fitted, chiefly because my faithful mother had worn both me and herself to a frazzle with just such drudgery before I was born.

Anna Howard Shaw, the minister and suffragist, also recorded the stringencies of pioneer life on her mother in her autobiography. Her father took up a 360 acre claim in Michigan nine miles from the nearest settlement. After clearing some timber and building a very crude cabin, Thomas Shaw returned to Massachusetts with his older sons, but sent his wife, their twenty-one-year-old son, and four young children back to take up the claim. The isolation and privations which they experienced there drove the mother into a mental breakdown and invalidism. After the older son became ill, the survival of the family for almost a year depended upon twelve-year-old Anna and a younger brother.[20]

In town, conveniences existed which were not available to isolated farm wives; still, housework included considerable physical exertion. *Queen of Home,* by Emma Churchman Hewitt, offers a glimpse of what keeping a house entailed in 1888. Hewitt, an associate editor of the *Ladies Home Journal,* discussed different domestic themes in the book, such as home decorations, home amusements, and occupations for women. In one section she examined the weekly household chores in an attempt to help women become more efficient and save on their energy. She talked about the work involved in the washing day, ironing day, cleaning day, baking, etc.--chores that are looked upon as several hours of work rather than a day's work in modern America. Hewitt also lamented that too many wives got prematurely old by working too hard; she urged a definite rest period every day. "Paterfamilias," of the birth control article, agreed that women of his youth aged prematurely. He stated in 1903:

> I have not forgotten the day when there were women of culture and refinement who had ten children, who did most of the sewing and housework, and when if there was more than a single servant in the family, it was a notable thing. I can remember that the lives of those women were lives of pain, anxiety and toil. I cannot remember in my youth a woman of thirty who was not accounted old, and I have verified this many times by looking over family albums.[21]

Servants were available, however, to families of sufficient means. The labor pool mainly consisted of Irish immigrants, concentrated in the cities of the East Coast, and blacks in the South. Prosperous families on the West Coast made use of Mexicans and Chinese for domestic work. Servants could often be found from within family groupings as well. Lucretia Longshore Blankenburg, the Philadelphia civic leader, remembered that a cousin of her father came to live with them as a housekeeper, while Harriot Stanton Blatch recalled that Susan B. Anthony, her mother's friend, would often come to care for the Stanton children and help with housework to free Elizabeth Stanton for writing speeches and articles.[22]

The amount of household help varied from occasional aid to retinues of full-time servants. An anonymous woman writing for *McClures* in 1912 said she was born to "well-to-do, conservative parents in a small city." She described the management of their household in the following manner:

> We had one servant whose duties I lightened by dusting the parlor, making my bed, setting the table for special occasions, and preparing sandwiches, chocolate, and fudge for my callers. I also helped Mother with supper on the night when the girl was out. Four times a year we had a dressmaker in the house by the week. . .

Obviously, neither this girl nor her mother regularly slaved over a washtub or hot stove. The author Isabella Alden recalled a less affluent situation in her autobiography. When she was growing up near Rochester, New York in the 1850's, her mother had one servant who only came certain days. Thus, her mother and her older sisters did almost all of the work. Albion Fellows Bacon, housing reformer, remembered that there were no servants in McCutchanville in rural Indiana, but that certain neighbors did cleaning and washing. Such limited uses of domestics can be contrasted with families like that of the doctor Sara Josephine Baker and that of Ethel Barrymore's grandmother which employed four full-time servants: a cook, maid, laundress, and nurse.[23]

As a result of the cyclical panics and other rigors of industrialization, economic uncertainty was relatively more common in the middle and late nineteenth century than it was in the early twentieth century. Thus, some families of relative financial means suffered extreme fluctuations in their financial situations during this era. Carrie Jacobs Bond, the composer, recorded that she was born with a silver spoon in her mouth in Janesville, Wisconsin, in 1862. When she was twelve, her father lost everything in a grain panic and died shortly afterward. The family was that suddenly reduced from affluence to dependence on relatives.[24]

Another unstable influence upon family fortunes was the lure of the West and the apparition of easy money which it held out to men. Anna Botsford Comstock, the entomologist and scientific illustrator, recalled the hardships which her husband, the noted entomologist John Henry Comstock, and his mother endured in such a case. John Comstock's parents were married in the East in 1848 and promptly migrated to a farm in Wisconsin. In 1849 after John Henry was born, his father departed for the gold fields of California. The father died of cholera in route, but his wife did not find out what happened to him until years later. Meanwhile, Susan Comstock was cheated out of the farm and was forced to work her way back East by being a housekeeper. She supported her son by nursing while he lived with relatives or foster parents. The background of the author Harriet Prescott Spofford affords another example. After her father, a lumberman and lawyer, suffered financial reverses in Massachusetts, he left for Oregon in 1849, leaving his wife and five children to shift for themselves. The family moved to where relatives could aid them. Six years later Joseph Prescott returned, penniless and in broken health. The grave economic circumstances of the family stimulated Harriet Spofford to begin her writing career as a way of earning money.[25]

The enticement of the West brought emotional hardships to families as well as economic deprivations. The suffragist Abigal Scott Duniway told how the family fortunes rose and fell in Illinois. Then when the family was living in comparative comfort and plenty in the early 1850's, her father "caught a new installment of Western fever" and decided to move to Oregon. Duniway poignantly described what leaving meant to her and her mother.

> How we regretted leaving the dear, familiar haunts, and how our mother grieved as she, for the last time, visited the hallowed spot in the pasture, where the remains of her first-born son were buried. . .I remember standing at the bedside, when another little sister came to our crowded home, and my mother said, through her tears: "Poor baby! She'll be a woman someday! Poor baby! A woman's lot is so hard!

On the way west, Duniway's mother died of cholera.[26]

Husbands did not think of themselves as tyrannical or arbitrary when they made important decisions regarding moving or financial investments without consulting their wives; they were merely doing their duty as the head of the family. The extent of the wife's frustration and resentment was probably in direct proportion to the wisdom of her husband's decisions. If the husband proved to be an astute businessman or shrewd investor, the wife probably felt little inclination to meddle in money matters and was content to be her husband's silent partner. On the other hand, erratic behavior in finances no doubt strained the marriage relation. Abigail Duniway described a scene in the early 1860's in which she could not help but feel resentment toward her husband's total authority in money matters:

> . . .a man came up from the village to our woodpile, where my husband was at work, and asked him to become surety for a considerable sum, with interest at two percent per month, to be compounded semi-annually until paid. The two men parleyed awhile and then went into the house. It dawned upon me suddenly, as I was picking a duck, that it would ruin us financially if those notes were signed. I tried hard to be silent, being a nonentity in law, but my hands trembled, my heart beat hard, and I laid the pinioned duck on its back and repaired to the living room to investigate. My husband had already signed two notes, and was in the act of signing the third, when I leaned over his shoulder and said tremulously: "My dear, are you quite certain about what you are doing?" The other fellow looked daggers at me, but said nothing, and my

husband answered, as he signed the last note: "Mama, you needn't
worry; you'll always be protected and provided for!" I wanted to
say: "I guess I'll always earn all the protection I get," but I
remembered that I was nothing but a woman; so I bit my lips to
keep silent and rushed back to my work, where for several minutes,
I fear that duck flesh suffered, for I didn't pluck the feathers
tenderly.

Hard times came, crops failed, a flood swept away a warehouse after the
harvest, and the unpaid notes fell due; the Duniways lost their farm.
The author Gertrude Atherton recorded similar resentment toward her
husband. While he forced her to beg him for spending money for every
small expenditure, he was himself a failure in every job he attempted
and ended up being supported by his wealthy parents.[27]

Females--both wives and daughters--did submit to the authority
of the male head of the household. The background of social economist
and university professor Jessica Blanche Peixotto provides another
example. She was the eldest of five children, all the rest being boys.
Jessica wanted to attend college, after graduating from high school in
1880, but her father disapproved. She stayed home for ten years,
participating in the family's social life, learning household management,
and taking music lessons, while her younger brothers gained their
education and went on to successful professional careers. When she was
twenty-seven years old, Jessica rebelled at this stultifying existence. She
enrolled in the University of California, eventually earned a Ph.D., and
launched her career as a professor of economics.[28]

The reaction of Susannah Graham Hunter, Mary Hunter Austin's
mother, to her widowhood clearly demonstrates how ingrained was
female deference to a male as head of the family. A crisis developed in
the family over four-minute eggs. Mary could not face a soft boiled egg
in the morning; hence, her request that her egg be put in the kettle a
few minutes earlier. This request appeared to challenge "the general
disposition to create, out of her brother's status as the Head of the
family, a criterion of how eggs should be served." Mary stated that her
mother was happily reconstituting the family around her eldest son.

It was to be for Jim as nearly as possible as it had been when the
whole affectional and practical interest of the family had centered on
Father having what he wanted and being pleased by it. To
remember Mary's egg became a constantly annoying snag in the
perfect family gesture of subservience to the Head, which all her
woman's life had gone to create.

Mary also had the nagging suspicion that her mother thought that a different sort of boiled egg "was more than a female had a right to claim on her own behalf." In the end, rather than capitulate to the soft boiled egg, Mary gave up eggs for breakfast.[29]

Of course, not all women were as acquiescent as Susannah Hunter to male authority figures. Gertrude Atherton remembered quite a different domestic scene: "My mother, although devoted to her husband, was high-strung and flared up on the slightest provocation; my stepfather was stubborn, superior, and provoking. . .I grew up in the firm belief that all married couples quarrelled incessantly and there was no such thing as happiness in the married state." Atherton's mother was hardly the typical Victorian wife and mother, however. She had had the audacity to divorce Gertrude's father after three years of marriage. In the 1860's divorce was a true scandal. In fact, Gertrude Franklin Horn may have been the first woman to apply for one in San Francisco.[30]

As a child then, the daughter Gertrude lived with her maternal grandparents, while her mother stayed in town among her admirers. Atherton, when writing about the topic years later, clearly thought her mother to be an anomaly, and male dominance, unchallenged in most marriages. While lamenting the intellectual vacuum in which most wives contentedly lived, Atherton gave a bleak description of marriage as she saw it to be in the 1870's and 1880's:

> That they [the wives] lived under male domination troubled them not at all, unless to be sure, the husband was subject to delirium tremens, or too utterly "incompatible," when they divorced him. But not often. Divorce left a social stigma on the woman, and she preferred to accept the role of the unhappy, complaining or embittered wife.

Atherton's only concession to marital bliss appears to be her statement that her two sisters-in-law, who were little younger than her mother, "took their husbands philosophically and were reasonably happy." While such pessimism about marriage was hardly universal, Atherton's recollections reinforce the idea that male dominance was not only prevalent but also accepted.[31]

The purity of Victorian wives is more difficult to assess than their domesticity and submissiveness. The ideal of the true woman demanded innocence in both knowledge and feelings. One might ascribe purity to the mothers by the fact that the daughters were kept ignorant of sex as long as possible. The data gathered by Dr. Clelia Mosher in the 1890's and early 1900's shows that it was typical for a woman reared in mid-century to know little of sex before marriage.[32]

The innocence of nineteenth century wives and mothers may be further verified by the myths they sustained of the "fallen woman," the woman who had attained knowledge of good and evil. Since all women were thought to be pure of heart by nature, it was only through the treachery of some man that a woman ended up with a baby out of wedlock or engaged in prostitution. One can easily see this image reflected in such novels as Corbin's *A Woman's Secret* and Blake's *Fettered for Life*. Of course, a woman could easily hasten her own bad end by thoughtlessness, carelessness, and lack of respect for social propriety. "Ruined women" were thus viewed sympathetically, but still not forgiven their error. In one novel, Eleanor Gates attacked the double standard vigorously. Yet, the unwed mother, for whom the author displayed so much sympathy, ended up comitting suicide, while her lover blithely departed for Europe with his mother. Blake's *Fettered for Life* provides a different example. One of her central characters was a prostitute with a heart of gold. She was naturally tricked into her profession in the first place. Although this poor woman did countless good deeds throughout the novel, her sin was only expiated when she died while saving the life of a "pure" character at the end.[33]

Thus, women of good status showed real ambivalence toward sexual impurity in other women. Pity and sympathy, strongly flavored with condescension was proper; tolerance of impropriety was not. These attitudes resulted from the asexual ideal held up for emulation and from the prevalent ignorance about social conditions in general and sex in particular among well-bred women.

Kate Waller Barrett, a genteel Virginian, found her whole life changed when she actually talked with one of these "fallen women." One stormy night a desperate unwed mother appeared at the Barrett's door wishing to talk with the minister's wife about her plight. Kate Barrett found her prejudices about "fallen women" dissolving as she realized how similar was her own upbringing to that of the other woman. She thenceforth dedicated her life to the establishment of the Florence Crittenton homes, where unmarried pregnant women could find a haven of help and understanding.[34]

Toward the end of the nineteenth century, groups of medical personnel and educated men and women began to argue that innocence should no longer be equated with ignorance. The doctors were primarily interested in educating the general public about the dangers of venereal disease. The layman who promoted sex education felt it to be a basic human right for men and women to understand the functioning of their own bodies. Such beliefs resulted in a new body of literature designed to educate the public about sex. Dr. Edith Lowry's books are good examples of the genre. *Herself,* published in 1913, was subtitled "Talks with Women Concerning Themselves." In the beginning, Lowry frankly stated, "Every woman should have some knowledge of the structure and care of her body. . . ." Although the book contains medical tenets which have since been disproved, it nevertheless spoke frankly about physiology, marital relations, and related matters such as abortions and venereal disease. Lowry wrote a similar book for men in conjunction with a male physician. In that work the emphasis lay much more on the dangers of venereal disease than upon providing general sexual knowledge. While promoting a healthy frankness about sexual matters, Lowry still allowed her moral reservations to influence her judgments on physiology. Both in her book for men and in her book for women, she encouraged regular marital relations as being beneficial physically and mentally; yet, in her book for men, she insisted that any sexual relations outside of marriage could be in no way good for the body.[35]

Sexual knowledge was undoubtedly at a low ebb in the nineteenth century, especially among women. What little scientific knowledge existed was often inaccurate and was locked in the possession of male gynecologists and obstetricians. The few women who braved social disapproval and male obstructionism to become doctors had little impact in disseminating medical knowledge to women. As the policy of silence came under increasing attack in the late nineteenth century, information about sex and bodily functions became more accessible to women. Actual sexual behavior practiced in the early to mid-nineteenth century is almost completely shrouded in mystery. We do know that there was a high marriage rate and a high birth rate. There was also a low rate of illegitimacy.[36] We know little else.

A sizable number of families failed to remain intact during the nineteenth century. Of the women recorded in both the *Woman's Who's Who* and in *Notable American Women*, about one-third suffered from the death of one or both of their parents while they were growing up, and numerous others sustained separations in their families.[37] Such deaths and separations affected the families in multiple ways.

Widowhood usually produced severe financial strictures for families, for rarely did men leave their families in a secure economic position when they died. At the same time, few women had training in a career nor were many occupations open to or proper for women as a means of self-support. The family of the author Eleanor Gates offers an example where hardship was not as terrible as it might have been. The father died in the same Dakota blizzard during which Eleanor was born. Fortunately for the mother and new baby, the three older sons could successfully run the farm in the father's absence. The reformer Isabel Barrows in her biography of her husband, the religious editor Samuel June Barrows, recalled the deprivation of his family when his father died.

His mother was left with five children to support. She did so by making and selling shoe blacking. Samuel himself went to work when he was nine years old to contribute to the family income. Frances Hodgson Burnett, the author of *Little Lord Fauntleroy*, experienced similar hardship as a child. Her mother tried to keep the family business going after her husband's death. When that failed, the family emigrated from England to a log cabin in Tennessee, where the two older boys barely supported the family. The increasing educational opportunities for women in the later nineteenth century allowed Susan Kingsbury's mother to support her and her brother by becoming dean of women at the College of the Pacific in Stockton, California. May Irwin's mother capitalized on the talents of her children. When the death of her husband left the family penniless, Jane Campbell secured variety hall singing engagements for her young teenage daughters.[38]

Separation had similar economic effects upon families. When fathers were called to fight in the Civil War, the burden of support would likewise fall to untrained women. Kate Barrett and her mother were reduced to following the Confederate Army during the war years. The father of Lutie Stearns, the librarian, served in the Union army as a surgeon while his wife supported their ten children by bleaching and braiding straw for the popular Tuscan hats. Responsibility for support eventually fell to Lutie after her father deserted the family and divorced her mother in the 1880's when Lutie was in high school. Miriam Folline Leslie's mother ran a boardinghouse in New York City while her father wandered around the country after his finances collapsed. Charlotte Perkins Gilman, the noted feminist writer, recorded a bleak picture of her childhood in her autobiography. Her father left her mother soon after Charlotte was born. Although Frederick Beecher Perkins had money, he contributed little to the support of the family. Consequently, Mary Perkins and her two children moved nineteen times in eighteen years in their efforts to survive dire poverty.[39]

Since poor widows with children were unlikely marriage prospects, the only resource often lay in dependence on relatives. Usually, the widow would return to her own parents' home if possible. Albion Bacon's mother took her three children to live in the country near her father's and brother's houses when she was widowed. The mother of Josephine Preston Peabody, the poet, also sought security at her mother's house when the death of her husband shortly after that of a daughter left her not only destitute but broken in spirit as well. In the absence of parents, other relatives would do. Sarah K. Bolton, the author, recalled living with her widowed mother, her brother, sister, and uncle in her grandmother's house after her grandmother's death. Eventually, Bolton lived with an uncle and aunt who paid for her education. More rarely, a widow and her family might live with her husband's parents, as in Harriet Laidlaw's experience. The mother of Charlotte Perkins Gilman lived with her children in the homes of her parents, her husband's parents, and her husband's aunts at various times after her husband left her.[40]

The necessity for such reliance on relatives naturally had psychological effects on those forced to be dependent. The composer Carrie Jacobs Bond remembered the repugnance she felt for living in her grandfather's hotel after her father died. The onus of dependency often stimulated the children toward early efforts at self-support or an early marriage. Bond married at eighteen, perhaps to escape her family circumstances, for the marriage was unhappy and ended in divorce. Both Sarah Bolton and Josephine Peabody began publishing poetry in their early teens. In addition, the widows themselves faced severe social adjustments. Mary Hunter Austin sensitively recorded the social plight of her mother on becoming a widow:

> Young as she was and wholly inarticulate in grown-up affairs, Mary suffered through her mother the strange indignities offered to widowhood by a society which made out of the wife's economic dependence on her husband a kind of sanctity which was violated by his death; dependence that made widowhood, when it happened, little less than improbity. At that time throughout America, the status of Wife and Mother, always spoken of in capitals, was sentimentally precious, a status of being treasured and apart. . .Then the blow fell and the treasured Wife became the poor Widow, the object of family bounty, not infrequently grudged, the grateful recipient of left-overs, the half-menial helper in the households whose husbands had simply not died.

Austin remembered that the moving direction of her adolescent life was the impression of her mother's widowhood. She began to feel the first "social resentment, the first conscious criticism of the organization of adult life" in reaction to the social stigma her mother faced.[41]

Widowers appeared to fare better than did widows. Frequently they remarried, thus providing the family with a stepmother. In the case of Jane Addams, her stepmother signified a positive influence, though no warm, loving relationship developed. Others, such as the historian Lucy Maynard Salmon and the sculptor Janet Scudder, had unhappy relations with stepmothers. Janet Scudder's mother died when she was five. Her father, a quiet, withdrawn man with seven children to support, made a bad second marriage, at least in Janet's eyes. So her mother-substitutes were a blind grandmother, who lived with them and a warm-hearted Irish servant, who served the family as nurse, cook, and housemaid no matter what the family fortunes.[42]

Even if a widower did not remarry in the family, he might make common cause with his wife's relatives. The mother of Cecilia Beaux, the painter, died at age thirty-three, only twelve days after Cecilia was born. The household in which Cecilia was reared came to be composed of her father, her widowed maternal grandmother, two of her mother's young sisters, her own older sister and a nurse. This menagerie provided a reasonably happy childhood for Cecilia.[43]

Occasionally, families broke up further after the death of the mother. Sarah Morgan Piatt, the poet, suffered almost constant insecurity after her mother died when she was eight. She lived first with her maternal grandmother for a while, then with friends. After being transferred to her stepmother, she finally ended up with a paternal aunt. The librarian Katherine Sharp and the socialite and suffragist Virginia Clay-Clopton also shared the fate of being left with relatives after their mothers died.[44]

Such examples of both widows and widowers demonstrates the extreme importance of relatives to family life in the nineteenth century. Relatives were not only sought in times of trouble, but their companionship was treasured in prosperity as well. Jeannette Gilder, the editor and author, described such close ties among kin in her account of her childhood. Her father ran a boarding school for young women in Flushing, New York. Besides the Gilder family, composed of parents and eight children, a sister of one of the parents plus her children also lived in the house. In addition, a brother with his family lived next door. Jeannette thus grew up amidst cousins, uncles, and aunts as well as siblings. In fact, one of her favorite activities as a child was visiting a maiden aunt who lived some distance away. The suffragist Harriot Stanton Blatch also recalled warm associations with relatives. Every summer she and her sister Margaret would stay with her grandparents and two aunts. These relatives, especially her vivacious abolitionist grandmother, made a lasting impression on Harriot.[45]

As shown by the accounts of widows and widowers, relatives often supported each other's children. Although the journalist Elizabeth Banks never said that she was an orphan in her autobiography, she grew up on the Wisconsin farm of a relative who also paid for her education. The Pittsburgh reformer Lucy Iams was reared by her grandparents after being orphaned. When Sarah Bolton's father died, some relatives wished to adopt her. Her mother refused the offer, but Sarah eventually lived with an uncle and aunt who sent her to Hartford Female Seminary. Harriot Stanton Blatch's parents were both alive, but an aunt paid for her college education.[46]

When people made a long move in the nineteenth century, it was often to join relatives. Abigail Duniway recounted that when her father arrived in Oregon with his family in 1851, he immediately made a visit to his brother-in-law and then settled down in Yamhill County among three cousins. Frances Hodgson Burnett's widowed mother emigrated from England with her family to a brother or brother-in-law in Tennessee who promised work for her older sons. Elsie De Wolfe was sent to school in Scotland for three years where she lived with her mother's relatives.[47]

Relatives also aided each other with psychological and emotional support in times of trouble and bereavement. Grandparents or aunts and uncles often provided the warmth and love of parents to bereaved children. Their encouragement was important to the widow or widower as well. Mary Hunter Austin remembered the happy evenings at Uncle Billy and Aunt Sophy's house. There her widowed mother could relax and forget her grief while the children enjoyed the companionship of their cousins. At times, however, the problems of dependency strained such warm relations, as was illustrated in Carrie Bond's case.[48]

C.   Conclusion

People in the nineteenth century possessed definite ideals regarding the family. Women were expected to be submissive and pure, while glorying in their roles as wives and mothers. Men were expected to provide strong leadership, as well as material support, and to represent the family to the world. Men and women did seem to accept these goals for themselves. Little public challenge to the ideas existed until the late decades of the nineteenth century.

Some of the basic facts of family life, however, conflicted with the picture of the perfect family. Not everyone married. Bachelors could still maintain a respectable place by contributing to society through some worthy profession. A spinster, however, was an anomaly in a society which defined a woman's place by her marital and maternal status.

Even for those who did marry, the responsibilities of a family could develop into an oppressing burden. Few women took the joy in unrestrained childbearing that was expected of them, nor did they view many of their household tasks as better than drudgery. The struggle to keep their families financially viable often caused husbands to abdicate their responsibilities in a search for easy fortune in the West.

Death shadowed most families. Infant mortality was simply a fact of life that struck with savage regularity. More serious to the viability of families was parental death which was also frequent. And it was in this respect that the ideal which society held up for women was the most negligent and damaging. Society did not sanction careers for women, because women were expected to be wives and mothers. Therefore women were not trained for earning a living, nor were many occupations open to them. As a result, a woman was helpless when she became a widow. She was not educated to be self-supporting; yet, a poor widow with several children made a poor marriage prospect. Widowers, in fact, remarried much more easily than did widows. As the nineteenth century progressed, more and more people, conservative in other respects regarding woman's sphere, urged that all women should be trained to be self-supporting as insurance for their futures.[49]

The ideal also failed to recognize the importance of relatives to most families. Relatives often provided companionship, monetary support, and incentives for long-range moves. It was common for a given household to be extended at sometime to include grandparents, or even uncles, aunts, and cousins. In times of crisis, especially in the case of widowhood, the aid of relatives often proved vital to the survival of a family.

A child growing up in the mid-nineteenth century could thus be expected to experience fluctuations in the family income; close contacts with relatives; death in the immediate family, most likely of siblings but possibly of parents; and the possibility of dependence on relatives.

The ideals and realities concerning woman's role in the family and the conflict between the two strongly influenced the young girls growing up in the mid-nineteenth century. Most of them never challenged the definitions of feminity which rested upon proper dress, manner and morality. (Even the rabid suffragists perpetually resented any slurs that they were "mannish" in appearance or behavior.) They did rebel at the notions of what was proper work for women, as they also revolted at other restrictions upon woman's sphere. They likewise struggled for control over reproduction and for greater autonomy within the family. Yet, the doctrine of separate and distinct spheres for men and women remained to haunt many notable Progressive women throughout successful careers and marriages.

NOTES

[1]The finest writing on ideals relating to women in the antebellum period is Barbara Welter's "The Cult of True Womanhood: 1820-1860," *American Quarterly*, 18 (Summer 1966), pp. 151-74. While the literature she explored only went to 1860, the ideas she described prevailed after the Civil War as well. I will therefore add my research of the postbellum period to hers of the antebellum period to extend the "cult of true womanhood" to the early twentieth century. See also the second chapter of David M. Kennedy's *Birth Control in America* (New Haven: Yale University Press, 1970) and the following dissertations: Kirk Jeffrey, "Family History: The Middle Class American Family in the Urban Context, 1830-1870" (Ph.D. diss., Stanford University, 1972) and Mary Patricia Ryan, "American Society and the Cult of Domesticity, 1830-1860" (Ph.D. diss., University of California, Santa Barbara, 1971).

[2]Caroline Fairfield Corbin, *A Woman's Secret* (Chicago: Central Publishing House, 1867). Abby Maguire Roach, *Some Successful Marriages* (New York: Harper and Brothers Publishers, 1906), p. 38. G. Stanley Hall, *Adolescence*, 2 (New York: D. Appleton and Company 1908), p. 610.

[3]Anna A. Rogers, "Why American Marriages Fail," *The Altantic Monthly*, 100 (September 1907), p. 292. It was around the idea of efficient household management that the concept of training in domestic science arose. An anonymous article, "Matrimony Our Most Neglected Profession" which appeared in *McClures*, 38 (April 1912) was one of many which supported training for efficiency.

[4]Thorstein Veblen, *Theory of the Leisure Class* (New York: The Macmillan Company, 1915), pp. 355-56. This theme also runs through some of the evidence cited by Hall in his chapter, "Adolescent Girls and Their Education," in *Adolescence*, 2:561-647. Henry T. Finck, quoted in Hall, *Ibid.*, p. 582.

[5]Lydia Maria Child, *The Mother's Book* (Glasgow: Richard Griffin & Co., 1832), pp. 151-52. Helene Adeline Guerber, *Yourself* (New York: Dodd, Mead, & Company, 1902). Rafford Pyke, "The Woman's Side," *Cosmopolitan*, 33 (1902) p. 328.

[6]Lucretia Blankenburg, *The Blankenburgs of Philadelphia* (Philadelphia: The John C. Winston Company, 1928), p. 104.

[7]Carl Degler described the conflicting evidence on this issue in his article "What Ought to Be and What Was: Woman's Sexuality in the Nineteenth Century," *The American Historical Review*, 79 (December 1974), pp. 1467-79.

[8]John Martin and Prestonia Mann Martin, *Feminism* (New York: Dodd, Mead and Company, 1916), pp. 153-154. Pyke, "The Woman's Side," pp., 324-325.

[9]Hall, *Adolescence*, 2: 582-83. Mrs. Theodore Birney, "The Twentieth-Century Girl: What We Expect of Her," *Harper's Bazaar*, 33 (May 26, 1900), p. 227.

[10]Lillie Devereux Blake, *Fettered for Life* (New York: Sheldon & Company, 1874). Corbin, *A Woman's Secret.* Ursula N. Gestefeld, *The Woman Who Dares* (New York: Lovell, Gestefeld & Company, 1892).

[11]See Mary Hallock Foote, *Edith Bonham* (Boston: Houghton Mifflin Company, 1917) and Eleanor Gates, *Apron-Strings* (New York: Grosset & Dunlap, 1917).

[12]Harriet Anderson, "Woman," *The Atlantic Monthly,* 110 (August 1912), p. 182. Martin, *Feminism,* p. 221.   Lavinia Hart, "Women as College Presidents," *Cosmopolitan,* 33 (1902), p. 78.   See also Hall, *Adolescence,* 2:611, 630.

[13]Katrina Trask, "Motherhood and Citizenship: Woman's Wisest Policy," *Forum,* 18 (1895), p. 614.

[14]Anderson, "Woman," p. 181.

[15]"Matrimony Our Most Neglected Profession," pp. 625-35.   Abigail Scott Duniway, *Pathbreaking* (Portland: James, Kerns, & Abbot Company, 1914), p. 14.

[16]Helen Hamilton Gardener, *Is This Your Son, My Lord?* (Boston: Arena Publishing Company, 1892).

[17]Gestefeld, *The Woman Who Dares.*

[18]For novels in which bachelors appear in a favorable light, see Gertrude Atherton, *Julia France and Her Times* (London: John Murray, 1912); Corbin, *A Woman's Secret;* and Gates, *Apron-Strings.*

[19]Harriot Stanton Blatch, *Challenging Years* (New York: G.P. Putnam's Sons, 1940), pp. 3-4. Paterfamilias, "'Race Suicide' and Common Sense," *North American Review,* 176 (June 1903), p. 895.   Mary Hunter Austin, *Earth Horizon* (New York: Houghton Mifflin Company, 1932), p. 101.

[20]Duniway, *Pathbreaking,* pp. 9-10.   Anna Howard Shaw, *The Story of a Pioneer* (New York: Harper and Brothers Publishers, 1915), pp. 20-31.

[21]Emma Churchman Hewitt, *Queen of Home* (Philadelphia: Miller Megee, 1888). Paterfamilias, "'Race Suicide' and Common Sense," p. 894.

[22]Blankenburg, *The Blankenburgs of Philadelphia,* p. 105. Blatch, *Challenging Years,* pp. 13-14.

[23]"Matrimony Our Most Neglected Profession," p. 626.   Isabella M. Alden, *Memories of Yesterdays* (Philadelphia: J.B. Lipincott Company, 1931), Albion Fellows Bacon, *Beauty for Ashes* (New York: Dodd, Mead and Company, 1914), pp. 11-12.   Sara Josephine

Baker, *Fighting for Life* (New York: Harper & Brothers, Publishers, 1925), p. 12. Ethel Barrymore, *Memories* (New York: Harper & Brothers, 1955), p. 10.

[24]Carrie Jacobs Bond, *The Roads of Melody* (New York: D. Appleton and Company, 1927).

[25]Anna Botsford Comstock, *The Comstocks of Cornell* (Ithaca: Cornell University Press, 1953), pp. 2-5. "Harriet Elizabeth Prescott Spofford," *NAW*, 3:337-39.

[26]Duniway, *Pathbreaking*, p. 8.

[27]*Ibid.*, 13-14. Gertrude Atherton, *Adventures of a Novelist* (New York: Liveright, Inc., 1938), pp. 82-84.

[28]"Jessica Blanche Peixotto," *NAW*, 3:42-43. See also Margaret Mead, *Blackberry Winter* (New York: Morrow, 1972).

[29]Austin, *Earth Horizon*, pp. 128-29.

[30]Gertrude Atherton, *Can Women Be Gentlemen?* (Boston: Houghton Mifflin Company, 1938), p. 38.

[31]Atherton, *Adventures of a Novelist*, p. 9. Atherton, *Can Women Be Gentlemen?*, pp. 40, 38.

[32]Clelia Mosher, "Statistical Study of the Marriage of Forty-Seven Women," volume 10, Mosher Papers, Stanford University Archives. The Mosher survey will be discussed in detail in Chapter IV. The data collected by Katherine Bement Davis in the 1920's and published in her book *Factors in the Sex Life of Twenty-Two Hundred Women* (New York: Harper & Brothers Publishers, 1929) support this view on the lack of sexual knowledge, although it is difficult to relate Davis's data to older women as a group.

[33]Gates, *Apron-Strings*.

[34]"Kate Harwood Waller Barrett," *NAW* 1:98. See also Clare E. Laughlin, *The Keys of Heaven* (New York: George M. Doran Company, 1918) for a surprisingly sympathetic view of Mexican border-town prostitutes. Another interesting contact with a prostitute is described by Anna Howard Shaw, *Story of a Pioneer*, pp. 15-18.

[35]See John C. Burnham, "The Progressive Era Revolution in American Attitudes toward Sex," *Journal of American History*, 59 (March 1973), pp. 885-908. Edith B. Lowry, *Herself* (Chicago: Forbes & Company, 1913), p. 6. Edith B. Lowry and Richard J. Lambert, *Himself* (Chicago: Forbes & Company, 1913).

[36]See Daniel Scott Smith and Michael S. Hindus, "Premarital Pregnancy in America, 1640-1971: An Overview and Interpretation," *Journal of Interdisciplinary History*, 5 (Spring 1975), pp. 537-70.

[37]See Peter R. Uhlenberg, "A Study of Cohort Life Cycles: Cohorts of Native Born Massachusetts Women, 1830-1920," *Population Studies*, 23 (November 1969), pp. 407-20.

[38]Eleanor Gates, *Biography of a Prairie Girl* (New York: Grossett and Dunlap, 1902). Isabell C. Barrows, *A Sunny Life* (Boston: Little, Brown and Company, 1913), pp. 2-8. Vivian Burnett, *The Romantick Lady* (New York: Charles Scribner's Sons, 1927), pp. 28-32. "Susan Myra Kingsbury," *NAW*, 2:335. "May Irwin," *NAW*, 2:257.

[39]"Lutie Eugenia Stearns," *NAW*, 3:355. "Miriam Florence Folline Leslie," *NAW* 2:393. Charlotte Perkins Gilman, *The Living of Charlotte Perkins Gilman* (New York: D. Appleton-Century Company, 1935), pp. 5-9.

[40]Bacon, *Beauty for Ashes*, p. 1. "Josephine Preston Peabody," *NAW*, 3:35. Sarah K. Bolton, *Sarah K. Bolton* (Boston: Thomas-Todd Company, 1923), pp. 9, 10, 21. "Harriet Burton Laidlaw," *NAW*, 2:358. Gilman, *The Living of Charlotte Perkins Gilman*, p. 9.

[41]Bond, *The Roads of Melody*. Bolton, *Sarah K. Bolton*, p. 15. "Josephine Preston Peabody," *NAW*, 3:35. Austin, *Earth Horizon*, pp. 91-92, 98.

[42]Jane Addams, *Twenty Years at Hull House* (New York: The Macmillan Company, 1910). "Lucy Maynard Salmon," *NAW*, 3:224. Janet Scudder, *Modeling My Life* (New York: Harcourt, Brace and Company, 1925), pp. 5, 19.

[43]Cecilia Beaux, *Background with Figures* (Boston: Houghton Mifflin Company, 1930, p. 13.

[44]"Sarah Morgan Bryan Piatt," *NAW*, 3:63. "Katherine Lucinda Sharp," *NAW* 3:272. "Virginia Caroline Tunstall Clay-Clopton," *NAW* 1:348.

[45]Jeannette L. Gilder, *Autobiography of a Tomboy* (New York: Doubleday, Page & Company, 1900). Blatch, *Challenging Years*, pp. 4-20.

[46]Elizabeth L. Banks, *The Autobiography of a "Newspaper Girl"* (New York: Dodd, Mead, 1902). "Lucy Virginia Dorsey Iams," *NAW* 2:249. Bolton, *Sarah K. Bolton*, p. 9, 21. Blatch, *Challenging Years*, p. 36.

[47]Duniway, *Pathbreaking*, p. 9. Burnett, *The Romantick Lady*, p. 29. Elsie De Wolf, *After All* (New York: Harper & Brothers, 1935), pp. 11-12.

[48]Austin, *Earth Horizon*, pp. 92-93. Bond, *The Roads of Melody*.

[49]Hewitt, *Queen of Home*, p. 404. Lowry, *Herself*, pp. 136, 191-93.

CHAPTER II

EDUCATION

The home environment in which a woman was reared in the nineteenth century determined the nature and extent of her education. The wealth of the family, parental values, and the location of the home were often more decisive in the choice of schooling for women than were the woman's own impulses. Of course, the attitudes of the family toward education often shaped the desires of the individual.

A.   The Development of Women's Education

In days when public education for boys was just developing in the United States, the availability of education for girls varied greatly from county to county and town to town. Public elementary education was established throughout the North before the Civil War. These schools were open to both boys and girls, but their quality differed greatly from one place to another and even from year to year. Teachers often had little more than an elementary education themselves. Public high schools were established in the decades after the Civil War. In 1860, only forty some high schools existed throughout the country; by 1870, the number had grown to 160. A city like Chicago had but one public high school in the early 1870's.[1]

Private schools were more readily available to women, and academies and seminaries dominated their education from the latter decades of the eighteenth century to the middle of the nineteenth century. Academies and seminaries gradually shifted the emphasis in girls' education from social accomplishments, like needlework, music, dancing, and drawing, to substantive subjects, like English grammar, Latin, Greek, arithmetic, geography, algebra, and history. Curiously, the study of French retained its popularity throughout this change. While it had been taught in a rudimentary way as a social grace, it found a new place in girls schools as a serious subject.[2]

Academies and seminaries thus offered to women the chance for a secondary education; yet, the quality of the schools was uneven. Sometimes college-educated men ran these schools, but the institutions were often supervised by women whose qualifications depended more upon "culture" and "refinement" than upon formal schooling.

While advanced education for women began with the opening of Emma Willard's Troy Female Seminary in 1821, the opportunity for a real college education received its impetus from the opening of Oberlin in 1833 and the founding of Mt. Holyoke in 1837. Oberlin is one of many examples of a seminary which transformed itself into a college. It was the first institution of higher learning to establish no barriers of sex or color for its students. At the same time, the first women students were required to take a shortened "literary" course which did not award the bachelor's degree. Eight years after its founding, the first woman graduated from the regular collegiate course pursued by men. The abolitionist and feminist Lucy Stone received her degree from Oberlin in 1847, the first woman from Massachusetts to graduate from college. She refused to write a commencement address, however, because it would have to have been read by a man. When a fellow rebel, Antoinette Brown, insisted upon taking the theological course after having finished the "literary" course, the college refused to allow her to graduate after she had completed the program in 1850. Nevertheless, Oberlin was hailed by women for its pioneering efforts in coeducation and in granting women an opportunity for higher education.[3]

Mt. Holyoke did not become an actual college until 1893, but the curriculum established by Mary Lyon in 1837 placed it well in advance of the best seminaries then in existence. After passing rigid entrance requirements, the student faced a strenuous three-year course which included classes in English grammar, geography, history, botany, rhetoric, physiology, philosophy, chemistry, astronomy, geology, logic, and theology, in addition to calisthenics, music, French, and domestic duties. In an important break with tradition, the sciences were given equal status with the liberal arts in the education of women.[4]

It was not until after the Civil War that a college education became more widely available to women. The path forged by Oberlin and Mt. Holyoke was expanded through the founding of the women's colleges in the East and the opening of the land grant colleges in the Midwest to coeducation. Vassar was established in 1865; Smith and Wellesley in 1875; the "Harvard Annex" (later Radcliffe) in 1879; and Bryn Mawr in 1885. The universities of Wisconsin and Iowa opened their doors to women in the 1860's, and Michigan, in 1870. While Cornell allowed women students in the 1870's, other schools waited several more decades before becoming coeducational. Neither Brown University nor the University of Alabama allowed women students until the 1890's. By 1900, women were admitted to over 70% of the colleges and universities in the country.[5]

B.   The Debate Over Women's Higher Education

    Higher education for women was surrounded by controversy throughout the nineteenth century. At the beginning of the century, society encouraged only elementary instruction for women in the basics-- reading, writing, arithmetic, spelling, geography--besides moral instruction in deportment and religious precepts. Girls who grew up in prosperous families also received training in art, music, and French. As Noah Webster stated about 1790, a good education for women was that which rendered them "correct in their manners, respectable in their families, and agreeable in society. That education is always wrong which raises a woman above the duties of her station. . . ."[6] Thus, the rationale for such limited instruction rested upon society's conception of woman's nature and woman's function--women did not possess the mental capacities of men, nor did they need intellectual training since their function was not decision-making but rather as guardians of morals and culture.

    Around the 1820's, these ideas were challenged in theory by women such as Hannah Mather Crocker and Frances Wright, and in theory and practice by Emma Willard and Catherine Beecher. The early reformers, such as Willard and Beecher, promoted advanced education for women in a conservative way. They did not demand equality for men and women. Rather they said that women needed more education, both to be better qualified as teachers in the expanding school system, and to be better wives and mothers when they married. Beecher and Willard did not demand an extension of woman's sphere. Such moderate ideas won acceptance fairly easily. But when women began to demand education the equal of men's, that is the opportunity for a college education, many people feared a social revolution in the making.[7]

    The debate over higher education revolved around the concepts of woman's nature and function which had limited women's educational opportunities in the first place. That women's brains were less capable than were men's brains was an almost universally held assumption at the beginning of the century. The few rebels who questioned this assumption stated that women were intellectually inferior to men in mental attainments because they were denied an equal opportunity for education. Still in the 1880's, medical science appeared to reinforce the notion of woman's mental inferiority. Elizabeth Cady Stanton remarked to the International Council of Women, meeting in 1888, that "men have decided that we must not enter the colleges and study very hard, must not have the responsibility of government laid on our heads, because our brains weigh much less than the brains of men." She then referred to a series of articles published in the *Popular Science Monthly* by Dr. William Hammond, a New York neurologist. The doctor attempted to prove that women's brains were physically inferior in size and quality, and thus inferior in intellectual capacity. In another article on the same topic, Hammond declared:

> No great idea, no great invention, no great discovery in science or art, no great poetical, dramatic or musical composition, has ever yet emanated from a woman's brain. There have been two or three second-rate female painters, and perhaps one first-rate female novelist,--and when that is said, all is said.[8]

A free-thinking feminist like Helen Hamilton Gardener was incensed at these charges. She undertook a fourteen-month study of the issue aided by another eminent New York neurologist, Dr. Edward Spitzer. In her article, "Sex in Brain," she noted that nowhere had mental capacity been definitely related to brain weight, and that in any case, the difference in size between male and female brains was very little. The variations in brain size among individuals in one sex group greatly exceeded the difference between an average male and an average female brain.[9]

As more and more women attended college late in the nineteenth century and early in the twentieth century, the arguments against female mental capacity lost their persuasiveness. M. Carey Thomas, president of Bryn Mawr, manifested her delight in the success of female college students in an address to the Association of Collegiate Alumnae in 1907.

> We did not really know anything about even the ordinary everyday intellectual capacity of women when we began to educate. . . .We were told that their brains were too light, their foreheads too small, their reasoning powers too defective, their emotions too easily worked upon to make good students. None of these things has proved to be so. . . .We should be only a little less good than men college students, but, tested by every known test of examination, or classroom recitation, women have proved themselves equal to men. . . ."

She went on to combat the charge that the first women students were a select group and therefore not applicable to the debate by using data from the University of Chicago. By 1907, Chicago had a student body almost equally divided between the sexes, yet the women still did as well as the men. Even the psychologist G. Stanley Hall conceded in 1908 that, "Her [woman's] academic achievements have forced conservative minds to admit that her intellect is not inferior to that of man."[10]

With charges of women's mental inferiority becoming more difficult to substantiate, opponents of women's higher education shifted their emphasis to the dangers education posed to woman's primary function--motherhood. They thought education threatened motherhood on two levels: the physical and the psychological. Since rigorous studying placed a strain on a person's physical capacities, advanced education was thought to damage a woman's child-bearing potential. The first major work to suggest this idea was Dr. Edward H. Clarke's *Sex in Education*, published in 1873. Clarke, a professor at Harvard Medical School, asserted that the choices for society lay between race suicide or uneducated women, for women could only be educated at the expense of their bodies. Even a woman doctor like Edith Lowry, who had progressive ideas on sex education, wrote in 1913 that girls should be guarded from too much exertion--either physical or mental--during puberty. She suggested that they should be taken out of school during these years and learn housekeeping, by implication not an exerting occupation, to avoid life-long invalidism.[11]

The race suicide scare of the early twentieth century, when nativists feared the demise of the Anglo-Saxon race, added fuel for the opponents of women's higher education. Since college women bore fewer children than did lower-class immigrant wives, a college education was blamed for promoting sterility. One man wrote: "Appallingly common are the cases of girls with tense nervous organizations and delicate brains whose latent maternity has been rendered a torture by the exhaustion following on their conscientious obedience to the demands of school and college, of social work and society."[12]

Some physicians refuted these ideas. In a letter on female invalidism, written in 1895, Dr. Mary Putnam Jacobi stated:

> It must, however, be noted, and contrary to what might theoretically be expected, that the influence of superior education, although occasionally seeming to be detrimental, is far less so than any other observed agency. Where there is to be trouble, this is always distinctly foreshadowed at or before the ages of sixteen, seventeen, eighteen, when the college education begins.

But Hall, after examining all the information as of 1908, seemed to resolve the issue in the negative. He stated:

> From the available data it seems, however, that the more scholastic the education of women, the fewer children and the harder, more dangerous, and more dreaded is parturition, and the less the ability

to nurse children. Not intelligence but education by present man-made ways is inversely as fecundity. The sooner and the more clearly this is recognized as a universal rule, not, of course, without many notable and much vaunted exceptions, the better for our civilization.

He then went on to propose a new plan for the education of women which would have as its purpose "to educate primarily and chiefly for motherhood."[13]

Advanced schooling also appeared to threaten maternity on the psychological level in that college women had a lower marriage rate than the rest of the population. Only half of the early women college graduates married, and 40% bore children. This compared with marriage rates of over 70% for Ivy League male graduates. So, although male college graduates had as low birth rates as female college graduates, the latter produced less children since fewer of them married. A college education, it was charged, lured women from their true calling and duty to the race with the prospects of a career and personal independence.[14]

While the controversy raged, social convention changed. M. Carey Thomas recalled the stigma attached to the early female college graduates:

> When. . .I went to Leipsig to study after I had been graduated from Cornell [in 1877], my mother used to write me that my name was never mentioned to her by the women of her acquaintance. I was thought by them to be as much of a disgrace to my family as if I had eloped with the coachman.

But as more and more women attended college, opinions softened. By 1911, almost 73,000 women were enrolled in institutions of higher education. As one opponent of the trend complained in 1916, "College training has become not merely respectable but fashionable."[15]

C.   The Education of Prominent Women

For women born about the time of the Civil War, three avenues existed for beginning their education--public elementary schools, academies and seminaries, and private tutoring. Depending upon the finances and values of the family, most young girls who acquired schooling experienced a combination of the methods. The South and East depended most heavily upon private means of education. Caroline Hazard, future president of Wellesley, had an education typical of a prosperous Eastern home. Born in 1856, she was tutored at home and attended Miss Mary A. Shaw's School in Providence, Rhode Island. She continued her education through private lessons and travel in Europe. The childhood of the author Constance Cary Harrison reflected a mixture of tutoring and private schools in the South. Born in 1843, she attended Miss Jane Kenah's day school in Cumberland, Maryland, while also studying Latin with a local minister. After her father died, she was tutored by a French governess at her grandfather's plantation in Virginia. Later she attended a boarding school in Richmond. Kate Barrett, with a Southern rearing in the 1860's and 1870's, was educated at home, except for a year at a neighborhood school and two years at the Arlington Institute for Girls in Alexandria, Virginia.[16]

As the Barrett example illustrates, some families relied almost completely upon tutoring for the education of their daughters. Born in 1855 and reared in Philadelphia, the artist Cecilia Beaux was taught at home by her aunts until she was fourteen, when she was enrolled in a fashionable girls school. Sarah Barnwell Elliot was educated solely by tutors and by her own reading in her father's library, although her father was a prominent Southern educator.[17]

In contrast, women reared in the Midwest made greater use of the public school system. Anna Howard Shaw attended a frontier schoolhouse in Michigan in the early 1860's, and Carrie Chapman Catt, attended village and country schools in Wisconsin and Iowa during the 1860's and 1870's. Both Jane Addams and Catharine Waugh McCulloch went to village schools in Illinois before attending Rockford Female Seminary.[18]

In the latter decades of the nineteenth century, public high schools became increasingly available. Shaw and Catt both attended them , although Shaw did not do so until she was eighteen and had moved to Big Rapids, Michigan to learn a trade. Katherine Lee Bates, the author of "America the Beautiful" and professor of English at Wellesley, graduated from two public high schools in the East before entering the newly founded Wellesley College in 1876.[19]

Normal schools were a distinct type of institution offering advanced education to women in the nineteenth century. The need for plentiful, inexpensive teachers for the expanding public school system occasioned their founding in the 1840's and later. State governments were the chief agency supporting normal schools, although some counties and cities had institutions of their own. In addition, normal departments were often established in public high schools and universities, and in private seminaries and colleges. The aim of the schools was strictly vocational. Students reviewed the subjects taught in the common schools, received some instruction in the higher branches of learning besides educational theory, and practiced teaching under supervision.

Prospective students had to be about fifteen or sixteen years old and had
to pass an entrance examination.[20]
    Normal schools enabled young women with few financial means
to obtain advanced educational training and to qualify themselves for a
respectable, if low-paying, profession.   Born the daughter of a
Massachusetts shoemaker, Fannie Fern Andrews graduated from the
Salem Normal School in 1884, when she was seventeen.   She taught
school for six years in her hometown of Lynn.   She later earned a college
degree from Radcliffe after she married.   The life of Elizabeth Powell
Bond affords another example of the utility of normal school training.
An older woman than Andrews, Bond was reared on a New York farm
before the Civil War.   After graduating from the State Normal School in
Albany at the age of seventeen, Bond taught for two years in public
schools, and then began a school of her own in her parents' home.   Her
career in education continued for over twenty years in a succession of
jobs, and reached an apex in 1886 when she became dean of Swarthmore
College in Pennsylvania.[21]
    Because of the widespread need for teachers on the elementary
level, few schools, either public or private, had rigid requirements for
their teaching positions.   Thus, women who had graduated from a
normal school were considered well-qualified for different kinds of
teaching jobs; at the same time, women with only a country school
education easily found employment teaching in similar schools.   In fact,
teaching was the easiest means for a woman to earn money, and women
who aspired to a higher education and other professions availed
themselves of its opportunities.   The sketch of Ella Hamilton Durley in
Woman of the Century offers an example.   The entry states, "It was in
the rude log schoolhouse of that locality [Davis County, Iowa] that the
young girl acquired sufficient knowledge of the rudimentary branches to
permit her to begin to teach at the age of sixteen."   Durley continued
teaching until she had the necessary funds to attend Iowa State
University.   She earned a bachelor's and a master's degree and eventually
became a journalist.   The daughter of a minister, Ida Joe Brooks was
born in Iowa in 1853, but was reared in St. Louis and Little Rock.   After
a public school education in those two cities, she taught school for
sixteen years before going on to medical school in Boston.   Thus, it was
very common for women to begin teaching at a very young age.
Elizabeth Bond, Henrietta G. Moore, Ada Chastina Bowles, and Anna
Howard Shaw all started teaching at fifteen, and Emily St. John Bouton
taught when she was only fourteen.   It was also very common for women
to use teaching as a stepping-stone to more education and different
professional careers.[22]

While normally a woman's formal schooling ended with her marriage, some women pursued advanced education despite familial responsibilities. Belva McNall Lockwood, who became the first woman to practice law before the Supreme Court, struggled long for her education. Born in Royalton, New York, in 1830, Belva attended the district school and the local academy. At fourteen years of age, she had to begin teaching during the summer to support her schooling during the winter. At eighteen years, she married a neighboring farmer who died five years later. As a young widow with a four-year-old daughter to support, Belva resumed teaching and went back to school. She attended an academy for a year, then a seminary, and finally Genesee College, which became Syracuse University, gaining her B.S. in 1857. After her second marriage in 1868, Belva Lockwood entered law school in Washington, D. C. and graduated when she was forty-three. The higher education of Janette Hill Knox came a little easier. Her father was an itinerant minister in New England, so her early education was gathered from town to town during the 1850's. She eventually attended a seminary for two years, from which she graduated in 1869 at the age of twenty-four. She married a minister, and after the death of their only son, they moved to Kansas where she went to college. After teaching several years, Janette Knox and her husband both attended graduate school at Boston University, where they received M.A. degrees in 1879.[23]

D.   Motives For a Higher Education

What prompted women to seek an education in the nineteenth century? Social convention was certainly important, especially in prosperous families. At first only basic instruction in substantive subjects besides instruction in the social graces was deemed sufficient for a well-bred young lady. Gradually, convention changed to include advanced education. By the second decade of the twentieth century, college degrees had become fashionable. As the editors of Woman of the Century put it when referring to English-reared Rhoda Holmes Nicholls, "She showed no talent for art in childhood, and entered the Bloomsbury School of Art in London merely to acquire the usual accomplishments." All over the United States during the nineteenth century, some women were educated "merely to acquire the usual accomplishments," but generally such education was limited to the academy and seminary level.[24]

Many others were prompted by a genuine desire for knowledge. One must especially credit such an impetus to the pioneers in woman's higher education who overcame numerous hardships and faced general

social disapproval to attain their goals. The attitudes of their families
toward education often inspired such women. When a woman was
reared in a home that placed a high value on learning, it was natural for
her to wish to develop her own intellectual potential. It was not unusual
in such cases for the families to provide substantial moral support for the
woman in her scholastic endeavors. In some cases, however, the
educational values of the family applied to males, and the young woman
would be forced to rely on her own emotional and even financial
resources to pursue her studies. Sophonisba P. Breckinridge, the noted
social worker, and Carrie Chapman Catt, the famed suffragist, afford two
diverse examples.

Sophonisba P. Breckinridge was born into a distinguished
Kentucky family in 1866. Her father, William Breckinridge, was a liberal
Southern Congressman who firmly believed in women's higher education.
He often encouraged Sophonisba to uphold the intellectual reputation of
the family. Toward that end, he sent Sophonisba back East to Wellesley
to get her college degree and encouraged her later pursuits in graduate
school. The pursuit of an education was more difficult for Carrie
Chapman Catt. Born in 1859, she was reared on the Iowa prairies. Catt
mastered the courses in the local public high school in three years, but
her father, a pioneer farmer, resisted her desire for a college education.
After teaching a year to earn money, she entered Iowa State College,
where she supported herself by washing dishes and working in the
library. Catt graduated in 1880 and began a short-lived career in
education before settling upon the suffrage cause.[26]

For a picture of sheer inward desire for learning, none can top
the description given by M. Carey Thomas, the famous president of Bryn
Mawr, of the emotional trauma she felt as a young girl when she thought
about her goals.

> I cannot remember the time when I was not sure that studying and
> going to college were the things above all others which I wished to
> do. I was always wondering whether it could be really true, as
> everyone thought, that boys were cleverer than girls. Indeed, I cared
> so much that I never dared to ask any grownup person the direct
> question, not even my father or mother, because I feared to hear the
> reply. I remember often praying about it, and begging God that if
> it were true that because I was a girl I could not successfully master
> Greek and go to college and understand things to kill me at once, as
> I could not bear to live in such an unjust world. When I was a
> little older I read the Bible entirely through with passionate
> eagerness, because I had heard it said that it proved that women
> were inferior to men . . . . I can remember weeping over the
> account of Adam and Eve because it seemed to me that the curse
> pronounced on Eve might imperil girls' going to college . . . .[26]

In comparison with men, women in the nineteenth century were motivated much more by such a general desire for knowledge than they were by specific career goals. Nevertheless, some women did know precisely what profession they wished to follow when they began their studies. Antoinette Brown Blackwell, the first ordained woman minister of a prominent denomination, apparently had definite intentions to pursue a ministerial career when she entered Oberlin in 1846. She wisely did not make her intentions known to parents or professors until after she had graduated from the literary course a year later, for she had anticipated their horrified reaction. She persisted in her efforts, completed the theological course at Oberlin, and was eventually ordained as a Congregationalist minister.[27]

The journalist Florence Finch Kelly was another woman who knew exactly what her career goals were in seeking an education. Florence, born in 1858, had decided in early childhood to become a writer. Since her father disapproved of her ambitions, she worked her way through six months at the county high school which qualified her for a teaching certificate. After two years of teaching, she had saved enough money to enter the University of Kansas. She finally won over her father, who supported her during her last three years. After graduation, she continued to develop her writing abilities while supporting herself as a journalist. Her journalistic career provided her with the opportunity to publish her own short stories and novels. But such women who pursued their education as a means to a definite career were rare in the nineteenth century.[28]

Straitened family circumstances forced some women to seek an education specifically in order to become self-supporting. One example, Sara Josephine Baker, grew up in a prosperous Eastern home. Her mother had been in the first class to attend Vassar, so Sara naturally intended to gain a liberal education there also. Her father died the same year she was to enter the college. With the necessity for earning a living facing her, Sara decided instead to go to the Women's Medical College in New York City to become a doctor. The life of journalist Elizabeth L. Banks provides another example. Apparently an orphan, she was reared by a relative on a Wisconsin farm. Elizabeth had a "college" cow and a "college" hen in order to save money for her schooling. She was eventually sent to Milwaukee-Downer College in order to equip her to support herself. During and after her college career, she acquired the skills for a career in journalism.[29]

Thus, women in the nineteenth century were motivated by diverse impulses in seeking advanced education. While many went to

school because of social convention, many others were motivated by a
sincere intellectual interest in learning. Career goals and the necessity to
be self-supporting likewise stimulated some women in their scholastic
careers.

E.   The Quality of Schools For Women

In evaluating the education received by women in the nineteenth
century, one must keep in mind the wide variations from place to place
and from year to year. Urban-rural differences were especially
important. Generally, country schools did not have the local tax base of
city schools; as a result, they offered low salaries and poor equipment.
The one-room school-house encompassing all elementary grades was
increasingly a rural phenomenon as the nineteenth century progressed.
Regional differences should be noted as well. The public school system
was much less developed in the South in comparison with the East and
Midwest; thus, families there were forced to rely upon private schools
and tutors. The West was sparsely settled, except for the Pacific Coast
regions, making much education highly problematical.

Despite such variability, some generalizations can be made about
the nature of a woman's education in the nineteenth century. Instruction
was given in the basic branches of learning besides such "ornamentals"
as music, art, and modern languages. Schools that were truly college
preparatory generally offered more science courses than ordinary
seminaries where the liberal arts were emphasized. Most schools aimed
at character development as much as the acquisition of intellectual
attainments. Toward that end, a strong Protestant religious orientation
was common in sectarian and nonsectarian schools alike. Often daily
Bible reading would be accompanied by Sunday church services and
regular lectures in moral precepts by the head of the school. Teachers in
the institutions were commonly recent graduates of the school. Although
such teachers may have extended their training through private study, it
was unusual for teachers and even directors of seminaries to have more
than a seminary education themselves. The quality of each institution
rested almost solely, however, on the talents of the person in charge, so
that there was little continuity of academic standards between different
administrations of the same school. The movement to have boards of
trustees replace owner-directors of schools was aimed at correcting such
problems, but even this reform did not always succeed. The fortunes of
Emma Willard's Troy Female Seminary offers an example. Founded in
1821, the institution became widely known for its high educational
standards. The school deteriorated after Emma Willard left in 1838 until
it became little more than a day school. It was revived as a college

preparatory high school in the early twentieth century under the direction of a vigorous new principal Eliza Kellas.[30]

The quality of women's colleges also varied across the country. In fact, most so-called female colleges were little better than seminaries. The high standards set by the Eastern schools--Vassar, Bryn Mawr, Smith, Wellesley--were not easily matched in other regions of the country.

One school, which was well-respected in its region, Milwaukee-Downer College, can be used to illustrate the kind of education received at good women's colleges. Milwaukee Normal Institute (later Milwaukee-Downer College), founded in the 1850's through the efforts of Catherine Beecher, had a preparatory seminary along with its college department. In the 1890's its college entrance requirements, for those students who had not graduated from accredited high schools, included a reading knowledge of Latin and Greek, along with a basic knowledge of mathematics, English, and a little science. Such requirements demonstrated the usual emphasis on a classical education in the nineteenth century. The students had their choice between four courses of study in the college: the Latin, ancient classical, modern classical, and scientific course. The major difference among the courses was in their requirements; actually, just about the same classes were offered to everybody at the same time. The scientific course had no over-abundance of science classes, but it lacked the emphasis on languages--Latin, Greek, German, French--of the other courses.[31]

Although the school was non-sectarian, it had the usual Protestant orientation. The catalogue of 1896-1897 stated that the aim of the college was "to make a Christian institution for the higher education of girls and women, not in the interest of any sect, but distinctly recognizing the value of the Christian religion as an essential element in a rightly developed character; and to offer an opportunity for a thorough and liberal training." The college girls were required to attend classes on the Bible and church history, besides regular chapel services. Boarding students were also obliged to attend a church on Sunday mornings. If the parents of a girl had not chosen a particular church, the president of the college would choose for them.[32]

By late twentieth century standards, the social atmosphere of such an institution was highly restrictive. Study hours were enforced and even the letter-writing of the students was strictly controlled by the president. While some girls gloried in the ivory-tower atmosphere evoked by such regulations, others chafed at being isolated from the world. Harriot Stanton Blatch recalled her despair at the apolitical atmosphere of Vassar in the 1870's. She had been reared in a highly political family where even the children took sides for or against their parents in debates on current affairs. Yet, at Vassar she found no courses in history or economics, which was not unusual for the day. She also rebelled at the "deadly atmosphere of disapproval of all participation by the student body in the public questions of our times." She mounted a campaign to transfer to Cornell where her brother was enrolled, but her Aunt Harriet, who was paying for her education, vetoed the idea. Harriot Blatch claimed that she was saved from a desperate end, "in the Vassar world of immature women" by playing whist once or twice a week with a favorite professor and two other faculty members.[33]

As with institutions for an elementary and secondary education, the West and South had fewer colleges and universities in the nineteenth century than did the East or Midwest. As state institutions were founded in the West, they were generally opened to men and women at the same time. The South, on the other hand, had a traditional view of woman's sphere which encouraged a mastery of the domestic arts much more than the liberal arts. This view, together with the economic problems which beset the South after the Civil War, handicapped the development of good institutions for women's higher education. According to the meticulous reports gathered by a southern college professor, Elizabeth Avery Colton, as late as 1912 only four accredited women's colleges existed in the region, while thirty-eight others offered bachelor's degrees for what amounted to only one year of college work. Colton's work to upgrade Southern women's colleges may have been a reaction to her own experience. After graduating with a B.A. from Stateville Female College in North Carolina, Colton was required to spend a year in preparation before being admitted to Mount Holyoke as a freshman in 1891.[34]

F.   Universities and Women's Education

When women first were allowed to attend state universities, they were generally shunted into special curriculums or female colleges attached to the institutions. One of the first women to attend the University of Wisconsin, Clara Colby, took both the philosophical and the Latin courses in 1865. The president of the university, who opposed coeducation, threatened to withhold her degree and those of five other young women because they had taken the regular men's curriculum rather than that of the university's female college. He relented, however, and Clara Colby graduated as valedictorian and a member of Phi Beta Kappa in 1869. It was not until 1872 that women were formally admitted as regular students, although they had always attended the same classes as men. Even then men and women were required to use the library on separate days, and women were not admitted to lectures if the class was already filled with male students.[35.]

Choosing an unorthodox major required a great deal of bravura. Grace Hebard attended the State University of Iowa in the late 1870's and early 1880's. She graduated with a Bachelor of Science degree in civil engineering in 1882, but she wrote of her college experience: "I met with many discouragements and many sneers, and much opposition to my enrolling in the scientific course which was then entirely a man's college. . . .All kinds of discouraging predictions were made that I would fail."[36]

Graduate work opened almost simultaneously to men and women in the United States. In fact, when many state schools allowed women to do degree work on the college level, they allowed women to enter their graduate and professional schools as well. Many women still had difficulties, however, in gaining admittance to particular programs. The first woman to receive a Ph.D. in the United States, Helen Magill White, earned her degree from Boston University in Greek in 1877. It was common, however, for women to go abroad for graduate work during the late 1870's and the 1880's. After receiving her A. B. from Cornell in 1877, M. Carey Thomas spent a frustrating year studying Greek privately at Johns Hopkins where she was not allowed to attend classes. She then went to the University of Leipzig in Germany where she was welcomed as an equal. But German universities would not yet grant the Ph.D. to women, so after three years she transferred to the University of Zurich where she graduated summa cum laude in 1882. It was not until 1893 that Johns Hopkins granted a Ph.D. to a woman, and in 1895 Harvard still refused to do so. Mary Whiton Calkins completed all requirements, including her dissertation, and was recommended by the department of psychology for the Ph.D., but the Harvard corporation would not relent.[37]

G.   Statistics on the Education of Prominent Women

By 1914, those women who were socially visible were very well educated. Over 60% (63.4%) had some kind of advanced education; over 40% (43.8%) had college degrees; and over 20% (22.7%) had done post graduate work. Broken down by ages, of those women younger than fifty-five years, over half (52%) had college degrees. Women over fifty-four, born before 1860, had more limited opportunities for a higher education. Less than one-third (29.9%) of this group had college degrees. (See Figure 1.)

A definite relation existed between marital status and the amount of education a woman had. A prominent woman who was unmarried in 1914 was almost twice as likely to have a college degree as was a married woman. The difference is even more striking regarding graduate work.

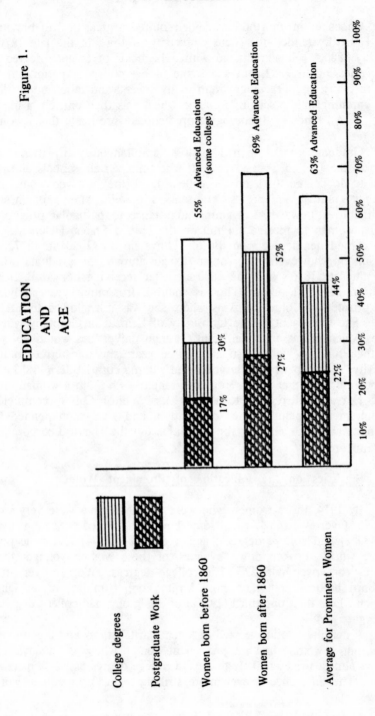

Figure 1.

EDUCATION
AND
AGE

College degrees

Postgraduate Work

Women born before 1860

Women born after 1860

Average for Prominent Women

55% Advanced Education (some college)

69% Advanced Education

63% Advanced Education

While over 40% of the single women had attended a graduate or professional school, only 14% of the married women had done so. It is difficult, however, to establish cause and effect between the two factors. Did a woman not marry because she wished to pursue an education and a career? Or did a woman continue going to school because she had no marriage prospects? The two variables were obviously interdependent.

When considering just the married women, the amount of education interacted with the marriage in a predictable manner. The more education a woman had, the more likely she married at an older age. The number of children a woman had made little difference in relation to her education, except for women with large families. Having five or more children decreased the likelihood of a woman having a college degree or having some advanced education and vice versa.

The statistics on education also reflected variations regarding region of birth and size of hometown. Women born in the East were the most likely to have a college degree and to have done graduate work, while women born in the South were the least likely to have done so. But of the younger women, those born in 1880 or later, there was much less of a regional variation, although those born in the East still outdistanced the others in degree work. Surprisingly, women reared in large cities were slightly less likely to have a college degree than women reared in rural areas or small or medium-sized cities. This variation stemmed from the fact that those who grew up in large cities were unlikely to choose careers in education, a career type characterized by a high amount of formal schooling for prominence. Women reared in large cities were most likely to become noteworthy for club or reform-work--activities which did not demand much formal schooling. These variations regarding education all disappeared when one considered a woman's current residence, both the region and the size of city, as of 1914.

H.   Conclusion

Women who became notable by 1914 had excellent educations, whether judged by the standards of their day or by those of later decades. Families in the South and the East made extensive use of private schools--day schools, academies, seminaries, and women's colleges--as well as private tutors. Families in the Midwest and West relied more heavily on the public school system--country schools, village schools, high school, and state universities. Often women began teaching in their mid-teens to help finance their further schooling. Evaluating the education received by women in the nineteenth century is difficult because of the lack of standardization in the teaching profession and in the educational system throughout the country. Nevertheless, the large number of eminent women with college degrees in 1914 had earned them at reputable colleges and universities.

Of what worth was such an education? Although the relation between schooling and social mobility is not always clear, advanced education provided an upward path to some women born in less than affluent circumstances. The normal school training and graduate work of Ella Flagg Young, the daughter of a sheet-metal worker, led to a highly successful career in public education and to a professorship at the University of Chicago. Higher education also aided the daughters of frontier farmers--women such as Carrie Chapman Catt and Anna Howard Shaw--to attain respected professional careers. More important was the role of education in broadening occupational opportunities for middle class women dissatisfied with a purely domestic role. By attending colleges, universities, and professional schools, they could qualify themselves for traditionally male professions as well as for new fields like library science and social work. In addition, women enjoyed the stimulation and development of their intellectual capacities, even if they had no career ambitions. Thus, for most of the women who achieved distinction in the early twentieth century, their education proved to be a vital element of their life cycles.

NOTES

[1]Eleanor Flexner, *Century of Struggle*, p. 28. Thomas Woody, *A History of Women's Education in the United States*, 2 (New York: Science Press, 1929), p. 229. Woody's two volume work is the best single source on the development of education for women. "Hannah Greenebaum Solomon," *NAW*, 3:324.

[2]See Woody, *Women's Education*, chapters 4-6 in volume 1.

[3]*Ibid.*, 2:231-36. "Lucy Stone," *NAW*, 3:387-88. Elinor Rice Hays, *Those Extraordinary Blackwells* (New York: Harcourt, Brace & World, 1967), pp. 109, 118.

[4]Woody, *Women's Education*, 1:357-62. Flexner, *Century of Struggle*, pp. 31-36.

[5]The 70% figure excludes technical schools and colleges for women. See Woody, *Women's Education*, 2:239-52 on the opening of universities to women students.

[6]Quoted in Woody, *Women's Education*, 2:151. On the opposition to higher education for women, see the same source, pp. 151-60.

[7]Flexner, *Century of Struggle*, pp. 23-31. See also Woody's chapter 7, "New Concept of Women's Education," *Women's Education*, 1:301-28; and Kathryn Sklar, *Catherine Beecher* (New Haven: Yale University Press, 1973).

[8]Elizabeth Cady Stanton to the International Council of Women, 1888, quoted in Helen Hamilton Gardener, *Facts and Fictions of Life* (Boston: Arena Publishing Company, 1895), p. 96. William Hammond, "Woman in Politics," *North American Review*, 137 (August 1883), p. 142.

[9]Gardener, "Sex in Brain," *Facts and Fictions of Life*, pp. 97-125. "Helen Hamilton Gardener," *NAW*, 2:11-13.

[10]M. Carey Thomas, "Present Tendencies in Women's College and University Education," quoted in *Up from the Pedestal*, ed. Aileen S. Kraditor (Chicago: Quadrangle Books, 1968), pp. 93-94. Hall, *Adolescence*, 2:612.

[11]Edward H. Clarke, *Sex in Education* (Boston: J. R. Osgood and Company, 1873). Lowry, *Herself*, p. 24.

[12]Martin, *Feminism*, p. 33.

[13]Mary Putnam Jacobi to Dr. Robert T. Edes, 1895, quoted in *Mary Putnam Jacobi, M.D.: Pathfinder in Medicine* (New York: G. P. Putnam's Sons, 1925), p. 481. Hall, *Adolescence*, 2:614, 635. On Hall's ideal education for women, see the same source, pp. 635-45.

[14]Martin, *Feminism*, pp. 124-25; pp. 137-38. George J. Engelmann, "Education Not the Cause of Race Decline," *Popular Science Monthly*, 63 (June 1903), p. 173. See Hall

for a summary of the various alumnae studies on the marriage and fertility rates of college women, *Adolescence,* 2:590-612.

[15]Thomas, "Present Tendencies," p. 92. Martin, *Feminism,* p. 123.

[16]"Caroline Hazard," *NAW,* 2:169. "Constance Cary Harrison," *NAW,* 2:146. "Kate Harwood Waller Barrett," *NAW,* 1:97.

[17]Beaux, *Background with Figures,* pp. 25, 26, 44. "Sarah Barnwell Elliott," *NAW,* 1:578.

[18]Shaw, *Story of a Pioneer,* p. 41. Mary Gray Peck, *Carrie Chapman Catt,* (New York: The H. W. Wilson Company, 1944), pp. 21, 23. Addams. *Twenty Years at Hull-House,* p. 30. "Catharine Gouger Waugh McCulloch," *NAW,* 2:459.

[19]Shaw, *Story of a Pioneer,* P. 56. Dorothea Lawrence Mann, *Katharine Lee Bates* (Reprinted from Boston Evening Transcript, 1931), pp. 7-9.

[20]See Woody, *Women's Education,* 1:109, 466-83.

[21]Fannie Fern Andrews, *Memory Pages of My Life* (Boston: Talisman Press, 1948). "Elizabeth Powell Bond," *WOC,* p. 104.

[22]"Ella Hamilton Durley," *WOC,* p. 265. "Ida Joe Brooks," *WOC,* p. 124. "Elizabeth Powell Bond," *WOC,* p. 104. "Henrietta G. Moore," *WOC,* pp. 516-17. "Ada Chastina Bowles," *WOC,* p. 110. Shaw, *Story of a Pioneer,* p. 45. "Emily St. John Bouton," *WOC,* p. 109.

[23]"Belva Ann Lockwood," *WOC,* pp. 468-69. "Balva Ann Bennett McNall Lockwood," *NAW,* 2:413-14. "Janette Hill Knox," *WOC,* p. 441.

[24]Martin, *Feminism,* p. 33. "Rhoda Holmes Nicholls," *WOC,* p. 535.

[25]"Sophonisba Preston Breckinridge," *NAW,* 1:233. Peck, *Carrie Chapman Catt,* pp. 21-35.

[26]Thomas, "Present Tendencies," p. 90.

[27]Hays, *Those Extraordinary Blackwells,* pp. 117-19.

[28]"Florence Finch Kelly," *NAW,* 2:323-24.

[29]Baker, *Fighting for Life,* pp. 2-25. Elizabeth Banks, *Autobiography of a "Newspaper Girl,"* pp. 1-3.

[30]"Eliza Kellas," *NAW,* 2:315

[31]*Annual Catalogue of Milwaukee and Downer Colleges, 1896-1897* (Milwaukee 1896).

[32]*Ibid.*, p. 41.

[33]Blatch, *Challenging Years*, pp. 34-36.

[34]E. A. Colton, "Report of Committee on Standards of Colleges," *Proceedings*, Southern Association of College Women, Bulletin 2 (1912), pp. 25-29.   "Elizabeth Avery Colton," *NAW*, 1:364-65.

[35]"Clara Dorothy Bewick Colby," *NAW*, 1:355. See also Woody, *Women's Education*, 2:239-44, and Merle Curti and Vernon Carstensen, *The University of Wisconsin, a History, 1848-1925* (Madison: University of Wisconsin Press, 1949).

[36]Quoted in "Grace Raymond Hebard," *NAW*, 2:173

[37]"Martha Carey Thomas," *NAW*, 3:446-49.   "Mary Whiton Calkins," *NAW* 1:278-79.

CHAPTER III

CAREERS

Few careers were open to middle class women in the early and mid-nineteenth century. Teaching was the only respected profession which welcomed them. Otherwise, taking in boarders, running a small shop, or accepting sewing were some of their options. Contributing articles and poems to periodicals, or even writing moralistic romantic novels was also considered genteel enough work for a lady, although clerking in a store was not. The seriousness of such concepts are illustrated by the entry of Emma Beckwith in *Woman of the Century.* It states, "At that time (1860's) it was not considered respectable for a young lady to stand behind a counter and measure off drygoods and ribbons for women, and possibly men customers." The unfortunate Beckwith had hoped to earn money that way to develop her musical talent, but she was dissuaded by friends and schoolmates from compromising her reputation.[1]

While many women eked out financial support for themselves or their families in the few acceptable ways, some women were forced into more masculine modes of endeavor by calamities like the Civil War. When husbands marched off to battle, not a few women found themselves running large plantations or small urban businesses.

Gradually, through the last third of the century, the idea of what was proper work for women expanded as their educational opportunities broadened. Traditional male professions, such as medicine and law were pried open by a few daring women, while new professions, such as social work and the fields of domestic and library science, gave women other new opportunities to earn a living. By 1914, two-thirds of all prominent women had had a career in which they earned a salary at some time in their lives. These varied from teaching for several years to life-long dedication to a profession.

Careers in which women were engaged in the early twentieth century can be roughly divided into three categories: *the professions,* including medicine, law, journalism, science, business, church and social work; *careers in education,* including teaching, school administration, and library science; and *careers in the arts,* including writing, painting, sculpture, art education, and the performing arts. In some cases, club work and reform activity also constituted careers. Exceptions existed. Two famous female mountain climbers, Annie Smith Peck and Fanny Bullock Workman, appear to defy all categories, although one might consider them reformers since they planted "Votes for Women" signs on peaks in the Andes and Himalayas. Nevertheless, the categories include probably 95% of the careers followed by middle class women at the time.

A.   Women in the Professions

Contrary to the stereotype of the spinster career woman, a majority (57.1%) of the women in the professions were married, and over half of those had children. In this respect, a famous woman such as Jane Addams might have been typical of settlement house workers, but she was not typical of most women engaged in a professional career. Besides being married, professional women were above average for prominent women in their educations and in their membership in career-related professional organizations. They frequently gave lectures and published articles or books either on technical subjects or on topics of social interest. They were active in reform work but were less interested in cultural activities. They lived predominantly in large cities but were also geographically mobile. In comparison with other prominent women, the professionals were highly politically aware and were active in political causes.

Women in the late nineteenth and early twentieth centuries showed a considerable propensity to dabble in the professions. For example, Anita Newcomb McGee studied medicine after her marriage and earned an M.D. in 1892 from Columbia University (later George Washington University) in Washington, D.C. She even took a postgraduate course in gynecology at the Johns Hopkins University, yet she practiced only four years, whereafter she expended her energies in women's organizations. Another woman offers an example of a varied professional career. Mary A. Ahrens, a mother of three, went from the study of medicine in her home, to teaching freedmen, to professional lecturing, to the study of law. She graduated from the Chicago Union College of Law in 1889, when she was fifty-three, and spent her following years as a practicing lawyer. Marion Marsh Todd left a busy law practice in San Francisco after two years to agitate for the Greenbackers and the Populist Party. Mary Baird Bryan became a lawyer to be "more companionable" to her husband, William Jennings Bryan, but she relinquished her practice as soon as he entered politics. Such examples might indicate a rather cavalier attitude toward serious professions. Yet those professions themselves were in considerable flux during that era. Many law schools and even medical schools consisted of two or three year courses with few entrance requirements. So a woman or a man who had invested only a few years of time in study did not feel the same sort of commitment to a profession that a person would after investing close to a decade of his life in preparation for practicing law or medicine. During the late nineteenth century, these professions raised their standards regarding entrance requirements to professional schools, the courses of study in the schools, and the state licensing examinations after graduation. This process served to eliminate much of the dilletantism which had characterized these occupations.[2]

An education in medicine first became available to women in the 1850's and 1860's. Here and there women were accepted as students in male medical schools, but at the same time several schools specifically for women were founded which trained the majority of early women doctors. The strongest of those schools were in Philadelphia and New York. Founded by a group of Quakers in 1850, the Female Medical College of Pennsylvania opened with a two-year course which grew to a four year course by 1893. The New York Medical College and Hospital for Women and the Woman's Medical College of the New York Infirmary for Women and Children were founded in 1863 and 1868 respectively.[3]

Female medical students did not have an easy time, however. Anna Manning Comfort recalled that the opposition to female medical students amounted almost to persecution, and it was manifested by the rude treatment they received from the men students and even some professors while attending clinics at Bellevue Hospital in New York. Because female medical students had difficulty in being admitted to clinical training in city hospitals, it was common for female medical schools to have their own hospitals associated with them. In addition to their clinical practice, many women with a real desire for adequate training followed their years at medical school with graduate course work at European hospitals and universities.[4]

Obtaining an education was not the only difficulty faced by women interested in medicine. Once they had earned their medical degrees, they had to establish a practice. Hostility to female physicians was common among both fellow doctors and many patients. Many women thus had great difficulty in setting up a practice. Hannah Longshore faced open hostility as the first woman doctor of Philadelphia in the 1850's, while Millie Jane Chapman had to struggle for acceptance in Pittsburgh during the 1870's.[5]

Sara Josephine Baker recorded her experiences as a new doctor in her autobiography *Fighting for Life*. After graduating from the New York Women's Medical College in 1898 and serving her internship in Boston at the New England Hospital for Women and Children, she and a friend nearly starved their first years of trying to establish a practice in New York City. Finally, as a way of increasing her income, Baker began doing public health work for the city.[6]

Other women with medical degrees also found it expedient to find work in public institutions or in new city health programs in lieu of private practice. In other cases, hospitals were especially founded to give clinical practice to female medical students and to give work to women with degrees. The New England Hospital for Women and Children, founded in 1863, and the San Francisco Children's Hospital, originally founded as a dispensary for women and children in 1875, were two such institutions of prominence.

Even if women could establish a successful practice, they were often isolated from their male colleagues by being denied admission to medical societies. Dr. Charlotte Brown was admitted to the California Medical Society in 1876, but was denied admission to the San Francisco Medical Society until after she had performed the first ovariotomy by a woman on the West Coast. Dr. Anna Broomall was a highly qualified doctor who was denied professional membership for almost two decades. After receiving her medical degree from the Woman's Medical College in Philadelphia in 1871, she spent three years gaining advanced training in obstetrics in Vienna and Paris. During her long tenure as instructor and professor at her alma mater in Philadelphia she brought the latest European advances to the practice of obstetrics in the area. Even though two of her papers were read before the Philadelphia Obstetrical Society and were published in their journal, Dr. Broomall was denied membership in the society until 1892, seventeen years after she began her practice.[7]

Women interested in practicing law in the late nineteenth century appeared not to face the kind of ostracism that women in medicine experienced. Perhaps this was because the legal profession had not yet attained the degree of organization that the medical profession had. Also, a knowledge of human physiology was more an affront to the prevailing ideal of pure womanhood than was a knowledge of legal principles.

Entry into the legal profession was still informal during the last half of the nineteenth century. One need not have attended law school, but one could merely "read" law with a practicing lawyer. To practice in court, it was still necessary however to pass a state bar examination. Yet, women who desired a thorough legal education met the same resistance to their entry into law schools that prospective women doctors faced. The experience of Belva Lockwood, the first woman admitted to practice before the United States Supreme Court, serves as a good example.

Both Georgetown and Howard Universities rejected her application to study law in the early 1870's. Columbia College also refused to admit her on the grounds that her presence would distract the young male students, although Lockwood was forty years old by then. The National University Law School finally admitted her in 1871, and she completed the course two years later. The administration forced her, however, to appeal to President Ulysses S. Grant, the ex-officio president of the school, to obtain her diploma.[8]

Ellen Spencer Mussey was another woman denied admission to law schools in the Washington, D.C. area, although she was eminently qualified. Mussey had taken over her husband's legal practice in 1876 when he became bedridden with malaria. Mussey displayed such an aptitude for her work that her husband, General Reuben Delavan Mussey, insisted that she continue as his partner after he had fully recovered two years later. Unfortunately, the Musseys neglected to have Ellen formally admitted to the bar. Sixteen years later, when she became a widow, Ellen Mussey faced grave problems because of that oversight. Mussey applied to various law schools, but was denied admission. The Board of Trustees of Columbia College firmly declared that women had not the mentality to study law. Even the National University Law School, from which Lockwood had graduated, had changed its charter by this time to prohibit women students. Finally several eminent judges took matters into their own hands and admitted Mussey to the bar in 1893 by an oral examination. Another Washington lawyer, Emma M. Gillet, and Mussey decided to open their own law school after six women students, who had studied with Mussey and Gillet for two years, were still denied admission to Columbia College in 1898. The two women founded the Washington College of Law that same year. The school, open to both women and men, eventually became affiliated with American University.[9]

Many other women followed the alternative course, as did many men, of taking a bar examination after private study with a practicing lawyer rather than pursuing formal schooling in law. The first woman lawyer of California, Clara Shortridge Foltz, offers an interesting case study. Born in 1849, she had three years of formal schooling between the ages of eleven and fourteen at a female seminary, after which she began teaching school. She eloped when she was fifteen years old and eventually settled in San Jose, California with her husband in the 1870's. By 1877, Foltz found herself with five children to support, having been left either a widow or divorcee. She began reading law with a local attorney, but had to draft an amendment to the state constitution and lobby it through the legislature before she was admitted to practice in 1878. Even then she was denied the right to enroll in the Hastings College of Law in San Francisco, a state institution. Foltz took the matter to court, but by the time she won her case before the California Supreme Court, her practice had grown so large that she had no time to continue in school.[10]

Clara Foltz and Belva Lockwood were unusual for women lawyers of the day in that they were both highly successful trial lawyers.

Most women shied away from the stridency of the courtroom, preferring to confine themselves to the dispensing of legal advice, preparing briefs for male colleagues, or to settling their clients' matters out of court. The first woman lawyer of Connecticut, Mary Hall, was admitted to the bar there in 1882, but she turned over all her courtroom work to male lawyers in her community. Laura Le Valley formed a law partnership with her husband, both graduates of the law department of the University of Michigan in the early 1880's. She too confined herself to office work, while her husband attended to courtroom matters. The Texas lawyers, Hortense Sparks Ward and William Henry Ward, had a similar arrangement. Ellen Spencer Mussey had also relied upon her husband to conduct their cases in court. When she became a widow, her male colleagues cajoled her into pleading her own cases.[11]

Besides the traditional professions, new professions such as social and settlement-house work attracted many ambitious women as well. Although mission houses had long existed in urban areas, settlement-house work had its real start when Jane Addams and Ellen Gates Starr founded Hull House in Chicago in 1889. The idea quickly gained popularity. It appealed to people's humanitarian impulses, giving them a direct way to aid the less fortunate. At the same time, it answered a deep-felt need among privileged young people, especially women, to escape a suffocating society life and to do something interesting and challenging with their lives.[12]

Many women who went into settlement work spent some time training at Hull House itself. For example, Cornelia Foster Bradford, founder of the first settlement house in New Jersey, had spent some time at the settlements in England, which had inspired Jane Addams. Then she resided at Hull House, before establishing Whittier House in Jersey City in May 1894. The career of Eleanor Laura McMain provides another example. After teaching school for several years, she became involved in Episcopalian kindergarten work in a poor area of New Orleans. She accepted the position as head resident of Kingsley House, a settlement incorporating the kindergarten with an Episcopalian mission, when it was founded in 1900. To prepare herself further for her work, she spent the summer of 1901 in Chicago, taking courses at the University of Chicago and spending time at Hull House and at Graham Taylor's Chicago Commons. McMain then began a thirty-year career in social service. Lillian Wald, founder of the Henry Street settlement in New York, was perhaps an exception in that she began her settlement work in 1893 without apparently knowing of Addams' pioneering work in Chicago. But the Hull House model may have exerted an influence even on the Henry Street settlement, for it soon broadened its exclusively medical orientation into an all-encompassing program characteristic of Hull House.[13]

Settlement work was not fostered only in the Midwest, however. The College Settlement Association, founded in 1890, was established by a group of women associated with the Eastern women's colleges, women like Katherine Coman and Vida Scudder of Wellesley, Jean Fine and Helen Rand of Smith, and Helena Dudley of Bryn Mawr. The group soon had successful settlement houses operating in New York, Philadelphia, and Boston. It also established a fellowship program which enabled young college graduates to spend a year or more at one of the settlements run by the association.[14]

Some women who began careers of social service by doing settlement work eventually expanded into different areas of social work, often under local or state government auspices. The career of Katherine Bement Davis serves as an outstanding example. She was born in 1860 and reared in a comfortable middle-class home in up-state New York. Davis graduated from an academy at nineteen, but taught school for ten years before entering college. She felt compelled to contribute to the family income after her father suffered business reverses. By continuing her studies at night by herself, she was able to enter the junior class at Vassar in 1890. After graduating and doing more teaching, Davis became administrator of the St. Mary's Street College Settlement in Philadelphia. Graduate work attracted her, so after three years of settlement work she began studying under Thorstein Veblen and George Vincent at the University of Chicago. By 1900, at age forty, she received her Ph.D. and embarked upon a highly successful career in penology. For thirteen years, she was superintendent of the Reformatory for Women at Bedford Hills, New York, making it one of the primary experiments in penal reform in the country. She left that post to become commissioner of corrections in New York City, under the reform administration of John Purroy Mitchel. Thereafter, Davis worked for the Rockefeller Foundation.[15]

The life of Grace Abbott offers another example. After being a resident of Hull House for nine years, during which time she served as the head of the Immigrants' Protective League, Abbott joined the staff of the federal Children's Bureau in Washington. She returned to Illinois to become director of the new Illinois State Immigrants' Commission in 1919, but moved back to Washington in 1921 to begin a thirteen-year service as head of the Children's Bureau.[16]

Women interested in social work did not have to overcome the difficulties of obtaining an adequate education or establishing themselves that the women faced in the traditional professions. Social work and settlement houses were new and therefore had no formal organization and no tradition of association with the male sex. In fact, women like Jane Addams, Ellen Starr, the Abbott sisters, Sophonisba Breckinridge, and Julia Lathrop helped to inaugurate many of the principles and methods of social work. It is therefore understandable that women would be so welcome in the profession.

A scattering of women found careers in other professions as well. The ministry or mission work, journalism, business, even science attracted some women. Those interested in such pursuits had to combat the same difficulties of obtaining adequate training and of forcing their way into a male world that women faced when interested in medicine or law.

By 1914, 68% of the prominent women had had a career, and of those, over 36% worked in a profession other than education. (See the graphs at the end of the chapter for a comparison of the career types.) The most popular careers for women within the professions were medicine, which accounted for almost one-third of the professional women; social work, with 29% of the professional women; and law, with 21%. The majority of professional women had married (57%) and almost one-third of all professional women had children. They lived in large cities but were also geographically mobile. They had good educations and joined professional organizations related to their careers. They published articles and books, and were leaders in women's clubs. They were not so interested in cultural activities, but were strikingly active in reform work. Regarding the latter, social work was a reform career by definition. Nevertheless, the link between women in the traditional professions and social activism is more complex. The most likely explanation is that women who attempted to enter a traditional profession faced a variety of social obstacles and even outright discrimination. Determined, intelligent women tended to react to such social injustice by working to reform the society which had presented the obstacles.

B.   Women in Education

Women with careers in education were quite different from women in the professions. (These are women whose predominant life work was in education, not those who just taught a few years and went on to another career.) First, they remained unmarried to a larger extent than women in other fields. Only 40% married, and 25% had children. As one would expect, women with careers in education had good educations themselves, and they did belong to career-related professional organizations, though not to the extent of women in the professions. Women in education were statistically low on community cultural interests, although they did belong to literary clubs and societies in larger numbers than women in other fields. They were also surprisingly low on humanitarian interests and social activism in comparison with women in the professions. Thus the college teachers who founded the College Settlement Association were distinct exceptions. Women in education were non-urban as well. The vast majority were neither born in large cities nor did they live in large cities in 1914. They moved from place to place often, and quite frequently changed states, but they did not move outside their home region as much as did women in the professions.

As the most popular occupation for middle-class women during the nineteenth and early twentieth centuries, teaching offered women unique possibilities for advancement. Even then, women often faced the same sort of discrimination on the higher levels of the profession that they did in other careers. Most women taught on the elementary school level, but women who became prominent as educators did so mainly as college teachers and administrators.

Nineteen percent of all college teachers in 1910 were women, yet most of them taught in women's colleges. Those colleges gave qualified women their best chance of a good job. The career of Mary Watson Whitney is an example of such a case. Whitney graduated from Vassar in 1868, where she had studied under Maria Mitchell, the famous astronomer. Whitney taught for a while, aiding her recently widowed mother, but she spent all her spare time studying mathematics and astronomy. Through Mitchell's patronage, Benjamin Pierce, the eminent Harvard mathematician, invited Whitney to take advanced courses with him on celestial mechanics, although Harvard was not open to women. In 1870 she worked for a while at the Dearborn Observatory in Chicago and graduated with a Master's degree from Vassar in 1872. From 1873 to 1876 Whitney did further graduate work at the University of Zurich in mathematics and celestial mechanics. Yet, when she returned to the United States, the only job she could find was teaching in her hometown high school. After five years of high school teaching, she became Maria Mitchell's private assistant at Vassar; and when Mitchell retired in 1888, Whitney succeeded her as professor of astronomy and director of the college observatory.[17]

In days when Ph.D.'s were still scarce in the United States, such highly qualified women as Helen Webster and Florence Bascom also found their best academic opportunities at women's colleges. Webster received her Ph.D. in comparative philology at the University of Zurich in 1889 and returned home to teach at Wellesley. Florence Bascom, a geologist, earned her bachelor's and master's degrees at the University of Wisconsin in the 1880's and became the first woman to be granted a Ph.D. by John Hopkins University in 1893. After teaching two years at

Ohio State as an assistant in geology, she was appointed to a regular position at Bryn Mawr, where she was eventually promoted to professor in 1906.[18]

A few women did find positions in coeducational institutions, often in places where they had themselves been students. Myra Reynolds and Edith Richert both eventually became professors of English at the University of Chicago after receiving their doctorates there in 1895 and 1899 respectively. Jessica Peixotto, the second woman to receive a Ph.D. from the University of California at Berkeley, also enjoyed a long academic career at her alma mater. New fields such as domestic science, library science, and sociology also opened coeducational schools to the hiring of women. Isabel Bevier became a veritable institution at the University of Illinois as founder of the department of Household Science, and Martha Van Rensselaer performed a similar function at Cornell University.[19]

Opportunities for women in college administration were almost totally limited to women's colleges, except for positions such as dean of women in coeducational institutions. The few women who gained the prestige of a college presidency ranged from M. Cary Thomas, with her Ph.D. from Zurich, to Caroline Hazard who had not even gone to college. Despite her lack of scholarly credentials, Hazard was hired to become president of Wellesley in 1899 because of her administrative and fund-raising skills. Emily Smith Putnam had a promising career as dean of Barnard cut short by becoming pregnant. After contributing substantially to the development of Barnard as an adjunct of Columbia from 1894 to 1899, Putnam was retained as dean only after some debate by the trustees when she married in 1900. Having a married dean was bad enough, but a dean who was also a mother would have been too much of a novelty for the board. So Putnam tendered her resignation, but she eventually returned to teach at Barnard fourteen years later.[20]

Other women achieved success as teachers or administrators in the public school system on the elementary and secondary levels. Ella Clara Sabin's distinguished career in education shows some of the possibilities open to talented women. Sabin was reared on a Wisconsin farm. After attending the district school, she began teaching at a similar school in 1866 when she was fifteen years old. At the same time, she started taking classes at the University of Wisconsin. Her success as a teacher led to her appointment to better teaching positions in the area and finally to a job as principal of a school in Madison. In 1872, Sabin moved with her family to Oregon where she began a one-room school of her own, charging fifty cents a week tuition. She impressed her colleagues so much with a paper presented at a teachers' conference that she was promptly hired to teach in a Portland school. A year later, she was promoted to principal, the first woman to hold such a job in the city. By 1887 her state-wide fame as a successful teacher and administrator led to her selection as the superintendent of schools in Portland. Four years later, Sabin began a thirty-year tenure as president of Milwaukee-Downer College.[21]

The life of Ella Flagg Young supplies another example of a highly successful career in the public school system. Young, the daughter of a sheet-metal worker, was born in 1845. Her attendance at elementary schools and high school was sporadic, but she entered the Chicago Normal School in 1860 at the age of fifteen and graduated two years later. After she began teaching in the Chicago public schools in 1862, her career advanced with the same rapidity which characterized Ella Sabin's. Young was promoted from primary school teacher, to head assistant of the school, to principal of the practice school associated with the Normal School--all within the space of three years. After six years with the practice school and a brief marriage which left her a widow, Young sought wider experiences as a high school teacher and then as principal of a grammar school. In 1887, Young was appointed assistant superintendent of the Chicago schools. She resigned her post twelve years later to teach education at the University of Chicago, where she earned a doctorate in 1900. Her association there with John Dewey was a great influence upon her as well as upon Dewey. At the apex of her career in 1909, she began a successful six-year term as superintendent of the Chicago public school system.[22]

Big city school systems were not the only ones to challenge the talents of prominent women educators. After successfully establishing and administering a progressive laboratory school for the Georgia State Normal School in Athens, Celestia Parrish accepted an appointment as state supervisor of rural schools for the North Georgia district in 1911. This job entailed the supervision of more than 2,400 rural schools and 3,800 teachers in forty-eight mountainous counties. Parrish expended her energy in this overwhelming job until her death in 1918.[23]

Such women as Sabin, Young, and Parrish had to display manifold talents and unceasing dedication to work their way up to prominent positions in the public school system. Women traditionally found it easier to rise to positions of responsibility in private schools. In fact, it was very common for women to open schools of their own during most of the nineteenth century when the public school system was as yet undeveloped. The life of Agnes Irwin is but one example of a successful career teaching in and administering private schools.

After attending a fashionable girls' school in Washington, D.C., Irwin began teaching in a private school in New York City in 1862 when she was twenty-one years of age. At twenty-eight years, she became principal of a seminary in Philadelphia, which was shortly thereafter renamed the Agnes Irwin School. For twenty-one years, Irwin directed this school, during which time it gained a fine reputation. She left the school in 1894 to become the first dean of Radcliffe. When she retired in 1903, she returned to Philadelphia and became the first president of the Head Mistresses' Association of Private Schools, a capacity in which she served until her death in 1914.[24]

Some well-educated women never did find a position appropriate for their talents. Helen Magill White, the first woman to earn a Ph.D. in America, suffered from this experience. After receiving her Ph.D. in Greek from Boston University in 1877, White sought further classical training at Cambridge University in England. She spent four years there where she won honors for her scholarship. Upon her return to America in 1882, she became principal of a private school in Pennsylvania. A year later, when she was thirty years old, she was contracted to organize a collegiate institute for girls in Massachusetts. Although the student body increased under her tenure, she resigned four years later because of family problems and disagreements with the trustees. After a short tenure teaching at Evelyn College, a temporary adjunct of Princeton University, White ultimately took a job teaching physical geography in a Brooklyn high school. What had promised to become a brilliant career had ended by the time she was thirty-five. She married and never went back to teaching.[25]

The field of library science emerged in the late nineteenth century as an outgrowth of the field of education. The career of Katherine Lucinda Sharp illustrates how an interest in library work could lead to a renowned academic career at the turn of the century. Born in 1865, Sharp was reared by relatives in Dundee and Elgin, Illinois after her mother died in 1872. After attending an academy, Sharp earned a bachelor's and master's degree at Northwestern University. She taught languages for two years at Elgin Academy, but discovered her real life work in 1888 when she accepted a position as an assistant librarian of the Scoville Institute in Oak Park, Illinois, the forerunner of the Oak Park Public Library. Sharp felt compelled to gain better training in her new profession; hence, she enrolled in the pioneering New York State Library School at Albany in 1890 and graduated with a bachelor of Library Science degree in 1892. Besides establishing libraries for two small towns, Sharp prepared an exhibit in behalf of the New York State Library School for the Columbian Exposition of 1893. In December of the same year, Sharp received an appointment from the new Armour Institute of Technology in Chicago to be its librarian and to head the first library school in the Midwest. Her success with this venture, together with her other professional activities, secured her offers from both the University of Wisconsin and the University of Illinois in 1897 to move her school to their campuses. Thus in September 1897, Sharp proceeded to the University of Illinois as professor of library economy, head librarian, and director of the Illinois State Library School. In this capacity, she not only maintained one of the foremost library schools in the nation, but she also helped to develop a strong university library. Family calamities and ill health forced Sharp to retire ten years later at the age of forty-two.[26]

Other librarians, such as Mary Frances Isom and Caroline Maria Hewins, secured their reputations for their work with public libraries. Isom organized the library of Portland, Oregon, noted for its county-wide services, and she founded the Oregon Library Association in 1904. Hewins did similar work in Connecticut as the director of the Hartford Public Library.[27] Although neither Isom nor Hewins had the connections with academic life that Sharp had, their life cycles corresponded closely with their other colleagues in the field of education.

For most women, education proved to be a fruitful field for their talents. Different levels of teaching and of administration were open to them, although the salaries commanded by women were not the equal of men in the same positions. Perhaps because of its manifold opportunities for women, the teaching profession seems to have been a self-contained, inward-directed occupation. Teachers were not the active social reformers that women in other professions were. They had little political consciousness, nor did they involve themselves to the extent of other career types in the wide spectrum of activities that interested most middle class women during this period. The reason for this probably lay in the very respectability of teaching as an occupation for women. Teaching was so eminently acceptable, that women did not have to face the obstacles in training nor the difficulties of becoming established that women interested in more traditionally male professions experienced. Hence, women in education did not feel the need to reform society that women felt who attempted careers in medicine, law, journalism, science, or the ministry. Also, teaching careers brought women into close contact with numerous female colleagues. Thus, women teachers did not feel the need to join the popular women's clubs to the degree that women in other professions or non-career women did. Regarding reform, the Progressive movement certainly touched many aspects of education. John Dewey challenged traditional educational theory, while others worked on more mundane matters such as the expansion of the high school curriculum. Interest in reform in one area generally led people to take an interest in reforming other aspects of society as well. Nevertheless, the social and political activists with careers in education were in a distinct minority in a relatively apolitical profession.

C. Women in the Arts

Women with careers in the arts were different from both women in the professions and women in education. They did not approach the level of formal education that women in the other two career types had. In fact, the majority of women in the arts had no advanced education; they had often received some technical artistic training, however, such as piano lessons or attendance at an art school. Two-thirds of the women in the arts were married and 38% had children. Their pattern for activities followed that of women in education. They were statistically low on humanitarian interests and on women's club leadership in comparison with women in the professions; they lacked political consciousness nor were they as active in reform causes. They were, however, interested in genealogy and in activities concerned with community arts. They tended to live in large cities, as did women in the professions, but they were not as geographically mobile as women in the other two career types.

Over 50% of the women in the arts were writers. In fact, this single occupation attracted more women than did any other except teaching. One can easily see why women were drawn to writing. It was a way to earn money from the safety and sanctity of the home. In addition, it was relatively easy. With a minimum of talent, it was not difficult to get articles, poems, even novels published in the late nineteenth and early twentieth centuries. But the attraction of writing was not strictly utilitarian. Most authors were genuinely inspired by the desire to create valuable literature. Unfortunately, Ellen Glasgow, Edith Wharton, and Sarah Teasdale cannot be considered typical of prominent women writers in the early twentieth century. Most of what ordinary authors published was second or third rate. But the shortcomings of the achievements should not obscure the artistic impulse which prompted most authors.

The writing career of Frances Hodgson Burnett may be considered fairly typical, although most authors did not achieve the financial success which marked her career. Burnett was born in England in 1849, but emigrated to America with her family when she was sixteen. Her widowed mother could no longer support the family in Manchester because the American Civil War had cut off the supply of cotton to the mills, causing an economic depression in the area. The family journeyed to Tennessee where a relative had promised work for the older boys. The poverty in which the family existed impelled Frances to seek a means of earning money. She opened a school for a year, and tried sending stories to magazines. The first two stories she sent were accepted by *Godey's Lady's Book*, and thus, her literary career was launched when she was about eighteen.[28]

Burnett first wrote story after story for second-rate magazines. Her fiction usually revolved around a hero who overcame numerous difficulties to win the heroine; that was the typical formula for popular novels during that era. Burnett finally had the courage to submit her efforts to *Scribner's*, the *Atlantic Monthly*, and *Harper's*, and there too she met with success. She married a young doctor in 1873, when she was twenty-four, and financed his advanced studies in Paris by writing articles. The royalties from her first novel, published in 1877 after being serialized in *Scribner's*, enabled the young couple to move to Washington from Tennessee. There her husband, Dr. Swan Burnett, successfully established his practice as an eye and ear specialist. While rearing her family of two sons, Burnett wrote voluminously for nine years, but in 1886 she struck a gold mine with her *Little Lord Fauntleroy*. Both the novel and the play she adapted from it enjoyed huge success in England and America. It made a rich woman of her at thirty-seven, and enabled her to spend many of her later years abroad.[29]

The life and works of Gene Stratton-Porter can serve as another example of a female author in the early twentieth century. Born on a prosperous Indiana farm in 1863, Stratton-Porter had little formal schooling until her teenage years when she attended high school. When she was twenty-three, she married a druggist twenty years older than she and had one child. Money was not a motivation for her writing career inasmuch as the discovery of oil on her husband's property insured the prosperity of the family. Stratton-Porter started writing fiction in her thirties, after achieving a little success as a photographer and writer of nature articles. She became popular with *Freckles*, published in 1904, and *A Girl of the Limberlost*, in 1909. In these books, she praised life in the country close to nature, and found moral virtue in the lives of animals. These sentiments were always expressed through a formula romance.[30]

Sentimental romantic novels comprised the majority of fiction written by female authors in the late nineteenth and early twentieth centuries. Occasionally, however, some of these same authors wrote novels to advance a social cause. Women wrote both for and against the movement to enlarge woman's sphere. Another favorite theme was an attack upon the double standard of morality. Other women authors used fiction to stir people's consciences regarding slum conditions and other social problems. Normally, a romantic plot was the vehicle for advancing the author's sentiments on any given topic. But authors were not, as a rule the social activists that women in the professions were. The amount of reform literature written by women authors was small. On the other hand, committed activists now and then ventured into the sphere of fiction in order to promote their ideas. Helen Hamilton Gardener, with her *Is This Your Son, My Lord?*, is a good example of the latter.[31]

The lives of painters, sculptors, and performing artists varied considerably from those of authors. Although the formal schooling of creative and performing artists was also limited, they generally had technical training in their artistic interest outside the normal educational system. In some cases, this meant attendance at schools of art or music; in many others, the aspirant would serve an apprenticeship with someone established in her field. Most young people seriously interested in an artistic career managed to travel to Europe for study, for European training was a precondition for a successful career in the United States.

The career of Janet Scudder offers a useful example. Born in Terre Haute, Indiana, in 1869, Scudder was reared in an unhappy home environment. After her mother's death when she was five, Scudder turned to her old blind grandmother and an Irish servant for maternal affection out of antipathy to her new stepmother. She demonstrated artistic proclivities early when she won prizes at county fairs when just a girl. After high school, Scudder attended the Academy of Art in Cincinnati for two years, where she developed skill as a woodcarver. Under the patronage of her brother, she found a job in Chicago at a woodcarving factory. Unfortunately, she was soon forced out of work by the male woodcarvers' union. An excellent opportunity opened to her, however, when Lorado Taft needed assistants to aid him in casting facades and other works for the Columbian Exposition of 1893. After working enthusiastically with Taft and gaining wide experience in sculpting, Scudder actually made two statues of her own for the fair, one for the Illinois building and one for the Indiana building. By working for the fair, she also made the contacts for further study in Europe. After several years of study in Paris, she found her niche in the designing of ornamental sculpture for gardens and residences. After her "Frog Fountain" made her reputation in New York City at the turn of the century, commissions poured in and she became well-established.[32]

The painter, Cecilia Beaux, had a similar career. Born in 1855, Beaux was tutored at home by her aunts and attended an exclusive Philadelphia boarding school for two years before concentrating on artistic studies. She took her first art lesson from a relative, but she also attended an art school as a teenager. Beaux exploited all available means for earning money, even though she despised such lucrative endeavors as her child portraits on china plates. She saved her money for a trip to Paris. In 1888, an uncle helped her to finance a trip. After a year of study, she returned to Philadelphia where she became renowned as a portrait artist.[33]

Musicians and singers were similar to painters and sculptors in that they too sought European training and performing experience before attempting to establish themselves in the United States. The singing career of Annie Louise Cary is illustrative of that. While she was growing up in Maine during the 1840's and 1850's, Cary's musical interests were encouraged by her parents, both amateur singers. After graduating from a seminary at nineteen, Cary began taking voice lessons in Boston. After studying for several years, she raised money for study in Europe by giving a special concert at the Boston Music Hall. Her year in Milan led to a debut in Copenhagen in 1868. She continued to perform and study in Europe until she joined a concert company in the United States in 1870. She became famous not only for her operatic roles but also for her performances in religious oratorios and at music festivals. Her career was cut short, however, when she married at the age of forty and retired from public performances except for occasional charity benefits.[34]

Not only European study but European birth was more common among performing musicians than among prominent women in other professions. While some of these women were reared abroad and made their reputations there before accepting jobs in the United States, others emigrated to America with their families while they were still small children. The operatic prima donna Ernestine Schumann-Heink is an example of the former while another opera star, Emma Juch, and concert pianist Fannie Zeisler are examples of the latter.[35]

The American dramatic theater was more independent of European influence, and American actresses tended to be native born and trained. Some famous actresses such as Ethel Barrymore grew up in families where the theater was a long tradition. Her grandmother owned a theater in Philadelphia and both of her parents were actors. Although Barrymore herself wanted to be a pianist, she was never consulted about her preferences. Her family got her a job on stage with her uncle when she was fifteen so she could help earn money.[36]

Mary Shaw, an American actress considerably older than Barrymore, became interested in acting after taking elocution lessons. Shaw had graduated from the normal school in Boston and had then taught school until her voice failed from constant use. When she turned to elocution lessons in her plight, she became drawn to the stage. Lacking the theatrical connections of a Barrymore, Shaw struggled unsuccessfully to join a professional company and began her career in amateur theatricals. A season with the Boston Museum stock company in 1879 led to her engagement by Augustin Daly's famous company in New York. It took her almost two decades, however, to gain starring roles, and her real fame only came when she helped to introduce the works of Heinrich Ibsen and George Bernard Shaw to American audiences in the first decades of the twentieth century.[37]

Art education also attracted many women, but it was generally a residual occupation rather than an end in itself. Young women who aspired to professional artistic careers often gave drawing or music lessons to help earn money for further study. Even after gaining professional status, women often supplemented their incomes by accepting private pupils. Of course, the many artistic aspirants who failed to achieve professional success could also turn to teaching as a means of support. In addition, teaching art or music was popular among married women who wished to supplement the family income or merely wanted to earn some money of their own.

D. Noncareer Women

Those women who were prominent in 1914 but did not have careers generally gained their recognition through reform work, women's club work, philanthropic activities, or their positions as socialites. In some cases reform work, club work, and philanthropy could be considered careers in and of themselves. May Wright Sewall, for example, went from a teaching career to almost full-time work for women's organizations. She helped found the National Council of Women and served as the president of the International Council of Women for five years. She also was a founding member and executive officer of the General Federation of Women's Clubs and the Western Association of Collegiate Alumnae, besides establishing numerous local women's groups in Indianapolis.[38]

Grace Hoadley Dodge, an heiress of Phelps, Dodge, and Company, foreswore a society life for social service and charitable work. She helped to form working girls' associations and supported other groups such as the Travelers Aid Society in New York. Dodge was also instrumental in the founding of the Industrial Education Association which eventually became the Teachers College of Columbia University. As the first treasurer of the trustees for the Teachers College, Dodge kept the new school solvent during her nine-year term. She also devoted considerable energy to administrative duties as president of the National Board of the Young Women's Christian Association. Though unsalaried, Dodge took such philanthropic work so seriously that she limited herself to a two-week vacation each year.[39]

Sewall and Dodge exemplify women who made full-time careers out of non-salaried work, and as such their life-patterns most closely resembled women in the professions. Most women without full-time occupations failed to compensate by making careers out of charitable or reform work, although they may have become prominent for the contributions they did make to clubs or other endeavors. These non-career women had their own characteristics distinct from women in education, the arts, or the professions.

Over 95% of these women were married and over 73% had children, indicating that if a prominent woman did not have a career, she would almost certainly be married and have children. Conversely, if a woman were single, she would very likely have a career. At the same time, most career women were married, and most married women had careers. Non-career women were the most poorly educated. They had neither advanced formal education, as did women in the professions and in education, nor did they have the technical training of women in the arts. They consistently displayed more interest in general women's activities--women's clubs, church groups, humanitarian endeavors--than did women in education or the arts. Yet, they could not compare in social and political activism with women in the professions. Non-career women were the most interested and active, though, in religious groups. The prominent women without careers generally lived in large cities and were less mobile than other prominent women.

E.   Conclusion

Career choices for middle class women expanded significantly from the mid-nineteenth to the early twentieth century. Thus, the women who were prominent in 1914 had seen considerable change during their lifetimes in the notion of proper work for women. The specific career choices made by these women had far-reaching ramifications for other aspects of their life cycles. Career type indicated not only a woman's educational level, but also a broad range of activities and interests. Since the opening of a variety of careers was in itself considered by women a great advance, the issue of equal pay for equal work did not receive the attention in the Progressive Era that it would command a half century later. Women, in general, did not receive the salaries or professional fees of men in the same occupations. This practice caused considerable complaining but no mobilization. Popular fiction was the only field in which women could be competitive with men on a monetary level. Thus, most of these women worked for more than financial rewards. Economic independence was indeed important for both single and married women, but more important was the sense of individual fulfillment in meeting challenges and making contributions outside the home to the development of American society.

NOTES

[1]Emma Beckwith," *WOC*, p. 69.

[2]"Anita Newcomb McGee," *NAW*, 2:465. "Mary A. Ahrens," *WOC*, p. 10. "Marion Marsh Todd," *NAW*, 3:470. "Mary Baird Bryan," *WWW*, p. 140. See Robert H. Wiebe, *The Search for Order, 1877-1920* (New York: Hill and Wang, 1967), pp. 113-117 for a description of the process by which the traditional professions organized themselves and elevated their standards.

[3]Woody, *Women's Education*, 2:353-57. See also the following sources: Gulielma F. Alsop, *History of the Woman's Medical College, Philadelphia, Pennsylvania 1850-1950* (Philadelphia: Lippincott, 1950). Hays, *Those Extraordinary Blackwells*. Kate Campbell Hurd-Mead, *Medical Women of America* (New York: Froben Press, 1933). Kate Campbell Hurd-Mead, *A History of Women in Medicine* (Haddam, Connecticut: The Haddam Press, 1938).

[4]"Anna Manning Comfort," *WOC*, pp. 196-97. See also Woody, *Women's Education*, 2:361-62.

[5]Blankenburg, *The Blankenburgs of Philadelphia*, pp. 103-4. "Millie Jane Chapman," *WOC*, pp. 168-69.

[6]Baker, *Fighting for Life*, pp. 44-54.

[7]"Charlotte Amanda Blake Brown," *NAW*, 1:252. "Anna Elizabeth Broomall," *NAW*, 1:246. See also Woody, *Women's Education*, 2:362.

[8]"Belva Ann Bennett McNall Lockwood," *NAW*, 2:414. On the entry of women to the legal profession, see the introduction by Dorothy Thomas in *Women Lawyers in the United States* (New York: The Scarecrow Press, 1957). On the status of women in law in the Progressive Era, see Elva Hulburd Young, "The Law as a Profession for Women," *Publications of the Association of Collegiate Alumnae*, 3 (February 1902), pp. 15-23.

[9]Grace Hathaway, *Fate Rides a Tortoise* (Chicago: John C. Winston Company, 1937), pp. 61-65; 80-83; 105-111. On the admission of women to law schools, see also Woody, *Women's Education*, 2:373-76.

[10]"Clara Shortridge Foltz," *WOC*, pp. 293-94. "Clara Shortridge Foltz," *NAW*, 1:641-42.

[11]"Mary Hall," *WOC*, p. 351. "Laura A. Woodin LeValley," *WOC*, p. 460. "Hortense Sparks Malsch Ward," *NAW*, 3:541. Hathaway, *Fate Rides a Tortoise*, p. 84.

[12]Addams, *Twenty Years at Hull House*. See also her address, "The Subjective Necessity for Social Settlements," and Allen F. Davis, *Spearheads for Reform* and *American Heroine: The Life and Legend of Jane Addams*.

[13]"Cornelia Foster Bradford," *NAW*, 1:218. "Eleanor Laura McMain," *NAW*, 2:474-75. Lillian D. Wald, *The House on Henry Street* (New York: Henry Holt and Company, 1915). p. 2.

[14]"Helena Stuart Dudley," *NAW*, 1:526-27. "Katherine Coman," *NAW*, 1:365-66. See also Vida Scudder, *On Journey* (New York: E. P. Dutton and Co., 1937) and Mercedes M. Randall, *Improper Bostonian* (New York: Twayne, 1964).

[15]"Katherine Bement Davis," *NAW*, 1:439-441.

[16]"Grace Abbott," *NAW*, 1:2-3.

[17]See Sophonisba P. Breckinridge, *Women in the Twentieth Century* (New York: McGraw-Hill Book Company, 1933), p. 190 for statistics on women's professional employment. "Mary Watson Whitney," *NAW*, 3.

[18]"Helen L. Webster," *WOC*, p. 756. "Florence Bascom," *NAW*, 1:108-09. "Florence Bascom," *WWW*, p. 81.

[19]"Myra Reynolds," *WWW*, p. 681. "Edith Rickert," *NAW*, 3:156. "Jessica Blanche Peixotto," *NAW*, 3:42. Lita Bane, *The Story of Isabel Bevier* (Peoria: Chas A. Bennett Co., 1955). "Martha Van Rensselaer," *NAW*, 3:513-14.

[20]Hart, "Women as College Presidents," pp. 72-79. "Emily James Smith Putnam," *NAW*, 2:107.

[21]Marie Adams, *Ellen Clara Sabin: A Life Sketch* (Madison: University of Wisconsin Press, 1937), pp. 5-13. See also Grace Norton Kieckhefer, *The History of Milwaukee-Downer College, 1851-1951* (Milwaukee; Milwaukee-Downer College, 1950).

[22]"Ella Flagg Young," *NAW*, 3:697-99. See also John T. McManis, *Ella Flagg Young and a Half-Century of the Chicago Public Schools* (Chicago: A. C. McClurg, 1916).

[23]Celestia Susannah Parrish," *NAW*, 3:18-19.

[24]"Agnes Irwin," *NAW*, 2:253-55.

[25]"Helen Magill White," *NAW*, 3:588-89.

[26]"Katherine Lucinda Sharp," *NAW*, 3:272-73.

[27]"Mary Frances Isom," *NAW*, 2:258-59. "Caroline Maria Hewins," *NAW*, 2:189-91.

[28]Burnett, *The Romantick Lady*, pp. 28-46.

[29]*Ibid.*, pp. 51-147, passim. "Frances Eliza Hodgson Burnett," *NAW*, 1:269-70. Frances Hodgson Burnett, *Little Lord Fauntleroy* (New York: C. Schribner's Sons, 1886).

[30]Jeanette Porter Meehan, *The Lady of the Limberlost* (Garden City, New York: Doubleday, Doran & Company, 1928).

[31]Gardener, *Is This Your Son, My Lord?*

[32]Scudder, *Modeling My Life.*

[33]Beaux, *Background with Figures.*

[34]"Annie Louise Cary," *NAW*, 1:297-98.

[35]"Ernestine Schumann-Heink," *WWW*, p. 721. "Emma Antonia Joanna Juch," *WWW*, p. 443. "Fannie Bloomfield Zeisler," *WWW*, p. 914.

[36]Barrymore, *Memories*, pp. 43-46.

[37]"Mary G. Shaw," *NAW*, 3:277-78. Mary Shaw, "Mary Shaw, "My 'Immoral' Play: The Story of the First American Production of 'Mrs. Warren's Profession,'" *McClures*, 38 (April 1912), pp. 684-94.

[38]"May Wright Sewall," *WWW*, p. 731. Bertha Damaris Knobe, "Mrs. May Wright Sewall: Leader of 5,000,000 Women," *Harpers Bazar*, 33 (June 2, 1900), pp. 269-71.

[39]"Grace Hoadley Dodge," *NAW*, 1:489-92.

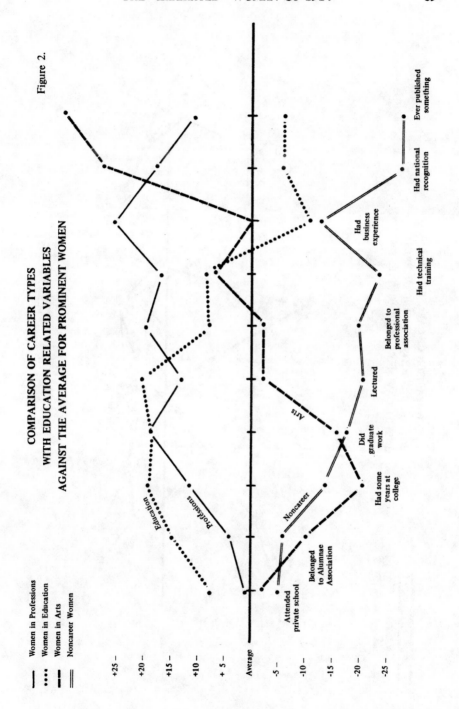

Figure 2.

COMPARISON OF CAREER TYPES
WITH EDUCATION RELATED VARIABLES
AGAINST THE AVERAGE FOR PROMINENT WOMEN

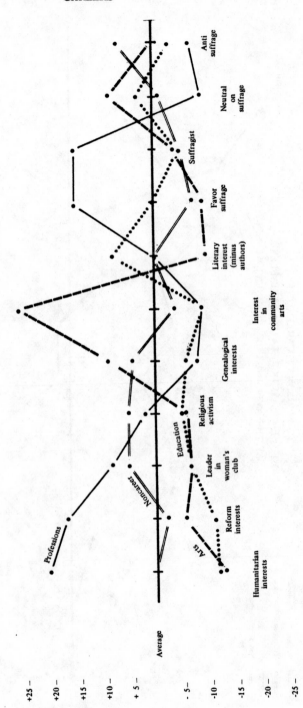

Figure 3.

COMPARISON OF CAREER TYPES
REGARDING ACTIVITIES AND INTERESTS
AGAINST THE AVERAGE FOR PROMINENT WOMEN

Figure 4.

CAREER TYPES WITH
MISCELLANEOUS VARIABLES
AGAINST THE AVERAGE FOR PROMINENT WOMEN

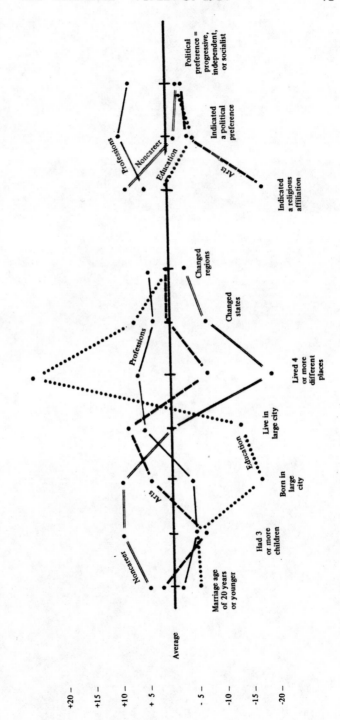

CHAPTER IV

MARRIAGE

The expanding opportunities for higher education and careers for woman challenged the ideal of woman as solely a wife and mother. Although proponents of higher education for women constantly reiterated that broader learning served to make women more competent as mothers, it could not be denied that college women did not have as high a marriage rate as lesser-educated women. In addition most college graduates worked for a while, even if they later married. The increasing career opportunities gave women respectable means of self-support and attractive alternatives to being purely housewives. While some people were alarmed at these trends, seeing in them the apocalyptic danger of race extinction, many others, even among conservatives, saw the wisdom of equipping women to be self-supporting in the face of possible spinsterhood or widowhood. Higher education came to be generally accepted for women in the early twentieth century as did careers for unmarried women and widows. However, the debate about careers for *mothers* continued to rage.

Woman's sphere expanded in directions other than education or career opportunities during the late nineteenth and early twentieth centuries. Women began to emerge as a potent political force in the life of the community. A small group of women had participated in the abolition movement during the first half of the nineteenth century, but it was not until the peak of the temperance movement, the growth of women's clubs, and the rise of the Progressive reform movement in the last decades of the century that significant numbers of American women emerged from their households to participate in political and social activity.

These activities will be discussed in some detail later, but it should be noted here that what had been unthinkable in the early nineteenth century--women "politicking"--became acceptable by the early decades of the next century.

A. Change in the Feminine Ideal

The widespread interest of middle-class women in careers and outside activities indicated a pervasive discontent among American women with the traditional sphere of hearth and home, as well as a new affluence and household innovations which allowed greater leisure time.

Writer after writer chastised women for their discontent. Amelia Barr, who did not begin her writing career until after she was widowed at 35 years, wrote:

> . . .There had never been a time in the world's history, when female discontent has assumed so much, and demanded so much, as at the present day; and both the satisfied and the dissatisfied woman may well pause to consider, whether the fierce fever of unrest which has possessed so large a number of the sex is not rather a delirium than a conviction; whether indeed they are not just as foolishly impatient to get out of their Eden, as was the woman Eve six thousand years ago.

She went on to excoriate the women who, she claimed, were dissatisfied with their duties, especially "the married women who neglect husband, children and homes for the foolish *éclat* of the club and platform, or for any assumed obligation, social, intellectual or political, which conflicts with their domestic duties." Barr even condemned the unmarried women who "having comfortable homes and loving protectors, are discontent with their happy secluded security and rush into weak art or feeble literature, or dubious singing and acting, because their vanity and restless immorality lead them into the market place, or on to the stage."[1]

Another popular writer, Margaret Deland, laid the blame for much of the prevailing discontent on the change in the feminine ideal. She contrasted the achievements of her mother's generation with the aspirations of the young women of the twentieth century:

> Who of us women in our comfortable living, dare compare ourselves to our mothers? They did not talk about their 'rights'; they fulfilled them--in taking care of their families. They did not talk about 'reforms'; they would have thought interference in municipal questions, and agitation for legislation, most unbecoming and unfeminine. . . .(That. . .would be the name of their ideal--selflessness.) Can we remember that selflessness, and see no difference between it and the present feminine individualism?

Deland maintained that the old ideals of selflessness and duty were being substituted by a new individualism, which was, in her opinion, merely another word for selfishness. Individualism manifested itself in the desire of women for careers and involvement in a variety of activities. She blamed the colleges for the propagation of this new ideal among women. Deland saw individualism as a direct threat to the institutions of marriage and the family. Deland said at one point.

> The individualist believes that happiness is the purpose of marriage--whereas happiness is only an incident of marriage. The purpose of marriage is the protection of the family idea. . .if the incident of

happiness is lost, duty remains! The obligation of contract remains; marriage remains. . . .Marriage is civilization's method of remaining civilized.

Deland's ideas were preceded in an article by Anna Rogers in which she stated, "The rock upon which most of the flower-bedecked marriage barges go to pieces is the latter-day cult of individualism; the worship of the brazen calf of Self." She saw the increase in divorce in the United States as an especially evil result of the changes occurring in the life styles of American women.[2]

Many other women who supported the broadening of women's opportunities countered such articles with their own propaganda. They ranged from radicals like Charlotte Perkins Gilman, to moderate social scientists like Anna Garlin Spencer, to conservatives like Emma Churchman Hewitt. Gilman demanded full equality between men and women, but feared this could never be reached so long as women were economically dependent upon men. She thus advocated, in her widely-acclaimed *Women and Economics*, that women become self-supporting and make use of centralized nurseries and cooperative kitchens to free themselves from domestic drudgery.[3]

The Unitarian minister and reformer Anna Garlin Spencer agreed that full equality was desirable, but could not accept the premise that women must be financially independent to attain equality. Spencer believed it was possible for married women to take part in the broader community life while still relying on their husbands for financial support. Her pragmatic and reasonable views of divorce saw no dire threat from it to the family as an institution. In fact, in *Woman's Share in Social Culture*, she declared, "In so far as greater freedom in divorce is one effect of the refusal of women to sustain marital relations with unfit men. . .it is a movement for the benefit and not for the injury of the family." At the same time, Spencer did not condone "selfishness, superficial and trivial causes of pique, of wounded vanity, of rash and childish whim, or even the mere suggestive power of newspaper scandals" as adequate reasons for the "termination of the most important of all human relationships, the marriage upon which the home is builded."[4]

Emma Churchman Hewitt, an associate editor of the *Ladies Home Journal*, wrote a popular book, *Queen of Home*, which discussed a wide variety of domestic themes from home decorations and the training of children to the organization of housework. Hewitt held surprisingly broad views on occupations for women. While she considered housewifery to be the noblest of all professions, she advocated a trade or profession for all women so they could be self-supporting if the need arose. She did not limit women to traditional female professions, such as teaching or writing. Hewitt encouraged women to consider business, arts, dentistry, medicine, architecture--a wide variety, in fact, of "male" endeavors. Although she ended the book with a paean to motherhood, Hewitt said that a woman could now take a prominent place in the world, perhaps as a scientist or philanthropist, and still be "Queen of Home." Such sentiments from one who considered the role of housewife to be the highest calling of womanhood demonstrate how acceptable the idea of a broadening sphere for women had become for many essentially conservative, middle class folk.[5]

In part, such attitudes may have been a mere pragmatic acceptance of contemporary American social reality. The real condition of married life and the role of prominent women in the family in the early twentieth century did represent a change from the ideals and realities of the mid-nineteenth century when the mothers of these prominent women had married and reared their families. What were the realities of married life among prominent women in the late nineteenth and early twentieth centuries? This chapter will examine not only basic marital statistics, but also career relations, sexual relations, and fertility. The end of the chapter considers the break-up of marriages through divorce and widowhood.

B.   Career Relations in Marriage

In general, marriage and birth rates had fallen among middle and upper class women in the United States. Higher education acted to lower those rates further. While two-thirds (67.6%) of the socially visible women in 1914 were married, this compared to a marriage rate of about 90% for the general population.

Most of the women (42%) married between the ages of 21 and 25. Another 28% married at a later stage, between the years of 26 and 30. This data resembles that of other studies, which fix the mean age of marriage at twenty-five years for women born in 1850.[6] Women who had done graduate work or had attended a professional school were naturally more likely to marry slightly later than the average--usually after the age of 26.

While most of the husbands of prominent women were in business or a profession, it was unusual for an entry in the *Woman's Who's Who* to identify herself in terms of her husband's position or career. Less than one-quarter of the group made a specific mention of their husband's occupation, although another 8% included an unspecific title when they gave their husband's name, e.g., Dr. Thomas Smith. Those husbands clearly identified in their wives' biographical entries represented a variety of professions, from law and medicine to artistic endeavors. Academic life received the most notice and included husbands who were either administrators or professors. Politics was the second most-mentioned field. Political husbands ranged from judges and governors to senators and Presidents, current and former. After academics and politicians, clergymen and military officers were specifically noted by their wives. Nevertheless, the great majority of prominent married women mentioned only their husband's name, and one even failed to do that, although she admitted she was married and had a son.[7] Clearly, married women identified themselves as individuals with their own interests and accomplishments; they did not look upon themselves as mere social extensions of their husbands.

At the same time, a husband's attitudes toward his wife's career and activities was often a crucial factor in her productivity and success. Sara Teasdale enjoyed her greatest poetic productivity during the early happy years of her marriage. Julia C. R. Dorr achieved her first publishing success when her husband submitted one of her poems to a magazine without her knowledge. The marriage of Amy Beach to a widower 24 years older than she ended her frequent appearances as a concert pianist, but began her career as the most prominent woman composer of her time. Although her husband, Henry Harris Aubrey Beach, was a member of the Harvard medical faculty, his knowledge of music enabled him to be one of her most helpful critics. Dr. Beach encouraged his wife to study composition independently so as to avoid teachers whose influence might impinge upon her freedom and originality. Her *Mass* in E flat major, first performed by the Handel and Haydn Society with the Boston Symphony Orchestra in 1892, and her aria "Eilende Wolken," introduced by the New York Symphony Orchestra also in 1892, were the first works by a woman composer ever performed by those musical organizations. The death of her husband in 1910 for some reason terminated the most prolific period of her career, even though Amy Beach was then only 43 years old.[8]

Some husbands sacrificed domestic amenities in order to encourage their wives' aspirations and interests. When Gene Stratton-Porter turned to writing fiction, Charles Porter insisted that the family eat their meals at the village hotel in order to relieve his wife of domestic responsibilities. Supporting the temperance work of his wife, Lillian Ames Stevens, Michael Stevens agreed that she should substitute her reform work for household duties. This resulted in leaving their daughter with a governess while Lillian Stevens traveled throughout the state as president of the Maine Woman's Christian Temperance Union, and subsequently throughout the nation as an executive officer of the National Woman's Christian Temperance Union.[9]

Other husbands sacrificed their own time in order to aid their wives' work. The Rev. Gustavus Rosinbury Alden, a Presbyterian minister, assisted his wife, Isabella Macdonald Alden, with her religious writing. He helped with the editing chores of her immensely popular children's Sunday school weekly, the *Pansy*, and he helped her to answer the correspondence of her many readers. May Wright Sewall's second husband, Theodore Lovett Sewall, closed his own boys' school to give more effective assistance to his wife's institution, the Girls' Classical School of Indianapolis. John H. DeVoe composed suffrage songs with which to embellish the lectures of his wife, Emma Smith DeVoe.[10]

Reformers like Lillian Stevens of the WCTU and the suffragist Emma Smith DeVoe received little if any monetary compensation for their hours of work and travel. Thus, financial support from their husbands was especially crucial for many such women. But marriages between female reformers and male feminists did not always produce idyllic relationships. Carrie Chapman Catt recounted to her biographer what she witnessed at the home of the president of the Iowa Woman Suffrage Association when Catt gave her first lecture for the organization in 1887. The husband of the president met Catt at the train and told her that he had personally made all the arrangements for the meeting. He impressed Catt with his enthusiasm for the suffrage cause, and she was relieved that his work was rewarded when her speech was well-received by the audience. The next morning, after the husband had gone to work, Catt complimented the wife on her liberal husband. After a pause,

> . . .the wife told her quietly that when Carrie's letter came asking her to arrange the meeting, she had read it at the breakfast table. She had no money of her own and had to ask her husband literally for every cent she spent. If he approved of the outlay, he gave her the exact sum required; if he did not approve, he withheld it. She, the president of the state suffrage association, did not possess even the small sum necessary for lights and janitor service for a church meeting. She passed the letter across the table to her husband, saying, "What shall I do about this?" He read it and replied cheerfully, "I'll attend to it," and had been as good as his word. His wife smiled as she recounted his labors for woman's rights the past week and his pride in his meeting.

As Catt's biographer recorded, the irony of that smile on the face of the penniless wife of a feminist husband was not lost upon Catt. Nor did Catt fail to make a mental note that "if the wife had been of tougher fiber in the first place, she would now be better off spiritually and financially."[11]

Catt's own second marriage was in decided contrast to the above scene. When Carrie Chapman married George William Catt in 1890, they signed a legally attested contract which provided that Carrie Chapman Catt would have two months in the fall and two months in the spring to do her suffrage work. Obviously believing in the cause himself, George Catt encouraged his wife to do the reforming while he earned a living for them both. His death fifteen years later left his wife financially independent and enabled her to devote her full time to the suffrage cause. Considering the crucial role that Carrie Chapman Catt was to play in the successful passage of the Nineteenth Amendment, it was certainly fortuitous for her to have found this kind of economic and emotional support from George Catt. No doubt her contribution to the suffrage cause would still have been considerable had she remained the self-supporting widow of Leo Chapman. Nevertheless, freedom from economic worries and the means to travel and to make financial contributions to the cause may have honed her talents and directed her energies in ways that would have been impossible before her second marriage.[12]

Many women profited from having husbands who shared their professional interests. Catherine Waugh met her future husband, Frank Hathorn McCulloch, in law school. After their marriage, they established a joint practice and renamed the firm McCulloch & McCulloch. Louise Blanchard, the first professional American woman architect, married her business partner, Robert Armour Bethune, their firm becoming R. A. and L. Bethune. The editors of the *Woman of the Century* recorded this tribute to the beneficial effects of shared marital interests in the entry of Elia Wilkinson Peattie:

> Her marriage, in 1883, to Robert Burns Peattie, a journalist of Chicago, was most fortunate. Nothing could have prevented her entering upon her career as a writer, but a happy marriage, with one who sympathized with her ambitions and who was also able to give her much important assistance in the details of authorship was to her a most important event. From that time she has been an indefatigable worker.[13]

In many cases, the husband actually introduced the wife to the area of interest which would become her life work. After Ada Chastina Burpee married the Rev. Benjamin Franklin Bowles, it was natural that she should take an active part in the parish work of her husband's church. Her initial success teaching an adult Bible class led her to deeper religious study, under the guidance of her husband. According to *Woman of the Century*, "Mr. Bowles desired that his wife should be in all things his companion, and, after giving her a thorough course in theology, he encouraged her to preach the gospel, which she had long felt called to declare." Ada Bowles was ordained some years later as a Universalist minister and embarked upon a career in her own pastorates.[14]

In the case of Fanny Bullock Workman, an avocation of her husband became a vocation for them both. Dr. William Hunter Workman introduced his wife to mountain climbing in the White Mountains of Vermont. After some years traveling throughout the Mediterranean region, India, and Southeast Asia on bicycles, the Workmans attempted their first important climb in the Karakorum range of the northwest Himalayas in 1899. Over the years, the Workmans developed an efficient mountaineering partnership. One year Dr. Workman would take charge of the general planning and organization, while Fanny Workman would attend to photographic and scientific research projects. The next year they would exchange responsibilities. The five volumes published by the Workmans about their expeditions in the Himalayas remain outstanding references for the Karakorum region, and attest to a remarkable marriage of shared interests.[15]

Of course, shared interests could place a strain upon marriages where there were discrepancies in talent. The artist Henry Brown Fuller was less gifted and less original than his wife Lucia Fairchild Fuller. Her greater success in their mutual profession led to a permanent separation. Hetty Howland Robinson Green and her husband were both millionaire financiers and entrepreneurs. But when Edward Green, a more daring speculator than his wife, went bankrupt in 1885, Hetty Green refused to underwrite his debts, thereby causing a separation.[16]

Even in cases where women were not in direct competition with their husbands through mutual careers, it was not unusual that a woman's determination to pursue her own interests and career would put a fatal stress on the marriage relation. As a consequence, the divorce rate among married prominent women (18%) was more than double the national rate (6-8%).[17] Divorce and separation will be discussed in detail later in the chapter, but it is worth noting some examples of clashes between women's careers and their marriages.

Rheta Childe Dorr's impulses to experience life beyond her home and to write about colorful people and events conflicted with her husband's conservative ideas of a wife's place. After some years of separate rooms and a formal relationship, the Dorrs separated permanently. Hortense Sparks Malsch Ward was too energetic and ambitious for her husband. After a period of marital discord during which Hortense Malsch became a public stenographer and notary, the couple was divorced. Hortense Malsch went on to study law and become a court reporter. Three years after her divorce, she married a lawyer, William Henry Ward, with whom she completed her legal studies and went into joint practice. Mary Coffin Ware Dennett's marriage was at first happy when she worked with her architect husband, William Hartley Dennett, as a consulting home decorator. Mary Dennett was not altogether sure of her artistic talent, however, and she became increasingly interested in reform causes. By the tenth year of their marriage, she was working full time for woman's suffrage. William Dennett failed to share these new interests, and estrangement and divorce soon followed.[18]

A number of other talented women relinquished flourishing careers when they chose to marry. The opera singer Emma Juch retired at the height of her career when she married at thirty-three. Vinnie Ream received a commission from Congress to execute a statue of the recently-assassinated Abraham Lincoln for the Capitol rotunda when she was just 18 years old. In her late twenties, Ream won a $20,000 federal commission for a bronze of Admiral David Farragut. But at thirty, Vinnie Ream married Lieutenant Richard Leveridge Hoxie, and gave up her professional artistic career in deference to her husband's wishes. Carrie Chapman Catt became engaged to Leo Chapman two weeks after meeting him. She resigned her high position as superintendent of schools in Mason City, Iowa, at the end of the term, and married Leo Chapman the following winter. Catt approached her second romance much more soberly. As we have seen, she consented to marry George Catt only after receiving legal assurance that she could continue her suffrage work.[19]

For other talented women, it was not simply marriage, but motherhood that interrupted or even ended promising careers. After coauthoring fifteen scientific papers with her husband, publishing twenty more of her own, and collaborating on the publication of a monograph, Rosa Smith Eigenmann, the first eminent woman ichthyologist, retired from active research to rear five children. The added burdens of a retarded daughter and mentally ill son preempted her social life and reduced her scientific work to the editing of her husband's manuscripts. After some debate, the trustees of Barnard College allowed Emily Smith Putnam to continue in her position as dean of Barnard after her marriage to George Haven Putnam. When she became pregnant, Putnam tendered her resignation without an argument.[20]

These last cases illustrate the range of differences between choice and coercion when women gave up careers after marriage. Ream retired from her career when her husband asked her to do so. Might she have continued had he been supportive or even indifferent to her work? Though the Eigenmann example is more complex, prominent women in 1914 generally did not have to abandon their work to rear a family. In days of inexpensive live-in maids and governesses, to concentrate one's energies solely on keeping house and rearing children was usually a matter of choice. Illustrative of that is the majority of prominent women who continued to pursue careers while caring for families.

Marriage and motherhood complicated the careers of women particularly in education, their principal outlet. In academic life women often confronted discriminatory laws or customs against marriage. Although Catt readily resigned her position, it is debatable whether she could have continued her position as superintendent of schools as a married woman. The questioned propriety of a married dean of Barnard College further illustrates the point. While laws regarding the eligibility of married women for public teaching positions varied from place to place, they negatively affected the careers of many women.

C.   Sexual Relations in Marriage

If career relationships within marriages are discernible with some ease, sexual relations between husbands and wives offer a greater challenge to historical investigation. Of the autobiographies and biographies consulted, none gave personal information on this important topic. Formerly, one was reduced to searching through novels and advice literature for clues relating to the sexual attitudes and behavior of women and men during this period. Now with the discovery of the Clelia Mosher questionnaires at Stanford University, a small amount of concrete data is available on marital relations in the late nineteenth and early twentieth centuries.

Clelia Duel Mosher, who appears in the *Woman's Who's Who*, gathered information over a twenty-year period on the sexual habits and attitudes of married women. She began when she was a college student at the University of Wisconsin in the early 1890's, but apparently discontinued her research during a decade of private medical practice. After 1910 she enjoyed unusual opportunities to collect data as a member of the Department of Hygiene and medical advisor to women students at Stanford University.[21]

In important respects the women whom Mosher interviewed appear to be closely similar to those found in *Woman's Who's Who*. The median age in both groups was about 50 as of 1914. The great majority (75%) in the Mosher survey attended prestigious colleges or universities, ranging geographically from the East to the Far West. Most of the women had married well-educated professional men. In fact, many of the husbands were college professors. The two groups also averaged about the same number of children (2.4 children per mother in the *WWW* compared to 2.7 for the Mosher women).

The major apparent difference between the women Mosher interviewed and the women in the *Woman's Who's Who* was their career orientation. While most of the Mosher women had taught a few years before marriage, hardly any of them pursued sustained careers. Nor were any questions asked regarding their current activities in the late 1890's and early 1900's. Thus, one cannot tell whether they belonged to the same kinds of clubs or whether they were active in humanitarian and reform work as were the women in the *Woman's Who's Who*. Nevertheless, the information about their backgrounds definitely places them in the same age group and social class as the women in the *Woman's Who's Who*. Their sexual attitudes and practices are thus relevant to the life histories of the *Woman's Who's Who* members.

The Mosher questionnaires are few in number (47), but rich in data. The questions asked of the women ranged from the backgrounds and medical histories of their families to the frequency of sexual intercourse in their marriage and the kinds of contraception they employed. Many of the women answered the twenty-five questions, with their multiple parts, in extreme detail, giving a unique glimpse into the sexual habits and beliefs of their day.

The women generally had little knowledge of sexual matters before their marriages. On one question, the women were asked, "What knowledge of sexual physiology had you before marriage? How did you obtain it?" Although seventeen out of forty-five women, or 38%, could be judged to have had considerable knowledge, even their knowledge did not always extend beyond female physiology to male physiology and sexual relations. The women with considerable information obtained it from other women, doctors, college courses, and medical books. One woman named three sources for her expertise: medical books; life on a farm, during which she witnessed animals breeding; and frank talks with her mother. Another woman described how her knowledge progressed from her sub-teen years to her marriage at about the age of 26:

> At 12 years my mother told me the facts about menstruation, and the physiology of childbirth. I knew nothing of sexual connection until I was perhaps 16 or 18 when I read about it in the textbooks to which we were referred when we studied physiology [at Cornell]. A few months before my marriage a wise woman friend told me about the various ways of "regulating conception" in use, theories concerning the sexual relations, etc., and referred me to one or two books on the subject. These books I read before I was married.[22]

The majority of the women were not so fortunate as the previous two examples. Of the women with slight sexual information, another Cornell graduate claimed her knowledge came from "plant reproduction and casual observation of animals." A woman with a high school education said she got her information from others girls. "Mother taught us that such things were not only not talked about but also not thought of. School child at 14 told what intercourse was. Was shocked and didn't believe it." Even a woman whose mother was a doctor suffered from ignorance on these matters. She said her knowledge of sexual physiology consisted of

> Vague ideas from fellow pupils at school. My mother was a physician but refused to instruct me when I asked questions. I remember well the first time I asked a question which showed that I already had the idea there was something shameful about child bearing. Yet she told me I would read books about it when I was older, and I never asked again.[22]

The women with some such slight knowledge of sexual matters comprised 31% of the sample, while the women with virtually no knowledge comprised another 31%. One woman, to illustrate her absolute lack of knowledge, stated that she ran away from her husband a month after her marriage, but that she was sent back by her parents and told to behave.[24]

Another of the questions asked, "Do you habitually sleep with your husband? What reasons for so doing or not?" Of those that answered the question, about two-thirds (64%) of the women replied in the affirmative, and almost one-third (32%) in the negative. Two of the women in the later group indicated that they had slept with their husbands until children came along. Then when waking babies disturbed their husbands, they discontinued the practice. Others indicated that it was more healthful to sleep alone, and two of the women feared the temptation that doing so would present to their husbands. One stated that she and her husband did not regularly sleep together, "Because sleeping on my guard made me nervous and irritable. It made the necessary control on my husband's part too hard." The other gave three reasons for sleeping separately: "More comfortable alone. Consider it more wholesome. To avoid temptation of too frequent intercourse."[25]

Other women appeared more ambivalent about the question. One even indicated that sleeping together was purely a matter of the season of the year. "Together in winter, apart in summer is what we found to be most comfortable." Another said that while they slept together for companionship, it was also a matter of economic convenience, presumably meaning that there was no other room. Case no. 24 stated bluntly, the "Chief reason for occupying bed is that we are yet in the phase of 'getting along.' Personally I prefer to sleep alone always." An older woman, born in 1832, said that she and her husband slept together "because it was the habit of people when I married to do so."[26]

Most of the women indicated that they shared their husband's bed for much more positive reasons. A woman who had graduated from the University of California with her husband in the 1880's said that they slept together for comfort and "because it keeps us close together. I suppose separate beds are more hygienic, but I believe people drift apart when they do not sleep together." Another woman expressed a change of heart about the matter. She said, "Yes, [we sleep together] when he is at home. I sleep much better and feel altogether more comfortable. The first year [of marriage]. . .I had a separate bed, believing that was the right thing; but I abandoned it entirely before the end of the year." A third woman gave this positive reason for sharing the same bed. "We sleep together from the choice of both of us and because of the companionship, rest, and pleasure which come with our being together."[27] If most women simply followed their personal inclinations in choosing their beds, a considerable number of them allowed factors such as custom, availability of space, and curious notions about hygiene to influence their conduct.

While a few of the women took little pleasure in sexual relations with their husbands, to most of the women sexual intercourse was both agreeable and desirable. In fact, most of the women with children maintained normal relations with their husbands during their pregnancies. Yet the frequency of intercourse reported by the Mosher women fell below the averages established decades later by the Indiana Sex Research Institute in *Sexual Behavior in the Human Female* (1953), commonly known as the Kinsey report. For example, average marital intercourse for the 20-30 year age group was 2.2 per week for the Kinsey women compared to 1.2 per week for the Mosher women. In the 30-40 age range, the Kinsey women averaged 1.5 per week while the Mosher women averaged .81 per week. The trend continued for those in the 40-50 age group. While the Kinsey women averaged 1.0 per week, the Mosher women were down to .64 per week. Then an aberration occurs. The Kinsey women in the 50-60 age group reported an average intercourse of about once in twelve days, which is .6 per week. Yet the Mosher women reported an average of 1.6 per week. Thus, the 50-60 year age group reported a higher frequency of intercourse than any other age group among the Mosher women, and even higher than the average for the 30-40 year old Kinsey women.[28]

Table 1. Sexual Frequency per Week by Age

	20-30 Years	30-40 Years	40-50 Years	50-60 Years
Kinsey group	2.2	1.5	1.0	.6
Mosher group	1.2 (6 cases)	.81 (12 cases)	.64 (6 cases)	1.6 (10 cases)

If that figure for the 50-60 year old Mosher women were correct, it could be interpreted as an indication of the general concern over birth control. In other words, once the women had passed their menopause, they made up for the lost time. Since, however, the figure is so out of line with the trends established both by the younger Mosher women and by the Kinsey women, it may well be unreliable. Another explanation that appears reasonable is that the women may have been thinking of their entire marriages rather than present conditions when they answered the question.

Why did the Mosher women in general maintain about half the rate of frequency as the Kinsey women? Their low rate could be interpreted to be as much a concern over birth control as to be a sign of low sexual interest. When contraceptive means were haphazard and unreliable, it is understandable that middle class men and women should turn to self-denial as a means of preventing unwanted conceptions.

Mosher also included an elaborate question on her survey regarding the purpose of sexual intercourse. She phrased the question in this way: "What do you believe to be the true purpose of intercourse? Necessity to man? Necessity to woman? Pleasure? Reproduction? What other reasons beside reproduction are sufficient to warrant intercourse?" As might be expected, Mosher received a wide variety of answers, some with detailed explanations.

The reason most frequently cited was, of course, reproduction. Thirty-eight of the forty-four women who answered this question, or 86%, felt reproduction was a legitimate reason for intercourse. But surprisingly, only 13 of that group (30% of the whole) indicated that reproduction was the primary purpose of intercourse, including only three women who felt that reproduction alone warranted marital relations. The vast majority of women who cited reproduction as a purpose of intercourse also cited other reasons as of seemingly equal importance.[29]

The second most popular reason for intercourse among the Mosher women was pleasure. Twenty-seven of the women, or 61%, thought a "true purpose" of intercourse was pleasure to both sexes. Another two women thought pleasure applied only to men. None of the women cited pleasure alone as a reason for intercourse; it was always given along with other reasons.

While many women thought intercourse was a necessity, more of the Mosher women thought it was a necessity to men than to women. Seventeen of the women, or 39%, thought intercourse was a necessity to both men and women. Another seven women stated that intercourse was necessary to men, without being necessary to women, bringing the total up to 55% for the women who felt intercourse was a necessity to men. Presumably, most of these women thought in terms of physical necessity, but at least one woman qualified her answer to be emotional necessity.

About a quarter of the women added comments that specified love, or the spiritual union between husband and wife, as a true purpose for intercourse. One woman stated it in this way: "I think to the man and woman married from love, it [intercourse] may be used *temperately,* as one of the highest manifestations of love granted us by our Creator." Other women, in asserting love as a primary reason, sought to counter the notion that reproduction alone warranted marital relations. Case No. 15 wrote: "The desire of both husband and wife for this expression of their union seems to me the first and highest reason for intercourse. The desire for offspring is a secondary, incidental, although entirely worthy motive but could never to me make intercourse right unless the mutual desire were also present." Another woman was more vehement. "I do not think this reason [reproduction] alone warrants it at all; I think it is only warranted as an expression of true and passionate love." A woman who had been married only a year said that her ideas on the subject had changed since her marriage:

> My ideas as to the reason for [intercourse] have changed materially from what they were before marriage. I then thought reproduction was the only object and that once brought about, intercourse should cease. But in my experience the habitual bodily expression of love has a deep psychological effect in making possible complete mental sympathy, and perfecting the spiritual union that must be the lasting "marriage" after the passion of love has passed away with years.[30]

Thus, while most of the Mosher women cited reproduction as purpose of intercourse, it was most commonly given along with other reasons. The majority of the women did not think of reproduction as the primary purpose of intercourse. On the other hand, no other reason--pleasure, necessity, love--was cited as often as reproduction as a reason for intercourse. And only one of the other reasons--love--rivaled reproduction as a primary reason for intercourse.

A common theme that runs through many of the women's responses is that marital relations should be strictly mutual. The idea was evident especially in the responses to the final question, "What to you would be an ideal habit?" One woman wrote, "No habit at all but the most sensitive regard of each member of the couple for the personal feeling and desires and health of the other. In fact, true and tender love, wide awake to the whole of life, should dictate marriage relations." In answer to the same question, several other women gave a figure, such as one time a week, qualified by phrases such as, "when both want it," "when acceptable to both," and "when desired by both." Case No. 18, a woman born in 1855, answered that the ideal habit would be one time a month after menstruation--which would keep alive "in me the sense of nearness which I regard indispensable to a happy marriage. But ideal must be compromise between two and must be best for both."[31]

There seemed to be some amount of criticism aimed at the husbands in regard to this mutuality. One older woman, born in 1844, felt that marital relations should ideally be a "special occasion each time" and that the "man should court [his] wife each time"--treatment she was apparently not used to getting. Another woman complained, "men have not been properly trained--seemingly in regard to eliciting the woman's full pleasure in marital relations." In drawing some rare conclusions from her studies, Mosher likewise criticized men for some of the sexual maladjustments she found in her patients. She said these maladjustments stemmed from:

    a) lack of consideration of the woman by too frequent coitus destroying psychologic sex impulse

    b) lack of understanding of slower time reaction in women making marital relations for the woman without the normal physical response. This leaves organs of woman overcongested.[32]

Besides mutuality, the risk of conception also concerned many women in regard to ideal marital relations. A woman born in 1868 expressed both ideas in her response to the last question about the ideal habit: "Occasional intercourse, with control over conception, everything to be absolutely mutual." A graduate of Radcliffe definitely separated sex for pleasure and sex for reproduction in her answer to the same question. She stated that the ideal habit would be "(1) four to six times a month when conception is least likely to take place--as expression of love, (2) once in a while for procreation." The response of a Cornell graduate, born in 1860, shows how serious the question of conception could become for marital relations among educated people.

> In general terms the ideal habit would be that which should most perfectly and completely serve as the physical expression of the spiritual union of husband and wife. My husband and I have not found yet what to us is an ideal habit. We believe in intercourse for its own sake—we wish it for ourselves and spiritually miss it, rather than physically, when it does not occur, because it is the highest, most sacred expression of our oneness. On the other hand there are sometimes long periods when we are not willing to incur even a slight risk of pregnancy, and then we deny ourselves the intercourse, feeling all the time that we are losing that which keeps us closest to each other.

Another woman, born in 1864, indicated that she and her husband had also practiced denial of marital relations in order to prevent pregnancy. In answer to question no. 24 about the method of contraception employed, she said that during the first ten years of their marriage they had sometimes gone two to three years at a time with no intercourse. She also added that she "would not do it again." Later in the marriage, the couple used the rhythm method as a means of birth control. The willingness of these last two couples to forego marital relations for long periods is indicative of the determination of educated middle class people in the late nineteenth century to plan their families and limit the number of their children. Such self-denial was no doubt common, although perhaps not to the extent of going two to three years without intercourse as had the last couple.[33]

The vast majority of the women (83%), including the two cases mentioned above, indicated definite methods of contraception they were employing to limit conception. Only four women failed to answer the question, and another four were currently using no means of contraception.

The most popular method was the douche. Eleven of the women mentioned using the douche in combination with other methods such as the rhythm method or withdrawal. Thus, nineteen of the thirty-nine women (49%) who used contraception used the douche. The formulas for these douches varied from warm water to cold water to soap and water to complicated recipes. A woman born in 1846 gave the following prescription: "a teaspoon of powdered alum to pint of water or alcohol 1/3 or 1/4 used as a douche." Another woman gave the weight of authority to her practice when she stated that a warm water douche was "recommended by a physician in good standing."[34]

The second most popular means of contraception was the rhythm method. Only four women used the rhythm method alone, but another eight used it in combination with other means, bringing the total to 31% who used the rhythm method. Most of the women who explained their calculations for the rhythm method had correctly determined the fertile period. For example, one woman stated that she never conceived "if intercourse was omitted for 14 days after menstruation." Another woman had misleading advice handed down from her mother. She stated that she "Practiced rule no intercourse ten days after menstruation and three days before which served my mother with douche immediately after. Did not answer in my case." She proceeded to add that "the French method" of prevention, probably the condom, was perfectly successful.[35]

The two means next in popularity were the condom and withdrawal. Both methods were used by 26% of the women. In each case, half of the women used the method alone, and half used it in combination with other measures. A couple of women mentioned avoidance of withdrawal as a means because it was detrimental to the husband. One of the women even stated that her doctor had fitted her with a pessary, or early form of diaphragm, "so as not to have withdrawal because bad for husband."[36]

Margaret Sanger claimed that the two most popular modes of contraception used by the middle classes, before her big campaign to introduce the douche and the diaphragm in the early 1900's, were withdrawal and the condom. While those two methods were in general use, they were not as popular as the rhythm method or the douche. It also appears that the douche was in widespread use already in the late nineteenth century.[37]

Of the four women who used the most advanced devices of birth control, the pessary, or cap over the uterus, three out of four used a combination of as many as three and even four methods of contraception. One woman mentioned using the pessary, condom, withdrawal, and rhythm methods, while another named the pessary, douche, condom, and withdrawal. They apparently wanted to leave little to chance.[38]

In summary, the Mosher survey suggests that the vast majority of educated middle class women in the late nineteenth and early twentieth centuries enjoyed sexual relations with their husbands in their marriages. This was demonstrated in their responses about the frequency of intercourse, the purpose of intercourse, and ideal relations in marriage. While reproduction was the most commonly cited rationale for intercourse, such motives as pleasure and love were as important to the majority of the Mosher women. One of the chief concerns of these

women regarding marital relations was that they be conducted on a
strictly mutual basis. Implied in that concern was a certain amount of
criticism of male attitudes and technique.   The other major concern,
which was probably the most detrimental factor affecting marital relations
in this era, was the risk of conception.   These women and their husbands
had such a will to regulate their families that it precluded sexual relations
at inopportune times. Such fear of unwanted children and the resultant
denial of normal relations no doubt placed severe strain at times on the
marriage relationship.   Despite these concerns, however, the women
welcomed sex as a healthy, normal part of their marriages.

D.   Fertility

        The fertility level of the women both in the *Woman's Who's
Who* and the Mosher survey demonstrates that the contraceptive
techniques and the self-denial employed by these women did aid them in
regulating their families.   The 879 women in the sample from the
Woman's Who's Who had 963 children, or live births. This averages to
2.4 children per mother, or 1.6 children per wife. For the prominent
women altogether, it is only 1.1. children per woman. Put another way,
every 1000 prominent women in the *Woman's Who's Who* gave birth to
only 530 daughters, many of whom died in infancy. They were not only
below zero growth rates; they were rapidly dying out.
        The fertility ratios for the women in the Mosher survey were
only slightly higher than those for the women in the *Woman's Who's
Who.* The forty-five women with complete answers had 102 live births.
This averages to 2.7 children per mother, or 2.3 children per wife. The
big difference between the Mosher women and those in the *Woman's
Who's Who* came in the number of childless wives. In the *Woman's
Who's Who,* childless wives represented over one-third (33.4%) of the
married women; whereas in the Mosher survey, childless wives
represented only 15% of that group.   This accounts for the similar
statistics for children per mother but very different statistics for children
per wife.
        Inasmuch as the Mosher women provided very detailed accounts
of their pregnancies, one can examine their fertility more closely than can
be done with the women in the *Woman's Who's Who.* Disregarding
three pregnancies in progress, of 127 conceptions mentioned in the
Mosher survey, there were 22 miscarriages, 3 stillbirths, and 102 live
births. Of the live births, 9 children died in infancy (before they reached
the age of 1 year), producing an infant mortality rate of 8.8%. This
compares favorably with a national infant mortality rate of 14.5% in 1900
for children under 1 year. Of the total 127 conception, 38 (30%) did not
result in living children past five years. For the thirty-eight mothers in

the Mosher survey, eighteen (47%) experienced miscarriage, stillbirth, or infant mortality--or combinations of the three. Seven of that group, or 18%, experienced infant mortality. This is actually low compared with the women who appeared both in *Notable American Women* and the *Woman's Who's Who;* of the 125 mothers in that group, 37% faced the death of one or more of their children.[39]

The statistics do not, of course, reveal the emotional trauma that such infant and child deaths often caused. One of the Mosher women wrote this poignant note of a son born in 1891: "A large child (12 lbs.), proclaimed the finest newborn child ever seen by doctor, nurse and alas! undertaker. He had an obstruction in breathing and lived only 10 hours." The following year the woman's two-year-old girl died during an operation; the child had been ill and retarded since she was 5 months old. The couple was then left with one son. Amelia Huddleston Barr, the novelist lost three of her first eight children before they were one year old. In a yellow fever epidemic in Galveston in 1866, her nine-year-old son, her three-year old son, and her husband all died. Three months later, another son was born, but lived only five days. Out of nine children, Amelia Barr was eventually left with three daughters.[40]

The deaths of infants and children affected the women in a variety of ways. The writer Ella Wheeler Wilcox and her husband turned to Spiritualism and studied under a Hindu mystic in the 1890's in an attempt to reach their infant son who had died only a few hours after birth. More typically, women gave a greater amount of their energy to careers and activities as an antidote to grief and as a way of filling their time. Kate Nichols Trask did not begin her career as a writer until after her fourth and last child had died. Although Maud Nathan had dabbled in philanthropic pursuits as a young mother, it was the death of her only child in 1895 that inaugurated her full-time career as a social reformer. For Alice Ames Winter, it was the loss of her 14 year old son that stimulated a greater interest in women's activities in Minneapolis.[41]

While the deaths of children gave some women a greater incentive to participate in activities outside the home, many others needed no such prodding to be active in careers, club work, and reform causes. Due to the availability and relative inexpensiveness of household help, most of the women had the aid of paid servants in caring for their children. A woman such as Clara Hampson Ueland, with seven surviving children, could not have participated in the broad range of humanitarian, cultural, and reform endeavors which interested her were it not for the retinue of servants she and her husband employed.[42] The extent to which women allowed the servants to rear their children depended, of course, upon personal preference.

Some women gave a high priority to guiding their children's development personally. Dr. Anna Manning Comfort relinquished her medical practice while her children were small. Ellen Axson Wilson, the first wife of Woodrow Wilson, educated her three children at home before they went to preparatory schools. As an outgrowth of a career in education, Martha Hillard MacLeish kept careful records of the early development of her children. She used the records to publish several articles on education in connection with the Illinois Child Study Society, of which she was president for five years (1904-09). She also studied the innovative ideas of John Dewey, which were being put to use in his progressive kindergarten, and applied those to the education of her own children.[43]

Other mothers left more of the care of their children to other family members or servants. Isabel Barrows first pursued a medical career and then shared fully in her husband's work as editor of the Unitarian weekly, the *Christian Register*. Meanwhile, she left the rearing of her daughter and adopted infant nephew to her sister and a maid. Lillian Ames Stevens substituted reform work for household duties, with the approval of her husband, and left her daughter with a governess while she lobbied throughout Maine for the Woman's Christian Temperance Union. After Rheta Childe Dorr separated from her husband, she was forced to leave her son with her sister-in-law for five years until she had a good enough job as a journalist to support herself, the child, and a governess.[44]

A few women foreswore responsibility for their children altogether. The musical comedy stars Anna Held and Lillian Russell sent their daughters to be reared in convent schools, although Russell took an active interest in her daughter's education. Another singer Alice Nielsen and the author Gertrude Atherton left their children permanently with their husbands' parents. Both pursued careers after the dissolution of unsuccessful marriages.[45]

E.   Divorce and Widowhood

Whether or not children were involved, marital failures were quite common among prominent women. Of the women found in both the *Woman's Who's Who* and *Notable American Women*, 22.4% experienced either divorce or permanent separation in their marriages. In that group, 18% took legal action and received divorces. A divorce rate of 18% was more than twice the national average (6-8%), figured for marriages over a twenty-year span beginning in 1887.[46]

As might be expected, women in the arts and women in the professions were more prone to marital failures than were women in education and noncareer women. Of the divorced women who appeared in both the *Woman's Who's Who* and *Notable American Women,* 57% were in the arts and 34% were in the professions. If one includes the marriages that ended in permanent separations, the proportions do not change. Of the women in education or non-career women, only minimal numbers experienced marital failures. Thus, the divorce rate for noncareer women (6.7%) and the marital failure rate for women in education (6%) would fit into the lower end of the national divorce rate (6-8%). For the women in the professions, the divorce rate (15.6%) was about double that of the national average, but slightly lower than the average for prominent women (18%). If one included the permanent separations, the figure rises to 19.4% compared to 22.4% for prominent women in general. Women in the arts led all categories, however. Their divorce rate was 22.4%, and their marital failure rate was 28.4%.

The high divorce rate for professional women reflected, in part, the damaging impact of their career aspirations. The cases of Rheta Childe Dorr and Hortense Sparks Malsch Ward were recounted earlier in the chapter.

Table 2.   Marriage Rates, Divorce Rates, and Marital
Failure by Occupation Type

	Marriage Rate	Marital Failure Rate (% of those married)	Divorce Rate (% of those married)
Professions	57%	19%	16%
Education	41%	6%	--
Arts	68%	28%	22%
Noncareer	94%	--	7%
Average for Prominent Women	67%	22%	18%
National Average	90%	--	6-8%

Both pursued professional careers which caused a permanent separation in the Dorr marriage and divorce in the Malsch marriage. Dedication to reform interests could be equivalent to pursuit of a career, and could thereby cause as many marital problems. Mary Coffin Ware Dennett's fervor for the suffrage cause provoked a divorce after ten years of marriage because her husband failed to share her new reform interests. In contrast, the marriage of Rose Harriet Pastor to James Graham Phelps Stokes was based upon mutual reform interests and socialist political inclinations. Rose Pastor Stokes became more and more extreme in her political views, however. By the 1920's, she was a dedicated worker for the communist party. Alienated by her radicalism, James Stokes sued for divorce in 1925.[47]

For women in the arts, the vigorous pursuit of a career also endangered or destroyed many marriages. The singer Alice Nielsen could not be contained in her marriage to a church organist. She broke with her husband and left her child with her in-laws in order to join touring choir and opera companies. Nielsen's example is illustrative of the mobility required of people in the performing arts. Singers and actresses were constantly touring the country, and this uprootedness, then as now, placed inordinate strains upon family life.[48] Yet, the artistic temperament must have been involved as well, for there were as many writers who experienced marital failures as there were performing artists. Careers in the arts may have promoted a degree of ego involvement that precluded the kind of give--and--take necessary for harmonious marital relations.

To be divorced or separated from one's husband in the early twentieth century was a social stigma for women, prominent or other wise. Some women in the arts, such as actresses, may have even profited from a certain amount of notoriety; but, for most women, divorce or separation was a social embarrassment. Josephine Woempner Clifford McCrackin fled from a paranoid husband who was threatening her life. When she turned to writing fiction to support herself, she portrayed her own experiences. She peopled her tales with heroines who had left bestial mates only to face earning a living in a society suspicious of women separated from their husbands. Even a powerful society matron such as Alva Erskine Smith Vanderbilt Belmont was affected by the criticism which greeted her divorce in 1895 from William Kissam Vanderbilt. It became a definite factor in her transformation from socialite to militant feminist. Belmont later wrote:

> I was one of the first women in America to dare to get a divorce from an influential man. Up to that time divorce had been the prerogative solely of actresses. Rich men could marry women, treat them in any way they chose, and ignore them. That is no longer

possible. I have gone down the aisle of the church when women I
had known since childhood drew back in their pews and refused to
speak to me. I have been the guest at parties where the hostess was
the only woman in the room who talked to me. Why? Because I
had dared to criticize openly an influential man's behavior.

Later in the same article Belmont added, "Someone must pay the price
in criticism, even in ostracism, for every advance which the world
makes. . . .Divorce was the cause of my first ostracism, then suffrage."
Although there was a general liberalization of public attitudes toward
divorce during the Progressive Era, most divorced women as individuals
faced the social disapproval or even ostracism that Belmont recounted.[49]

The dissolution of other marriages came by means of death
rather than separation or divorce. The death of a husband at any point
in the marriage could be a devastating experience for a woman, but
young women with small children were left especially vulnerable after
such a tragedy. Of the married women in the *Woman's Who's Who* and
Notable American Women, 12.5% became widows before they were forty
years old. Two-thirds of these women (66.5%) were left with children to
support. Most of the widows were not so fortunate as Josephine
Marshall Jewell Dodge who had married into one of the wealthiest
families in New York. When she was left with five children to care for
at the age of forty-one, she did not have to seek a means of earning a
living. Kate Harwood Waller Barrett was left with six children and
limited financial resources when her minister husband died at forty-five
years. Fortunately, however, Kate Barrett had entered upon a career
before her husband's death. She had become interested in her husband's
work with local prostitutes. Thereafter she attended medical school and
then established one of the early Florence Crittenton homes. She
continued that work after her husband's death, becoming vice-president
and general superintendent of the National Crittenton Mission.[50]

Many women had neither financial resources nor training in a
career when they became widows. Amelia Barr thought of starting a
girls' school or keeping a shop when she was forced to support herself
and three daughters. She settled upon running a boarding house for
genteel professional men. After several years of trying to eke out a
living, she went to New York where she did some teaching. Eventually
she found success as a novelist. Carrie Jacobs Bond and her son nearly
starved and were behind six months on rent at times after the insurance
money left by her husband had run out. She tried taking in boarders,
painting china, and performing songs she had written to earn their living.
A growing circle of sympathetic friends, including a number of
professional singers, helped to publicize her compositions. Songs such as

"I Love You Truly" and "Just a Wearyin' for You" became national favorites, and eventually enabled Carrie Bond to establish her own publishing company.[51]

As the last two examples illustrate, self-reliance was characteristic of the prominent women who became widows. Neither Barr nor Bond turned to relatives for aid. It may have been a question of practicality for Barr, since both her family and her husband's family resided in the British Isles. Bond, however, probably made a conscious decision not to seek help from her relatives in Wisconsin, although she lived as close as Chicago. Her own mother had been widowed when she was twelve, forcing the family to survive from the largesse of relatives. Bond clearly resented that dependence in her childhood, so it is understandable that she chose to rely on her own resources when she herself became a widow. Another striking example of this was Lasell Carbell Pickett, the widow of General George E. Pickett of Civil War fame. In the words of *Woman of the Century*, after the general had died,

> The sympathy of the South was aroused, and a subscription was started with eight-thousand dollars from one State, and pledges of thousands more from the devoted comrades of her dead hero. Hearing of that plan to put her above the anxiety of temporal want, Mrs. Pickett resolutely declined to accept financial aid, and soon secured a small government position sufficient to support herself and son.

Even after she was threatened with total blindness in 1891, Pickett retained her clerical position and still refused any aid.[52]

If one includes the women who became widows in their forties in the discussion of young widowhood, then age difference at marriage becomes a definite factor or consideration. A sizable number of women (18%) married men who were nine years or more older than they were, and half of that group married men 17 or more years older. The most extreme examples included Amy Beach, who at 18 years became the second wife of a man twenty-four years her senior; twenty-two-year-old Frances Folsom married forty-nine year-old Grover Cleveland; and Marilla Ricker, at twenty-three, married a man of fifty-six. These marriages of young women with older men seemed successful enough for the most part. Their rate for divorces and separations (14.7%) was slightly less than that for prominent women in general. In some cases, the older husbands proved to be emotional and financial patrons for their wives' work. On the other hand, the age difference also produced a high rate of widowhood. About 40% of the women who married older men were left widows while in their forties or younger. At the same time, the older men generally left their wives in better financial conditions than did the men who died young.

Of the married women found in both the *Woman's Who's Who* and *Notable American Women*, almost one-third (30%) were widowed or divorced at a young age (before 46). In that group, almost half (43%) had families to support, but over half (53.5%) of the women remarried. Quite a different picture emerges, however, if one looks at divorcees and widows separately in relation to remarriage.

For the widows in their twenties and thirties, only 29% remarried at a young age. (This is discounting four cases who remarried from 15 to 42 years after their husbands had died.) Adding in the widows in their early forties, the remarriage rate of young widows would rise to 31%. The total remarriage rate for young widows, including those who remarried later in life, was 44%.

The total remarriage rate for young divorcees was much higher 65%. Subtracting the divorcees in their early forties, the remarriage rate for those in their twenties and thirties was 74%. What dramatizes the difference between the two groups even more are the cases where children were involved. Divorcees with young children had a remarriage rate of 50%, while widows with young children had a remarriage rate of only 23%. Such figures demonstrate the affection and fidelity that the widows held for their late husbands, for a widow with small children should have been no less a marriage prospect than a divorcee with young children. Nor was it the case that divorcees knew their prospective second husbands before their first marriages terminated; generally, several years intervened between the first marriage and second marriage.

A survey of the topics discussed in this chapter--career relationships, sexual relationships, fertility, divorce, and widowhood--demonstrates that much had changed regarding marriage and the family from the mid-nineteenth century, when these women were reared, to the early twentieth century. In comparison with the data presented in the second chapter on the childhood of the women, the biggest difference revolved around the role of women as wives and mothers in the families. By the late nineteenth and early twentieth centuries, prominent women were well-educated and most of them had careers. This was not true of their mothers. These advantages apparently made the women more assertive and more independent in relation to their husbands and their role in the family. While marriage characteristically altered the circumstances of their lives, very few of them relinquished their careers or outside interests for lives of domesticity. And few of the women tolerated the total male dominance which characterized many mid-nineteenth century marriages. When these women did find themselves with inconsiderate or tyrannical mates, they did not allow themselves to be stifled forever; they escaped through separation or divorce, or they asserted themselves within their marriages.[53]

The fertility statistics also demonstrate the amount of control that these women desired and exercised over their lives.[54] The size of their families was very small, much smaller than the generation of their mothers, as a result of contraceptive techniques and probably of self-denial. The aspect of family life which these women could not control was the still virulent rate of infant and child mortality. Medical science had not advanced to the point where these women were spared the sorrows their mothers had known.

These women and their families also evidenced less dependence on relatives than had earlier families. One reason for this may have been the heightened prosperity of the late nineteenth and early twentieth centuries. Financial insecurity did not seem to be so omnipresent as it had been earlier. But even more important, perhaps, were the changing opportunities for women and the changing ideas about woman's place in the home. Many of the women helped support their families during times of financial difficulties, and, strikingly, their husbands were not averse to accepting their aid. Wives helping to support families had been regarded as a lower class phenomenon, and certainly had not been accepted practice in the middle classes. The fact that careers for women had become respectable therefore allowed families to utilize their own resources fully before seeking outside aid. The widows among this group also exhibited the same degree of self-reliance. They persisted in efforts to support themselves rather than falling back upon their families or other sources of aid.

All these characteristics of the prominent women--their independence, assertiveness, self-reliance, and desire to control their lives--indicate that they were moving in the direction of equality with their husbands and with men in general. Even in their sexual relations with their husbands they evidenced a desire for mutuality that would have been unseemly in their mothers' day.

NOTES

[1]Amelia Barr, "Discontented Women," *North American Review*, 162 (1896), pp. 201, 208. See also Thorstein Veblen's *Theory of the Leisure Class*, pp. 356-58.

[2]Margaret Deland, "The Change in the Feminine Ideal," *The Atlantic Monthly*, 105 (March 1910), pp. 291-292; 296. Anna A. Rogers, "Why American Marriages Fail," pp. 292; 289-297.

[3]Charlotte Perkins Gilman, *Women and Economics* (Boston: Small, Maynard & Co., 1898).

[4]Anna Garlin Spencer, *The Family and Its Members* (Philadelphia; J.B. Lippincott Co., 1923). Anna Garlin Spencer, *Woman's Share in Social Culture* (New York: Mitchell Kennerley, 1912), pp. 259-260.

[5]Emma Churchman Hewitt, *Queen of Home.*

[6]Peter R. Uhlenberg, "A Study of Cohort Life Cycles," p. 412.

[7]This example was the journalist and author Rheta Childe Dorr who had separated permanently from her husband.

[8]"Sara Teasdale," *NAW*, 3:436. "Mrs. Julia C. R. Dorr," *WOC*, p. 253. "Amy Marcy Cheney Beach," *NAW*, 1:117-19.

[9]"Gene Stratton-Porter," *NAW*, 3:404. See also Jeanette Porter Meehan, *The Lady of the Limberlost.* "Lillian Marion Norton Ames Stevens," *NAW*, 3:370-71.

[10]Isabella Alden, *Memories of Yesterdays.* "Mrs. May Wright Sewall," *WOC*, pp. 643-44. "May Eliza Wright Sewall," *NAW*, 3:269. "Mrs. Emma Smith DeVoe," *WOC*, p. 239.

[11]Mary Gray Peck, *Carrie Chapman Catt*, pp. 47-48.

[12]*Ibid.*, p. 59.

[13]"Catherine Gouger Waugh McCulloch," *NAW*, 2:459. "Louise Blanchard Bethune," *NAW*, 1:140. " Mrs. Elia Wilkinson Peattie," *WOC*, p. 562.

[14]"Ada C. Bowles," *WWW*, p. 119. "Mrs. Ada Chastina Bowles," *WOC*, p. 110.

[15]"Fanny Bullock Workman," *NAW*, 3:672-74.

[16]"Lucia Fairchild Fuller," *NAW*, 1:677. "Hetty Howland Robinson Green," *NAW*, 2:82

[17]Bulletin 96, Bureau of the Census, 1907.

[18]Rheta Childe Dorr, *A Woman of Fifty* (New York: Funk & Wagnalls Company, 1924), pp. 52-56, 69-72. "Hortense Sparks Malsch Ward," *NAW*, 3:540-41. "Mary Coffin Ware Dennett," *NAW*, 1:463-64.

[19]"Emma Johanna Antonia Juch," *NAW*, 2:294-95. "Mrs. Vinnie Ream Hoxie," *WOC* pp. 398-99. "Vinnie Ream," *NAW*, 3:122-23. Peck, *Carrie Chapman Catt*, pp. 38-39; 59.

[20]"Rosa Smith Eigenmann," *NAW*. 1:565-66. "Emily James Smith Putnam," *NAW*, 3:106-07.

[21]The questionnaires, entitled "Statistical Study of the Marriage of Forty-Seven Women," are found in volume 10 of Mosher's unpublished work, "Hygiene and Physiology of Women," Mosher Papers, Stanford University Archives. Sixteen of the questionnaires were collected from 1892 to 1897; fourteen, in 1912 and 1913; and five in 1920. The rest of the questionnaires were undated. For more information, see Carl N. Degler, "What Ought To Be and What Was: Woman's Sexuality in the Nineteenth Century," *American Historical Review*, 79 (December 1974), pp. 1467-90.

[22]Mosher, "Statistical Study," case nos. 18 and 15. This assignment of cases to the three categories of sexual knowledge--considerable, slight, and none--differs from the distribution reported in the Degler article. See Degler, "Woman's Sexuality," p. 1483. I assigned the cases to the three categories based upon my own judgment of their answers. If a woman said "slight" or "none," I accepted her judgment at face value. If however, she said "slight" and went on to name books she had read or college courses on physiology which she had taken, I placed her in the group with considerable knowledge.

[23]Mosher, "Statistical Study," case nos. 5, 35, and 41.

[24]*Ibid.*, case no. 27.

[25]*Ibid.*, case nos. 13 and 25; 2; and 22.

[26]*Ibid.*, case nos. 6, 34, and 21.

[27]*Ibid.*, case nos. 41, 12, and 15.

[28]Indiania University Institute for Sex Research, *Sexual Behavior in the Human Female* (Philadelphia and London: W.B. Saunders Company, 1953), pp. 348-49. Degler discussed the actual quality of the marital relations in the section on orgasm in his article. The question he used for his data was phrased thus by Mosher, "Do you

always have a venereal orgasm?" Stated in that manner, the question led to vague and confusing responses. I felt the question and responses to be too unreliable to be very useful. See Degler, "Womans Sexuality," pp. 1483-84.

[29]These figures differ from those cited by Degler. See Degler, "Woman's Sexuality," pp. 1485-86.

[30]Mosher, "Statistical Study," case nos. 10, 15, 12, and 22.

[31]Ibid., case nos. 12, 35, 40, 42 and 44; 18.

[32]Ibid., case nos. 28, 40. Mosher, Ibid., introduction, p. 1.

[33]Ibid., case nos. 10, 22, 15, and 23.

[34]Ibid., case nos. 19 and 36.

[35]Ibid., case nos. 27 and 41.

[36]Ibid., case nos. 41 and 45.

[37]Margaret Sanger, My Fight for Birth Control (New York: Farrar & Rinehart, Inc., 1931), p. 53.

[38]Mosher, "Statistical Study," case nos. 45 and 51.

[39]Note that out of the 9000 some American women in the Woman's Who's Who, 366 were also in Notable American Women. Of those 366, 192 were married and 125 were mothers. On the infant mortality rate in 1900, see Margaret Mead and Frances Balgley Kaplan, ed., American Women, Report of the President's Commission on the Status of Women and Other Publications of the Commission (New York: Charles Schribner's Sons, 1965,) p. 79. By 1967 the infant mortality rate for children under one year had declined to 22.1 per 1000. See Sam Shapiro, Edward R. Schlesinger, and Robert E. L. Nesbitt, Jr., Infant, Perinatal, Maternal, and Childhood Mortality in the United States (Cambridge: Harvard University Press, 1968), p. 3. Although for the NAW and WWW women, the deaths of children past infancy were included, one can compare their rate directly with that of the Mosher women. Only one of the Mosher women recounted the death of a child past 5 years, and she was already counted among the nine who had experienced infant mortality.

[40]Mosher, "Statistical Study," case no. 24. Amelia E. Barr, All the Days of My Life (New York: D. Appleton and Co., 1913).

[41]Ella Wheeler Wilcox," NAW, 3:608. "Kate Nichols Trask," NAW 3:477. "Maud Nathan," NAW 2:608. "Alice Ames Winter," NAW 2:632.

[42]Clara Hampson Ueland," NAW, 3:498.

[43]Mrs Anna Manning Comfort," *WOC* pp. 196-97. "Ellen Louise Axson Wilson," *NAW,* 3:627. "Martha Hillard MacLeish," *NAW,* 2:473-74.

[44]Isabel C. Barrows, *A Sunny Life,* pp. 111, 121. "Lillian Marion Norton Ames Stevens," *NAW,* 3:371. Rheta Childe Dorr, *A Woman of Fifty.*

[45]"Anna Held," *NAW,* 2:178. "Lillian Russell," *NAW,* 3:213. "Alice Nielsen," *NAW.* 2:632.

[46]Walter F. Willcox, *Statistics of Marriage and Divorce in the United States,* printed privately, Paris, 1909, pp. 13-15. See also Bulletin 96, Bureau of the Census, 1907.

[47]"Mary Coffin Ware Dennett," *NAW,* 1:463-64. "Rose Harriet Pastor Stokes," *NAW,* 3:384-85.

[48]"Alice Nielsen," *NAW,* 2:632.

[49]"Josephine Woempner Clifford McCrackin," *NAW,* 2:455. "Alva Erskine Smith Vanderbilt Belmont," *NAW,* 1:126-27. Mrs. O. H. P. Belmont, "Women as Dictators," *Ladies Home Journal,* 39 (September 1922), p. 7. See also William L. O'Neill, *Divorce in the Progressive Era* (New Haven: Yale University Press, 1967). O'Neill does not discuss facts and figures about divorce, but confines himself to the public debate over divorce in the Progressive years.

[50]"Josephine Marshall Jewell Dodge," *NAW,* 1:492. "Kate Harwood Waller Barrett," *NAW,* 1:98.

[51]Amelia E. Barr, *All the Days of My Life,* pp. 291-308. Carrie Jacobs Bond, *The Roads of Melody.*

[52]Bond, *The Roads of Melody.* "Lasell Carbell Pickett," *WOC,* pp. 570-71.

[53]For example, see the autobiographies of Mary Austin, Gertrude Atherton, Rheta Childe Dorr, and Abigail Duniway.

[54]See Daniel Scott Smith, "Family Limitation, Sexual Control, and Domestic Feminism in Victorian America," pp. 119-36.

myriad of women's organizations which flourished in urban centers. Membership in women's clubs was very high in the South, however, so the most important reason for the high degree of religious activism lay in the ethos of the region. The culture of the South was more conservative than that of the other sections regarding woman's sphere. While church work was eminently respectable, other forms of female activism, such as suffrage agitation, were more questionable. Therefore, religious activism was a means, besides women's clubs and reform work, for Southern women to go beyond the home in a socially acceptable way.

D.   The Young Women's Christian Association

For the thousands of women interested in religious activity, a variety of societies provided means for such work. Women were by and large excluded from direct participation in the governing of churches; thus they founded ladies aid associations, prayer circles, and missionary societies. The functions of these groups differed from church to church and from denomination to denomination. Ladies aid associations often took responsibility for housekeeping chores connected with church property as well as maintaining an interest in local charitable work. The missionary societies endeavored to raise money and supplies for domestic and foreign missions, with some ambitious groups directly supporting a missionary in the field. It was common for these groups to participate in relief work in their communities. Even missionary societies saw the need of dispensing food, clothing, and the Gospel in their own locales, especially if that were a quickly growing city.

The strongest and most dynamic group which embodied the precepts of Christian social activism was the Young Women's Christian Association. Springing out of the great revival of 1857-58 and modeled on the somewhat older Young Men's Christian Association, the YMCA began as an urban movement of middle class women directed toward young women who were self-supporting. The first groups were formed in New York and Boston in 1858 and 1866 respectively. By 1871, representatives of eight groups attended a convention at Hartford, Connecticut, while thirteen other organizations sent reports of their work. Two years later, the number of Women's Christian Associations had grown to thirty-six in as many cities.[9]

For most urban YWCA's, the vague goals of helping women and girls first took concrete form in the establishment of boarding houses. The growth of white collar and blue collar jobs for women stimulated an influx of females into cities after the Civil War. Many commercial boarding houses at first refused to take them. Thus the YWCA's met a real need with their establishment of cheap, clean, and respectable places for women to live. Almost from the beginning, the associations determined that these boarding houses should be self-supporting, not the objects of charity.[10]

Besides sponsoring boarding places and evangelical activities like prayer meetings and Bible study, YWCA's offered educational opportunities and employment services. The Boston group exemplifies how associations approached different classes of women regarding these functions. Since there was a strong demand for domestic servants in late nineteenth century Boston, the YWCA first established an employment bureau to try to find girls for places. When the bureau could not meet the demand for household help, the association set up a three to six month training course for lower class women interested in domestic service. By the 1880's, representatives from the YWCA began meeting the boats of immigrants as they came into Boston harbor in order to secure girls for household help. At the same time, the YWCA had setup a business register to seek white collar jobs for middle class girls, while offering training in business skills such as bookkeeping and typing.[11]

The first growth of the YWCA movement was in the cities of the East. The second level of development was on the coeducational college campuses of the Midwest. The Young Men's Christian Association established student associations which were often coeducational. From these beginnings, a strong network of campus women's associations developed into the conservative American Committee of the YWCA.

For a long time the American Committee represented a rival group to the urban Eastern association, loosely organized under the International Board of the YWCA. The American Committee influenced by the YMCA wanted membership in YWCA's restricted to members in good standing of evangelical Protestant churches. The International Board had long fought against any kind of membership restriction. By 1906, the two groups came together under the leadership of Grace Hoadly Dodge, the wealthy New York philanthropist. Although the International Board supposedly capitulated on the membership issue, restrictions were never strictly enforced. Proof lies in the entry of Anna Goodman Hertzberg in the *Woman's Who's Who*. Hertzberg, of San Antonio, Texas, listed membership in the YWCA and the YMCA Auxiliary Association, at the same time recording her religion as Jewish. It should also be noted that, at all times, the programs, activities, and services of the YWCA's were open to all women regardless of creed or class.[12]

Even on the question of color, the YWCA's were ahead of their time. Although associations were not integrated at the turn of the century, by 1906 a policy had been adopted that branches for black women should be associated with the local YWCA's; there should not be separate associations for each race. It was common for women of both branches to work together on projects, and leadership development among Negro women was directly encouraged by the associations.[13]

The YWCA movement was unique with its combination of evangelical Christianity and social activism. It appealed to middle class women as an organized way of doing religious work across denominational lines. At the same time, there was friction between the movement and organized churches. From the beginning, Protestant clergymen were divided about the merits of such an organization. In fact, the Boston association was delayed in its founding from 1859 to 1866 by the city's clergymen. After having helped to found a YMCA, the ministers thought the undertaking too great for women to handle, and thus discouraged the idea when the women wanted to begin their own association in 1859. Publications of the YWCA demonstrate that the association felt a continual need to justify its existence, at the same time finding fault with the churches for their lack of effort among young women. It is thus easy to infer that many ministers and male-run churches felt threatened by such an inter-denominational woman's religious organization, and had attacked the YWCA as being superfluous. At the same time, the YWCA invariably used Protestant ministers for their outside speakers, indicating that some of the groups strongest supporters were also among the clergy.[14]

As with other women's organizations, the YWCA movement provided specific opportunities to middle class women: an excuse to meet together on a regular basis, a place of their own to meet, worthwhile charitable work to do, and challenges to their organizational abilities. But the YWCA's went beyond these features. They also provided training in leadership and full-time work for women in ways that few other women groups did. Women were hired to run boarding houses. They were also hired to give sewing classes and manage employment bureaus. Charlotte Drinkwater, one of the first women hired on a full-time basis by a YWCA, was given these instructions by the Boston association on becoming head of the group's new two-hundred-woman residence in 1874: "Build it up by your own originality; no one can tell you how to do it, and the men's prophecy of women's failure must not be fulfilled." Mabel Cratty, one of the real molders of the modern YWCA, reluctantly taught school for fourteen years until she found her metier in working for the national organization of the YWCA. Association work became almost a quarter-century career for Cratty. The national YWCA instituted its own training school for leadership about 1906 where a B.A. or its equivalent was required to enter. This was in itself a pioneering effort in training for social work.[15]

Association endeavors also provided middle class women with the opportunity, albeit limited, to cross class and race barriers in contacts with members of their sex. The boarding houses provided rooms for both white collar and blue collar workers. The question of women's wages and working conditions appeared often in YWCA publications, and in the early 1900's, some associations were formed in factories proper. By 1920, working women were actually strong enough in the YWCA to push through a resolution supporting unions and the principle of collective bargaining. Likewise, the city associations with their branches provided occasions for white women and black women to have contact with each other.[16]

E.   Humanitarian Interests

Religious activism failed to attract as many notable women as did general humanitarian endeavors. Fully 62.4% of the *Who's Who* women displayed an interest in such extensions of the maternal role as hospitals, charities, juvenile work, and settlements. The women typically pursued such concerns on the local level, but a few national organizations, such as the Red Cross, also drew support from prosperous women.[17]

Women in the professions outdistanced all others in their interest in humanitarian activities. A surprising 83.4% of the professional women exhibited such interests, while almost two-thirds (62.7%) of the noncareer women did so. Both women in education and women in the arts fell below the average, with about half of their numbers engaged in charitable work. (See figure 7.)

For many professional women, humanitarian activities became extensions of their careers. This was true especially in the case of physicians, but also for other occupations. Nancy Dryden Richards, for example, had a private medical practice in Washington, D. C. for a while, during which she also extended her services to the Florence Crittenton Home, the Women's Christian Home and the Woman's Hospital and Clinic. Katherine Porter, a physician in Orange, New Jersey, was not only chairman of the Public Health Education Committee of the Essex County Medical Society, but she was also physician to the Children's Aid and Protective Society and the medical inspector of the Orange public schools. In addition, Porter found time to be on the boards of directors of the Anti-Tuberculosis League and Fresh Air Work of Orange. In her entry in the *Woman's Who's Who*, lawyer Bertha Stull Green declared herself "interested in movements to better the condition of laboring women, and in laws for the protection and benefit of women and

Figure 7.

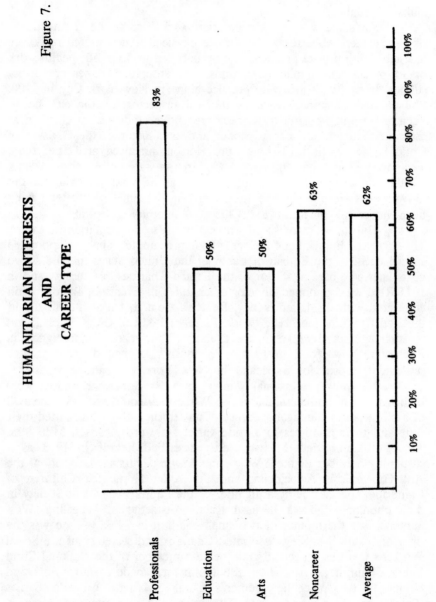

HUMANITARIAN INTERESTS
AND
CAREER TYPE

children." To advance such interests, Green compiled a booklet, "Laws of Idaho, Concerning Women and Children, " for use in the women's clubs of Idaho.[18]

For some women, humanitarian work became the central thrust of their careers. Because many female physicians encountered resistance in establishing private practices, they proceeded to do public health work or to practice in public institutions. S. Josephine Baker could not support herself with a private practice alone in New York City in 1900. She secured an appointment as medical inspector for the city health department and went on to pioneer preventive medicine for children as assistant to the health commissioner and as director of the Division of Child Hygiene. In 1913, Jane Lord Hersom practiced medicine at the Temporary Home for Women and Children, a state institution in Maine. At the same time, Eva Charlotte Reid was assistant physician at the Government Hospital for the Insane in Washington, D. C., after having been house physician at the Chicago Maternity Hospital.[19]

The life work of social workers was also humanitarian in nature. The career of Edith Shope Reider offers an example. She was appointed special agent of the Bureau of Labor of the United States in 1908. Two years later, she became visitor of the United Charities of Chicago, and in 1911 Reid was appointed director of charities in Evanston, Illinois. Still connected with the latter agency, Reid was sent to Ohio in 1913 to aid the Red Cross in flood relief work. Florence Ledyard Cross Kitchelt was registrar and social worker in the evening public school for foreigners in Rochester, New York, in 1914. Previously, she had directed various settlement houses for a decade in New York City and Rochester.[20]

Not only professional women, but also noncareer women were highly active in humanitarian work. While they could not offer the skill of a physician or the legal expertise of an attorney, they contributed their time and their resources to a wide variety of worthy causes. Mrs. John Amee of Cambridge, Massachusetts, described herself in 1913 as a sustaining member of the YWCA, the Visiting Nursing Association, the Anti-Tuberculosis Association, and the Avon Home for Children of Cambridge, besides being a member of the Ladies Benevolent Society in their church. Rebecca Barnard Raoul Altstaetter of Wheeling, West Virginia, was the mother of two small children in 1913; yet she was the director of the Wheeling Associated Charities and secretary of the Social Worker's Club in Wheeling while being a member of the National Child Labor Committee. Altstaetter also found time to do suffrage work and belong to the Wheeling Women's Club. Mariette Amanda Barnes Knight, an older women than Altstaetter, had two grown children in 1913. She busied herself as an officer of the Board of Lady Visitors of the Children's Hospital of Columbus, Ohio, plus active membership in the District Nursing Association, Kindergarten Association, Humane Society, West Side Social Centre, and the Home and School Association all in Columbus.   In addition to her humanitarian activities, Knight belonged to a variety of women's clubs, alumnae associations, and civic art groups.[21]

As with most of the other variables, the regional variation on humanitarian interests was not nearly so great as the variance among career types.   Western women had the highest percentage, with 71.6% indicating an interest in charitable activities.   Lifelong Southerners had a 68.2% interest, but the women who had moved into or out of the South brought the overall percentage down to 65%, compared to the average of 62.4%. The Eastern and Midwestern women likewise hovered around the average for prominent women, with around 60% manifesting humanitarian interests.

Humanitarian work appealed to large numbers of middle and upper class women in 1914. It enabled them to use their time and skills in genuinely useful and interesting ways. It was also socially respectable work. While the variety of charitable endeavors open to women in 1914 represented a real enlargement of woman's sphere of activities, such work had evolved gradually from women's church organizations.   And the nature of the work too was thought to be an expression of women's natural maternal inclinations to aid the needy and unfortunate in society.

F.   The Temperance Movement

Religious and humanitarian impulses among women also found expression in the temperance movement of the nineteenth century. For many, this movement was a bridge. from religious activism to the more radical sphere of politics.   In fact, the strongest single woman's organization of the nineteenth century was the Woman's Christian Temperance Union.   But it had already passed its peak by 1914.

Sentiment for temperance can be traced back to the reforming wave in the early nineteenth century, but the movement was revitalized in the 1870's through a spontaneous crusade generated in Midwestern women's prayer meetings. On the crest of this movement, the Woman's Christian Temperance Union was founded in 1874. It soon reached into every state and included a dues paying membership of almost a quarter of a million American women. Its success was attributable to its dynamic leader, Frances Willard, who was its president from 1879 to 1898. Willard diverted the strong impulses for temperance among women into more political channels. She led the WCTU into an espousal of a wide variety of reforms, including woman's suffrage, prison reform, helping unwed mothers and prostitutes, and child labor laws. While thousands of women were thereby drawn into political activity, a conservative wing within the WCTU chafed at the leftist direction of Willard's leadership. After her death in 1898, this group reasserted itself, and brought the emphasis of the WCTU back to working for prohibition alone. By 1914, the organization no longer appealed to women as a wide-ranging reform movement; thus, only 6% of the prominent women at that time identified themselves as members of the WCTU or as temperance advocates.[22]

G.   Political Preference

Although political activity among women dated back to the agitators against slavery in the 1840's, few prominent women identified themselves with a political party as of 1914. This apparent lack of political consciousness was understandable since few women had the right to vote. Of the 18% who did give a party preference, more women identified themselves as Progressives, independents, or socialists (8.4%) than as Republicans (5.8%) or as Democrats (4.0%). Women in the professions were the most political of the career types. Over one-quarter (28%) of their number declared a political choice, with over half (57%) of that group aligning themselves with the Progressives and independents. The women in education, the arts, and noncareer women were all below average on political indication, with rates of 14%, 14%, and 17% respectively. (See figure 8.)

The four regions varied considerably in their responses to this variable. Women of the West were by far the most political, with a rate of fifty-two percent (52%). But it should be noted that most Western states had granted women complete suffrage by 1914, and those that did not had at least granted women partial suffrage. Thus it was natural that Western women would identify themselves with a party for voting purposes. The Midwest had the second highest rate for party preference, with an average of 25.5%. Both the South and the East were below average, with rates of 15% and 14% respectively. In each case, the rates for those who were born in and still living in a region were lower than when the in- and out-migrants were averaged with them. Thus, the rate for lifelong Easterners was the lowest of all at 10.3%. (See figure 9.)

H.   Reform Interest

While relatively few prominent women indicated a party preference, a majority of the socially visible women did indicate a general political and social interest in the current events of their day. This interest was evidenced in a variety of ways, from civic work to suffrage activity, from membership in the Women's Trade Union League to

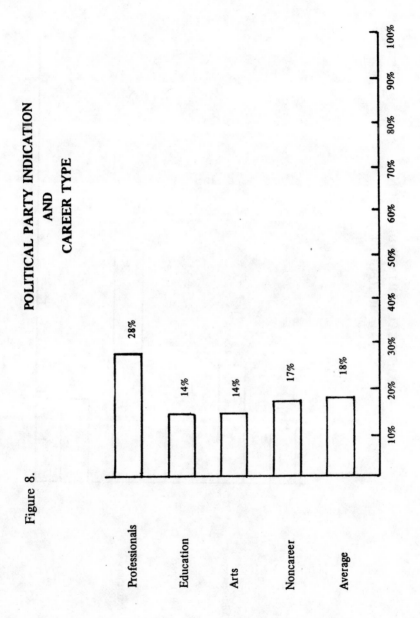

Figure 8.

POLITICAL PARTY INDICATION
AND
CAREER TYPE

Figure 9.

POLITICAL PARTY INDICATION
AND REGION

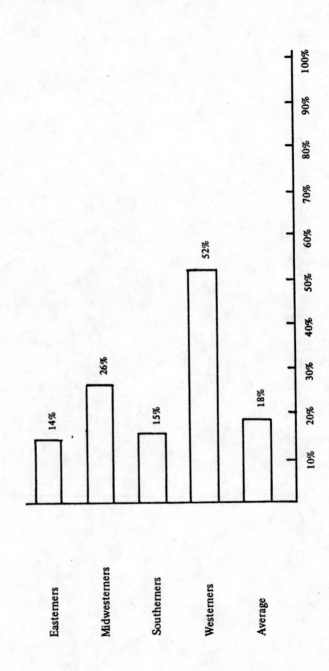

doing sociological studies of immigrants.   The Progressive reform movement had captured the imaginations of prominent women as it had those of their male counterparts.

It is not surprising that women became as interested and as active in reform efforts as did men, although this was the first instance in American history when large numbers of women took an active part in public affairs.   La Follette wrote in his *Autobiography*: "In all my campaigns in Wisconsin, I had been much impressed with the fact that women were as keenly interested as men in the question of railroad taxation, reasonable transportation charges, direct primaries and indeed in the whole progressive program."[23]   Women, in fact, contributed notable leaders to the movement: the muckraker Ida Tarbell; social workers Jane Addams, Lillian Wald, Mary McDowell, the Abott sisters, Julia Lathrop, first head of the Children's Bureau; Florence Kelley, head of the National Consumer's League; Margaret Dreier Robins, head of the Women's Trade Union League.   Their individual careers tell us little, however, about the relation between women of their class and reform activity in general.   Nor can they necessarily serve as models of typical female reformers.

The most useful characteristic for examining reform proclivities among prominent women is current events interest.   The variable was defined to include local civic work as well as membership in national organizations like the National Consumer's League; it included investigative sociological work and interests in women's rights.   In fact, the variety of ways in which the variable measured current events interest paralleled the variety of levels of the progressive reform movement. Thus, this variable, current events interest, will be considered tantamount to reform activity.

The rate for current events interest was highest among women in the professions (71%) compared with the average for prominent women of 54.6%.   Noncareer women were slightly under the average, with 53% of their numbers engaged in reform work.   Women in education and women in the arts trailed with 44% and 49% respectively.   If one considers just those women who evidenced an interest in current events, almost one-third (32.3%) were professional women, and almost another third (30.8%) were noncareer women.   Only 19.2% were in the arts, and 17.5% were in education.   (See figure 10.)

The regional variation paralleled the rates for party preferences to some extent.   The West was again the highest, with 72.6%, and the East was the lowest, with 52.0%.   The rates for the South and the Midwest were very close together, but the South was surprisingly high in relation to its rate for party preference.   Fully 60.5% of the Southern women indicated current events interest, while 58.8% did so in the

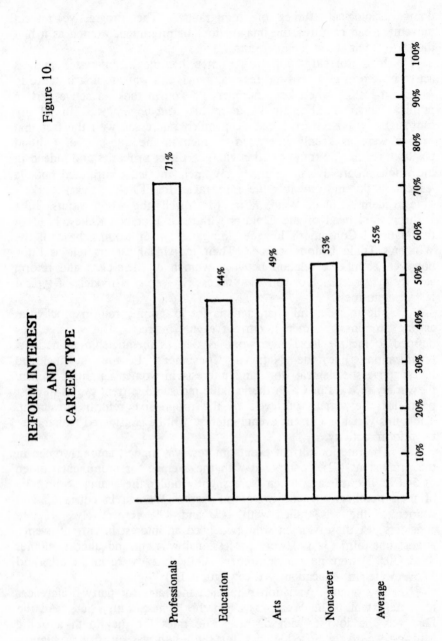

Figure 10.

REFORM INTEREST
AND
CAREER TYPE

Professionals — 71%
Education — 44%
Arts — 49%
Noncareer — 53%
Average — 55%

Midwest. Again, the rates for the natives, those born in and still living in a region, were lower than the average rate for the region. Thus, the rate for lifelong Easterners was the lowest at 51.3%. As with membership and leadership in women's clubs, the more. conservative women in the East appear to have been out of step with their sisters in other regions, and women in the South appear to have been more active than their reputation had admitted. (See figure 11.)

The women who were interested in current events have an interesting profile. In marital status, they were quite close to the average for prominent women--69.1% married and 45.6% were mothers. Thus, reformers were more likely to be married and to be mothers than were professional women, but less likely than noncareer women. Surprisingly, there was a positive correlation between age and reform activity. The older a woman was, the more likely she was to engage in reform work. While there is a tendency to picture reformers as idealistic young adults, the young women were actually below average, with 44.5% of their numbers interested in current events. Evidently, the greater experience a woman had in living, the more she became interested in correcting the defects she saw in society.

There was also a definite correlation between humanitarian work and current events interest. A very high 85.6% of all reformers also engaged in humanitarian work. That rate is even higher than the one for professional women interested in humanitarian work (83.4%). A partial explanation for the high correlation is that some activities fell into both categories by definition. For example, work with the Protective Agency for Women and Children, a legal aid society sponsored by the Chicago Woman's Club, was considered both humanitarian and reforming in nature. Most settlement work also fell into both categories. Nevertheless, even when defined separately, the two phenomenon--an interest in humanitarian causes and in current events--typically attracted the same women. (See figure 12.)

Similarly, those women interested in current events also belonged to and led women's clubs in large numbers. A total of 88.7% of the reformers belonged to women's clubs, and 65.6% were leaders in them, compared with the average of 77.1% and 48.7% respectively. The rates for reformers were higher in both cases than those for professional women and noncareer women. Looking at it the other way, 63% of the total women's club members and 73.6% of the leaders had an interest in current events, compared with the average of 54.6%.

Reformers strongly favored women's suffrage. Seven out of ten (70%) did so compared with an average of 53.5% for all prominent women. Almost four out of ten reformers (39.9%) were active

Figure 11.

REFORM INTEREST
AND REGION

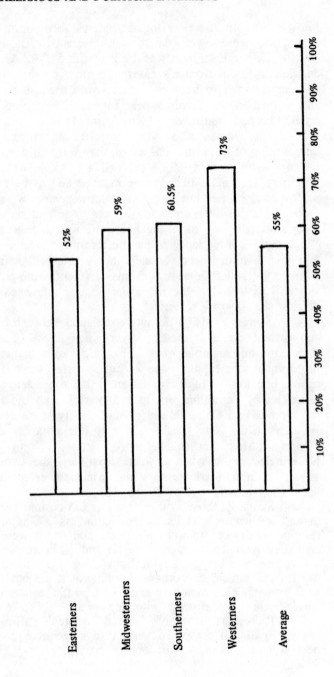

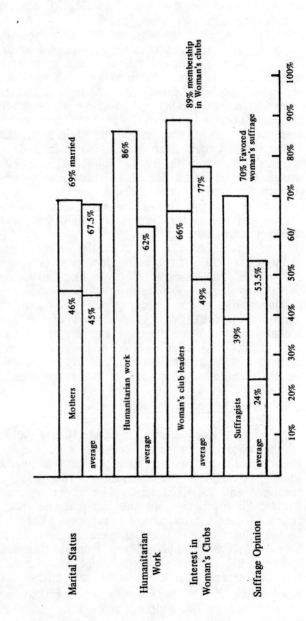

Figure 12.

CHARACTERISTICS OF REFORMERS
WITH THE AVERAGE FOR
PROMINENT WOMEN

campaigners for suffrage. This was about the same rate for suffrage activity as professional women had (38.7%), but much higher than the rate for noncareer women (18.9%).

Reform activity was not related to environmental conditions. There was no correlation between the size of a woman's hometown or the size of a woman's current residence and current events interest. Thus women living in large metropolitan areas and women living in small towns in 1914 were equally likely to be engaged in reform work. Nor was geographical mobility related to current events interest. Women who had moved about a great deal were little more inclined to reform activity than were women who stayed in their homestate or even in their hometowns all their lives. Even education had no relation to reform interests. Women with little schooling were as likely to be reformers as women with advanced degrees. Other variables which did not relate to concern for current events included genealogical interest, involvement in community arts, and membership in an alumnae group. Reformers were slightly higher than the average on religious activism, but the difference was not significant.

A reformer who was a socially visible woman in 1914 was thus likely to have either a profession or to have no career. She was probably married and had children. She was likely to be middle-aged or old as opposed to young. She belonged to a woman's club in which she was holding or had held an executive position at some time. She engaged in humanitarian work besides or as part of her reform interests. She probably did not belong to the Daughters of the American Revolution or other patriotic societies, to a community arts group, or to an alumnae association. She favored woman's suffrage, and might well have worked for suffrage in addition to her other activities.

I.   Profiles of Reformers

The life of Lucretia Longshore Blankenburg illustrates the profile of the noncareer woman who was a reformer. The daughter of Philadelphia's first woman physician and namesake of woman's rights leader Lucretia Mott, Blankenburg was reared in a heady atmosphere of feminism and social concern. She chose not to follow her mother's footsteps in medicine, but she did graduate from a local commercial college. When she was almost twenty-two, Lucretia Longshore married a German immigrant, Rudolf Blankenburg, who established a successful business in Philadelphia and was eventually elected as a reform mayor there in 1911. Though their marriage was marred by the deaths of all three of their children, husband and wife worked closely together whether for his business or for civic endeavors.[24]

Lucretia Blankenburg entered her long career as a reformer when she helped to found a woman's club, the New Century Club, after the Centennial Exposition held in Philadelphia in 1876. Being a clubwoman was in itself somewhat remarkable at that time, and Blankenburg helped to propel the club toward civic work almost from its inception. The club began by offering night classes for working women, and Blankenburg taught the bookkeeping class. When she noticed that one woman with little aptitude came to her classes as an opportunity for a social outing, Blankenburg helped to stimulate the founding of the New Century Guild, a club for working women, as an adjunct of the New Century Club. Through her club work, Blankenburg also caused the introduction of police matrons to the city's police inspectors and the appointment of women to the Philadelphia school board. In addition, Blankenburg worked for the Woman's Health Protective Association, the Good Citizens' Club, the Woman's City Party, and the Tenth Ward Woman's City Improvement Society.

Blankenburg's feminism could be traced to the days when she was teased as the daughter of an "improper person," a woman doctor. No doubt the reform spirit of the Quaker Longshore household also affected Lucretia. At any rate, she spent long hours of her adult years working in the cause of woman's suffrage. As president of the Pennsylvania Woman Suffrage Association for sixteen years, Blankenburg often testified before legislative and Congressional committees. Upon being elected auditor of the General Federation of Women's Clubs in 1908, she resigned her position in the state suffrage group in order to devote her time to influencing the General Federation to support woman's suffrage. She served the General Federation as first vice-president in 1912 to 1914, and in 1914 her resolution endorsing woman's suffrage was finally passed by the body.

The career of Albion Fellows Bacon is another that illumines the characteristics of a typical woman reformer of the progressive era. Bacon grew up in rural Indiana where she lived with her widowed mother and older sisters. Although she never knew her father, a Methodist minister, Bacon was influenced by the social concern of the Methodist church. She did not know what she wanted to do when she grew up, but she stated, "a career never occurred to me, for it would have seemed as impossible as walking on the ridge pole or driving a locomotive, and as unattractive." After Bacon attended high school in Evansville, Indiana, she worked there as a secretary for an uncle who was a judge. At twenty-three, she married Hilary Bacon, a banker and merchant who was fifteen years older than she. During the first ten years of her marriage, Albion Bacon reared four children and suffered from a long illness. She had no interest in civic matters and refused to join her friends who worked for civic improvement and charitable organizations. Her concern for her daughters roused her from her apathy when she visited their school and saw its alarming conditions. When the daughters contracted scarlet fever from their schoolmates, Bacon declared herself ready to serve on the sanitation committee of the Civic Improvement Society. When the children were ready to go back to school, she said, "the house was so lonely that I was glad to have some outside interest to take up even a small part of my leisure."[25]

Bacon began her reform work by reading Jacob Riis's *How the Other Half Lives* and by investigating conditions in Evansville. She was amazed to find slums as terrible in Evansville as Riis described in New York City. As a Friendly Visitor, Bacon came into direct contact with certain poor families. The pathos of their situations prompted Bacon to organize a circle of men visitors in her home. She joined a group that sponsored a visiting nurse, and she helped to organize a Working Girls' Association which eventually maintained a dormitory, lunch room, and library, and sponsored social evenings. Bacon's important contributions to social improvement, however, lay in her work for housing reform.

What began as her proposed housing ordinance for Evansville grew into a bill for a state law regulating tenements. Bacon sponsored statewide investigations into housing conditions. She talked and wrote for months to support her bill. She won endorsement from the State Conference of Charities and the Indianapolis Commercial Club. Finally her bill was passed in March 1910 by the Indiana legislature, but amendments limited its coverage to Indianapolis and Evansville. Bacon began another campaign to extend the coverage, and in 1913, the legislature passed a law regulating all residences in the state except single family dwellings. An important element in the passage of the second bill was the support of the State Federation of Women's Clubs, whose housing committee Bacon chaired.[26]

Neither Blankenburg nor Bacon had advanced educations. Although Blankenburg had some training at a commercial college, she always spoke, "from the standpoint of the housekeeper." "I have no other," she said. "I am not a college woman. Few colleges were open to women in my day; so mine is purely the home viewpoint."[27] Both women entered civic work after about ten years of marriage and child rearing. Both women worked through women's clubs and charitable and civic organizations. Both Blankenburg and Bacon were reared in atmospheres of social concern. They both favored woman's suffrage, although Blankenburg extended her conviction into considerable concrete work.

One last example, that of Caroline Bartlett Crane, illustrates the involvement of a professional woman in reform work. Though her interest in the liberal ministry stemmed from her teenage years, familial disapproval kept Caroline Bartlett from a ministerial vocation until she was twenty-eight. After graduating from Carthage College in Illinois, Bartlett taught school, homesteaded a claim in Dakota, and did newspaper work, until she was called to a struggling Universalist church in Sioux Falls, Dakota Territory, in 1886. Bartlett received formal ordination when she began her pastorate at a Unitarian church in Kalamazoo, Michigan, in 1889. The metamorphasis she worked in that church foretold her civic work to follow. Bartlett instituted a comprehensive program of practical Christianity through the establishment in the People's Church of a kindergarten, a gymnasium for women, a manual training department, and a domestic science department, all innovations to the progressive town of Kalamazoo. When Bartlett was thirty-eight, she married Augustus Warren Crane, a noted physician ten years her junior. (This was as rare an age match then as three-quarters of a century later.) In 1898, after two years of marriage, Caroline Crane resigned her pastorate following an illness and differences with her board. She remained an active member of the People's Church.[28]

Crane had already made notable contributions to her community through her work at the People's Church, but in her early forties, Crane inadvertently discovered a talent for municipal reform work. When failing to secure a speaker on meat inspection for the Twentieth Century Club of Kalamazoo, of which she was an officer, Bartlett took it upon herself to inspect the seven slaughter houses supplying Kalamazoo. The revolting conditions she found impelled her to more action than delivering her speech at the Twentieth Century Club. When Crane discovered that the conditions in Kalamazoo were typical for the state, she single-handidly induced the Michigan legislature to pass a law allowing for local meat-inspection ordinances. Then after several years of agitation, she prevailed upon the Kalamazoo city council to pass a model ordinance which she had authored.

Crane also organized the Women's Civic Improvement League during these years, around 1903-1904, which prompted the city to inaugurate a modern system of street cleaning. As a branch of the League, Crane established a Charity Organization Board as a central municipal agency for all charity cases.

As Crane's reputation spread as an expert in municipal sanitation, her talents came into demand nationally. Soon Crane had to put a fee on her services, and she developed a professional plan which she called a sanitary survey. Cities as disparate as Erie, Pennsylvania, and Montgomery, Alabama, contracted for her surveys as did the entire states of Kentucky, Minnesota, and Washington. Usually it was the women's clubs in a given locale, in cooperation with Boards of Health, that prompted her hiring. Her surveys covered the food and water supply, the sewer system, and public institutions. She made a detailed preliminary study of each community before she arrived, and she sent back a printed report of her findings after she left.

For all of her interest in urban reform, Crane placed a premium on her home life, refusing to spend more than two months of any year away from home. When she was fifty-five she and her husband adopted two children. In contrast to Bacon and Blankenburg, Crane seems to have had no background of social concern during her childhood. Rather her inspiration for social activism came from the contemporary trends within liberal Protestantism. Typical for a professional woman, she had a good education, including a college degree and postgraduate work at the University of Chicago. But like Blankenburg, the direct stimulus for her reform work came from her involvement in women's clubs. Her innovative pastoral work began after she was thirty years old, and her real municipal reform work did not begin until her forties. Like Blankenburg, Crane worked avidly for suffrage, and served on the executive board of the National American Woman Suffrage Association.

J.   History of Suffrage Agitation

Woman suffrage was a respectable reform favored by a majority of prominent women in 1914, but not many years earlier it was the radical cause of the militant feminists. Suffrage activism dated back to the famous woman's rights convention held at Seneca Falls, New York, in 1848. There Elizabeth Cady Stanton's resolution, "that it is the duty of the women of this country to secure to themselves their sacred rights to the elective franchise" passed by a small margin. Throughout the 1850's frequent woman's rights conventions were held, but no feminist organization developed. The leaders of the new movement were as interested in the abolition of slavery as the equality of women, and spent much of their time working for the anti-slavery cause. And when such women as Lucy Stone or Lucretia Mott did speak for women's rights, suffrage as an issue took a back seat to property rights and other elements of woman's inferior legal status such as divorce, guardianship, the rights to one's earnings, and equal opportunity to education and employment.[29]

Two suffrage organizations were founded in 1869. The National Suffrage Association, led by Stanton and Susan Anthony, was the more radical. It saw the lack of the franchise as only one of the many wrongs suffered by American womanhood, and it did not fear raising such controversial issues as divorce, woman's role in the family, the unionization of women laborers, and destroying prostitution and the double standard. The conservative American Woman Suffrage Association, under the guidance of Lucy Stone, Henry Blackwell, Julia Ward Howe, and Mary Livermore, feared the alienation of important sections of society if controversial issues such as divorce came to be connected with suffrage. The two organizations went their separate ways for two decades. By then, the conservative approach of the American Association appeared to be the more popular alternative, and this organization invited the National Association to merge with it. In 1890, the two groups came together to form the National American Woman Suffrage Association. The membership of NAWSA grew from 13,150 in 1893 to 45,501 in 1907 to 100,000 in 1915. Only two years later, the numbers rose to 2,000,000.[30]

Despite the merger, a question of tactics divided the suffrage agitators. Some women, like Susan Anthony, maintained that a federal amendment would be the only means for securing suffrage to all American women. Others maintained that the road to suffrage lay through amending state constitutions. With the union of the two suffrage groups, the emphasis came to fall on the latter method, with singularly poor results. There were 483 campaigns in thirty-three states between 1870 and 1910, and these were just to get the issue before the voters in the form of a referendum. Of these campaigns, only seventeen succeeded in inducing referenda, and in only two, Colorado and Idaho, did the referenda pass. The achievements seemed out of all proportion to the energy expended.[31]

Suffrage activity thus appeared to be in a state of paralysis in the first decade of the twentieth century. The NAWSA was suffering from poor leadership, poor organization, and defeat after defeat in state campaigns. The credit for revitalizing the suffrage movement goes to two talented women, Alice Paul and Carrie Chapman Catt. Fresh from working with England's militant suffragettes, Paul used a flair for the dramatic to bring new life to the federal amendment. Beginning in 1913, she organized marches, circulated petitions, and began bombarding Congress and President Wilson with suffrage delegations all as chairman of NAWSA's Congressional Committee. Friction between the static NAWSA and Paul's dynamic committee was inevitable, and Paul eventually departed, forming first the Congressional Union and then the Woman's Party. Paul succeeded in organizing followers in all forty-eight states. Her groups kept up constant pressure upon Congress and the President and gained untold publicity for the federal amendment.[32]

The moribund NAWSA was revitalized by Carrie Chapman Catt after she assumed the presidency in 1915. She began by studying the situation of the suffrage forces in each state. She too realized the bankruptcy of solely relying upon state amendments. She therefore formed a comprehensive plan of action for the association calling for a reorganization and renewal of state campaigns in conjunction with a renewed national effort for a federal amendment. She even prepared for the battles over ratification in the individual states to be put into effect after the amendment passed Congress. Years of intensive effort by Catt, Paul, and their thousands of coworkers were rewarded when the federal amendment was passed in June 1919 and when ratification was accomplished in August 1920.[33]

K. Suffrage Attitudes of Prominent Women

Since suffrage was a very current issue when John William Leonard was preparing his *Woman's Who's Who*, he specifically included a question regarding opinion on woman's suffrage on the data sheet which entrants were to fill out. This means that those women who were silent on suffrage took a stand of sorts on the issue; they had to make a definite decision not to answer the question. A few women with views on the topic asked the editor not to include their opinions for business or personal reasons. One women wrote, "I'm in favor of it, but don't put that in, for my husband forbids it." According to Leonard, this was "the only Woman-Afraid-of-Her-Husband" disclosed in his entire editorial correspondence with more than 10,000 women.[34] But the vast majority of women who did not answer can be rightly adjudged as taking a public stand of neutral.

A majority, or 53.5% of all prominent women favored suffrage, with 23.8% being active suffragists. Over one-third were neutral (37.0%), and only 9.5% of the women were against woman suffrage. The activists against suffrage were a minute 1.5% of the total.

Occupation type was the best predictor of suffrage opinion, with region being second. Professional women favored and worked for suffrage more than any other group, with 69.3% of their number favoring the cause and 38.7% actively working for it. Women in education were in second place with 52.8% favoring suffrage and 18.7% as active suffragists. With women in the arts, the women who were neutral (44.9%) almost equaled those who favored suffrage (45.5%). The noncareer women, with slightly more favoring suffrage (47.1%) than those in the arts, had the highest percentage for those against suffrage (16.4%). (See figure 13.)

The small number of women who were full-time paid suffrage workers were defined as professionals because their characteristics and life history most closely matched those of professional women. Nevertheless, the number of full-time suffragists do not distort the fact that women in the professions strongly favored woman suffrage and frequently agitated for it. This was no doubt due to the obstacles they had faced in gaining their educations and establishing themselves in their professions. Elsie de Wolfe, the first American interior decorator, claimed that her suffrage views were a result of her professional endeavors. "I was in business, and through contacts in the business world I realized how women were handicapped by the many discriminations against them in the matter of pay and promotion and the kind of work they were permitted to do."[35] De Wolfe's experiences were shared by many other professional women.

While professional women and noncareer women worked together on humanitarian causes, reform work, and in women's clubs, they appeared to diverge on the issue of suffrage. Controlling for current events interest, however, shows that a majority (58.1%) of the noncareer women who were reformers also favored suffrage, and almost one-third (31.1%) worked for it. The number of those neutral among noncareer women went down, from 36.4% to 27.0% for the noncareer reformers. It is interesting, though, that the number of antis remained high even for those noncareer women who were reformers. For all noncareer women, the percentage was 16.4, while for those who were

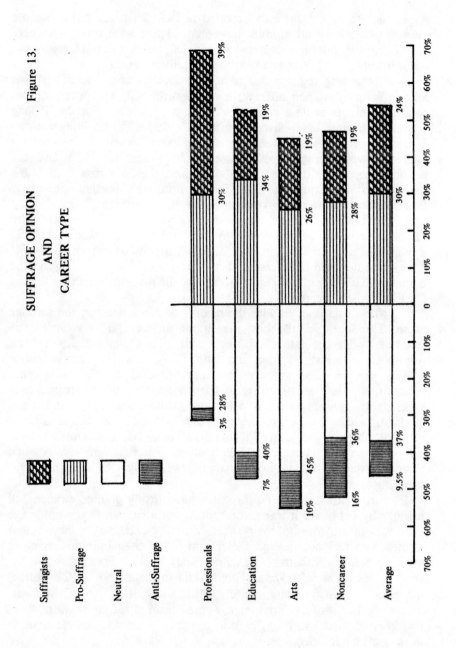

Figure 13.

SUFFRAGE OPINION
AND
CAREER TYPE

reformers, the percentage only dropped to 14.9. That was still above the average of 9.5% for all prominent women. There were therefore a core of antis among noncareer women who did not alter their suffrage views even when they participated in other reform work.

Regarding regional variation, the South was the area that was least in favor of woman suffrage; it was also the only area where the in- and out-migrants made a difference in the percentages. For the lifelong Southerners, only 39.4% favored suffrage, with 58.2% remaining neutral. These two percentages almost interchanged exactly when the in- and out-migrants were averaged in. Those in favor rose to 47.2% and the neutrals dropped to 39.3%. At the same time, the antis rose from 11.8% for lifelong Southerners to 13.2% for the total with Southern residence. Eastern women were also lukewarm on the issue, with 48.8% favoring the cause. In contrast, Western women were fervid suffrage supporters, with 71.6% favoring the reform, and almost one-third of the women (32.6%) actually working for it. The West also had the lowest percentage (4.2%) for women opposed to suffrage. The Midwest was above average in the numbers that favored suffrage (66.2%) and in the number of suffragists (28.1%). (See figure 14.)

These statistics fit with the records of the regions on the suffrage cause. The South was the most recalcitrant, for there suffrage came to be connected with the issues of Negro voting and states rights. Even women such as Kate Gordon and Laura Clay, both one-time executive officers of NAWSA, bitterly fought ratification of the Nineteenth Amendment. It meant suffrage at the price of federal dominance over states rights. The East was also a laggard on the issue. As late as the fall of 1918, when the Senate rejected the suffrage amendment after a personal plea by President Wilson, the *Woman Citizen* wrote: "New England and the Democratic South stood together, and the Atlantic seaboard from Maine to Louisiana cast twenty-eight of the thirty-four opposing votes."[36]

In contrast, ten Western states had already granted women full suffrage by 1914, and it was natural for Western women to champion the extension of suffrage to their sisters across the country. Even those women who had not favored the reform found their opinions changing once the ballot was theirs. The author Mary Hallock Foote stated in her entry in the *Woman's Who's Who*: "Anti-suffragist, but as Cal(ifornia) has given women franchise, expects to live up to it."[37] In the Midwest, where two-thirds of the prominent women favored the cause, most states had granted partial suffrage, such as the vote in presidential elections or in school board elections.

There was no correlation between marital status and suffrage opinion. Although the women who opposed suffrage were mothers as

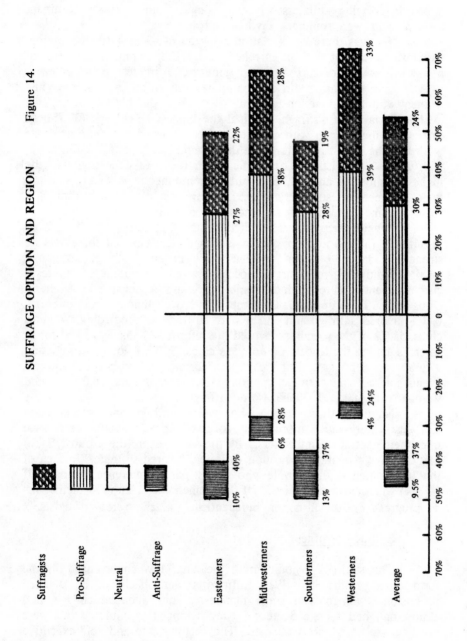

SUFFRAGE OPINION AND REGION

Figure 14.

Suffragists

Pro-Suffrage

Neutral

Anti-Suffrage

Easterners

Midwesterners

Southerners

Westerners

Average

opposed to being childless wives or single women, most prominent women who were mothers favored suffrage.

Nor was there a correlation between age and suffrage opinion. Other variables that did not correlate with suffrage opinion were size of hometown or size of current home, genealogical interest, or art interest.

Even education did not correlate with suffrage opinion. While women who had done postgraduate work had the highest percentage (59.6%) in favor of suffrage and had the highest percentage (32.7%) of suffragists, the women with college degrees who had not done graduate work had the lowest percentages in those same categories (47.6% in favor, with 16.2% suffragists). The women with the least education had the highest number of antis (13.6%), but their number in favor (48.4%) and their number of suffragists (19.9%) were slightly higher than the corresponding percentages for the women with college degrees.

Religious activists had a slightly higher percentage both in favor of suffrage (56.9%) and opposed to suffrage (13.1%). But there was no strong correlation between religious activism and suffrage opinion.

Positive correlations did occur between humanitarian interests, current events interests, and membership and leadership in women's clubs and suffrage opinion. Of those women with humanitarian interests, 63.0% favored suffrage and 31.8% were suffragists. Regarding women's clubs, 53.0% of the members favored the reform and 15.6% worked for it, whereas among the leaders of women's clubs, 66.0% favored suffrage and 37.6% were suffragists. But the highest correlation was between current events interest and suffrage opinion. Of the reformers, 70.0% favored woman suffrage and 39.0% were suffragists.

Naturally, those women who favored suffrage, and especially the suffragists, were much more likely to give a political party preference than their neutral or anti sisters. By the same token, the group (18.2%) that did give a political indication definitely favored suffrage. In fact, of the 160 women in the sample who gave a party preference, almost half (47.5%) were active suffragists. Of the women who identified themselves as progressives, socialists, or independents, 62.2% were suffragists.[38]

L.   Suffrage Profiles

The statistics become more meaningful when arranged in the form of a profile. In 1914, suffragists were likely to be married professional women with small families. They attended college, and almost half had college degrees. They belonged to churches but were not likely to be religious activists. They belonged to and held executive positions in women's clubs. They did humanitarian work and were likely to engage in other reform work besides their suffrage activity.

This profile of the typical suffragist looks quite similar to that for reformers. In fact, Caroline Bartlett Crane, the previous example of a professional woman who was a progressive reformer, fits the suffragist profile very well. But there are some major differences between the two groups. A reformer was almost as likely to be a noncareer woman as she was a professional woman; suffragists were professional women. Although young women were the least likely to be suffragists, there was no positive correlation between age and suffrage opinion as there was between age and reform interests. While this was also true for education, suffragists were in general college educated. This matches their professional career type. The percentage of suffragists who were religious activists was about the average (30.4%), while that for reformers was somewhat higher (36.9%). In general, one might say that a reformer who was a professional woman might also fit the suffragist profile, but a reformer who was a noncareer woman could not be considered a typical suffragist.

The life of Catharine Waugh McCulloch, an Illinois lawyer and suffragist, demonstrates the suffragist profile. Born in New York in 1862 Catherine Waugh was reared on an Illinois farm. She graduated from Rockford Female Seminary and then from the Union College of Law in Chicago, a forerunner of Northwestern University Law School. After her graduation in 1886, when she encountered difficulty in establishing a legal practice in Chicago, she began a practice in Rockford. At the same time, she continued her studies at Rockford Seminary, receiving her B.A. and M.A. in 1888 after completing a thesis on woman's wages. Two years later Catharine Waugh married Frank Hathorn McCulloch, whom she had met in law school, with the Reverend Anna Howard Shaw officiating at the wedding. She went into joint practice with her husband whose legal firm was renamed McCulloch & McCulloch. Their family of four children was larger than the typical for suffragists or prominent women in general. It is interesting, though, that all four of the children had their mother's maiden name as their middle name. But despite McCulloch's rather large family, she continued with her flourishing practice and became actively involved in the suffrage movement.[39]

McCulloch worked on the state, regional, and national levels for woman suffrage. As legislative superintendent of the Illinois Equal Suffrage Association, she yearly submitted a bill to the Illinois legislature providing for woman suffrage in presidential and certain local elections. After twenty years of lobbying, McCulloch's bill was passed in 1913. McCulloch not only wrote articles and plays, and gave speeches for the suffrage cause, she also served as a legal adviser and executive officer of NAWSA. When she became unhappy over the Eastern orientation of that body, she helped to found the Mississippi Valley Conference in 1912 to hold regional suffrage conventions.

True to the suffrage profile, McCulloch also engaged in a variety of humanitarian and reform work, and belonged to women's clubs. In 1913, she was a member of the Chicago Woman's Club, the Evanston Woman's Club, the Frederick Douglass Center, and the Immigration Aid Society, besides a variety of suffrage organizations. She led a campaign to get Lucy Flower, reformer and Chicago Woman's Club member, elected to the previously all-male board of trustees of the University of Illinois. She publicized the legal disabilities of women in her book *Mr. Lex*. McCulloch also continuously sponsored reform legislation. In 1901, the Illinois legislature passed her bill granting women equal rights in the guardianship of their children, and in 1905, it passed another which raised the age of consent for women from fourteen to sixteen.[40]

Such well-known national leaders of the suffrage movement like Carrie Chapman Catt and the Reverend Anna Howard Shaw deviated from the norm mainly in their all-consuming devotion to the suffrage cause. They had no time for the multiplicity of humanitarian interests and reform work which engaged most suffragists in 1913. Alice Paul had been active in settlement work, but she, like Shaw, was unmarried and she apparently took no interest in women's clubs--both unusual qualities for suffragists.

Those women who opposed suffrage, or the antis, had different characteristics. They were noncareer women who were married and were mothers. They were likely to have larger families than the average; 38.7% had three or more children, compared with 28.3% for the average prominent woman. They were not college-educated. The majority of the antis did humanitarian work, but they were less likely to do so than the average prominent woman (57.3% for the antis as opposed to 62.3% for the average). They were as likely to be religious activists (42.2%) as they were to be mere church members (43.4%). They were not likely to do reform work, although they belonged to women's clubs at a higher rate (80%) than average (77%). Almost half (48.2%) of all antis were leaders in women's clubs, which was about the average (48.7%) for prominent women.

The biography of Lena Wooten Schackleford, as found in the *Woman's Who's Who*, illustrates the profile of the anti-suffragist. Born in Woodburn, Kentucky, in 1862, Lena Wooten was educated in public and private schools. She graduated from Logan Female College in Russelville, Kentucky, which was probably the equivalent of an academy. In 1888, Lena Wooten married Thomas M. Schackleford, who became chief justice of the Supreme Court of Florida. The Schacklefords had three children. In 1913, Lena Schackleford claimed that she had been identified with religious, social, and philanthropic affairs in Florida for twenty years, although her real forte seemed to be club work. She was president of the Whittier Club of Brooksville, first vice president of the

Tampa Women's Club, and president of the Tallahassee Women's Club. From 1908-10, Schackleford had been president of the Florida Federation of Women's Clubs. She belonged to the Christian Church, and she stated that she was against woman suffrage.[41] In connection with Schackleford's biography, it should be noted that while antis were likely to be club leaders, only 9.4% of all women's club leaders opposed suffrage and 66.0% favored it. So while Schackleford was a typical anti, she was not a typical woman's club leader.

The entry of Edith Mitchel Bradner provides another example of an anti-suffragist who fits the profile. Born in Flushing, New York in 1870, Edith Mitchel Murray married the Rev. Lester Bradner when she was fifteen years old. She gave no data on her schooling, which leads one to believe that it was sporadic and certainly did not include attendance at a college. The Bradners had three children. Edith Bradner declared her interests to be education, teacher training for Sunday schools, child welfare, and ornithology. An Episcopalian, she belonged to the Rhode Island Sunday-school Alumnae Association and the Girls' Friendly Society. Bradner also held membership in the Audubon Society, Shakespearian Society, Providence Mothers' Club and something called the Rhode Island Clerica. She declared herself against woman suffrage. Bradner thus displayed the typical anti interest in religious activism and women's clubs without a comparable interest in reform activities.[42]

No detailed study has been made as to why such women as Schackleford and Bradner opposed woman suffrage. They may have feared for the sanctity of the home, thinking it in sure danger of collapse if women were to become involved in politics. They may have believed that women were to be subservient to men according to God's immutable law. It is quite likely, though, that the basis for such anti-suffragism among prosperous women lay in their own elitism. These women had power already by virtue of their own position in society and that of their husband's. They feared that an extension of the franchise would mean a dispersal of that power to other women--whether they were black women in the South, immigrant women in the East, or merely other native white women in a lower class than theirs. Margaret Deland expressed such anti-democratic attitudes very succinctly when she stated:

> We have suffered many things at the hand of Patrick; the New Woman would add Bridget also. And . . . to the vote of that fierce, silly, amiable creature, the uneducated Negro, she would add . . . the vote of his sillier, baser female.
>
> I hope I am not understood as being opposed to woman suffrage. I am only protesting against suffrage for all women; just as I would

protest (if there was any use in doing so) against suffrage for all men. In other words, I protest against any extension of the suffrage.[43]

Unable to repeal universal manhood suffrage, the anti-suffragists were determined that it should not be extended to all women as well.

The women who took a public stand of neutral were characterized mainly by negatives, things in which they were not interested compared with suffragists and anti-suffragists. Almost 70% of the neutrals were married, and 43.4% had children. They were fairly evenly distributed over the career types, with 31.5% being noncareer women, 25.9% in the arts, 24.1% in education, and 18.5% in professions. The neutrals were likely to have some years in college, though not necessarily a degree. They were less inclined to church membership than the average prominent woman. Almost 40% of the neutrals failed to give a denominational preference compared to 27.4% for the average. This group of women failed to do either humanitarian work or reform work. Although a majority (60%) of the neutrals belonged to women's clubs, they were well below the average membership rate of 77%. In addition, they failed to command leadership positions in the clubs. The neutrals thus present a picture of noninvolvement in the activities that interested most prominent women. Refusing to take a stand on the suffrage question was but another part of their noninvolvement. In some cases these women were totally taken up with their professional lives. In other cases, the women may have participated in some activities, but only gave professional information for the *Woman's Who's Who*.

The entries of Gabrielle DeVeaux Clements and Bessie Faunce Gill illustrate the profile of the typical neutral. Born in Philadelphia and educated at Cornell University, Clements took postgraduate training in art at the Pennsylvania Academy of Fine Arts and the Academie Julian in Paris. Other than this educational information, Clements admitted only that her chief works as of 1914 were mural paintings in Baltimore and Washington. Bessie Faunce Gill graduated from Smith College in 1887, and after a year of graduate work at Smith, took a teaching position in Miss Capen's School, Northampton, Mass. Twenty-six years later she was still there, although by then she was the associate principal. Like Clements, Gill gave no indication of church membership, club membership, activities, interests or suffrage opinion.[44]

M.   Conclusion

By 1914, socially visible women pursued a wide variety of public activities. Of particular import is the inter-relatedness of several types of interests and the unrelatedness of others. Humanitarianism and reform proclivities were correlated with each other and with membership and leadership in women's clubs.   Other kinds of activities, such as community arts groups, patriotic societies, and alumnae associations, appealed to distinct and separate minorities of the women.   The three central concerns then--reform work, humanitarian interests, and women's clubs--comprised the core of public activities for prominent women in 1914. Pro-suffrage opinion also correlated with these three interests, but actual suffrage agitation was not characteristic of most publicly active women.

Surprisingly, the two groups that dominated the major women's activities--noncareer women and women in the professions--were quite divergent.   One group was poorly educated; the other, very well educated.   One had active religious interests; the other apparently had none.   And while the two groups worked together on humanitarian projects, reform work, and in women's clubs, they separated on the suffrage question.

NOTES

[1]Muriel Beadle and the Centennial History Committee, *The Fortnightly of Chicago: The City and Its Women: 1873-1973* (Chicago: Henry Regency Company, 1973), p. 34. Knobe, "Mrs. May Wright Sewall," p. 280. De Wolfe, *After All*, pp. 98-99.

[2]See Scott, *The Southern Lady* and Mary Elizabeth Massey, *Bonnet Brigades* (New York: Alfred A. Knopf, 1966).

[3]Flexner, *Century of Struggle*, p. 179.

[4]J. C. Croly, *The History of the Woman's Club Movement in America* (New York: Henry G. Allen & Co., 1898), p. 8.

[5]*Ibid.*, p. 8.

[6]*Ibid.*, p. 8.

[7]James, "Introduction," *NAW*, 3:26.

[8]Hannah Greenebaum Solomon," *NAW* 3:324-25.

[9]Elizabeth Wilson, *Fifty Years of Association Work among Young Women: 1866-1916* (New York: National Board of the Young Women's Christian Associations, 1916), pp. 23.

[10]Wilson, *Fifty Years*, pp. 25-38. Mary S. Sims, *The Natural History of a Social Institution--The Young Women's Christian Association* (New York: The Woman's Press, 1936), pp. 29-30.

[11]Wilson, *Fifty Years*, pp. 38-45.

[12]Sims, *History*, pp. 21-25. "Anna Goodman Hertzberg," *WWW*, p. 384-385.

[13]Sims, *History*, p. 193.

[14]Wilson, *Fifty Years*, pp. 29-32. Sims, *History*, pp. 95-120.

[15]Quoted in Wilson, *Fifty Years*, p. 38. Margaret Burton, *Mabel Cratty: Leader in the Art of Leadership* (New York: The Woman's Press, 1929), pp. 15-27. Sims, *History*, p. 55.

[16]Sims, *History*, pp.. 165-69; 208-09; 173.

[17]This figure includes the women who belonged to mission societies or the YWCA, but it goes beyond religious humanitarian work to include those who engaged in secular charitable efforts.

[18]"Nancy Dryden Richards," *WWW*, p. 685.   "Katherine Porter," *WWW*, p. 654.

[19]Josephine Baker, *Fighting for Life.*   "Jane Lord Hersom," *WWW*, p. 384.   Eva Charlotte Reid, *WWW*, p. 679.

[20]"Edith Shope Reider," *WWW*, p. 679.   "Florence Ledyard Cross Kitchelt," *WWW*, p. 461.

[21]"Mrs. John Amee," *WWW*, p. 47.   "Rebecca Barnard Raoul Altstaetter," *WWW*, 47. "Mariette Amanda Barnes Knight," *WWW*, p. 464.

[22]Flexner, *Century of Struggle*, pp. 181-186.   O'Neill, *Everyone Was Brave*, p. 35. "Frances Elizabeth Caroline Willard."   *NAW*, 3:613-19.

[23]Robert La Follette, *La Follette's Autobiography* (Madison: The University of Wisconsin Press, 1960), p. 43.

[24]Lucretia Blankenburg, *The Blankenburgs of Philadelphia.*   Helen Christine Bennett, *American Women in Civic Work* (New York: Dodd, Mead and Company, 1915), pp. 207-227.   See also "Lucretia Longshore Blankenburg," *NAW*, 1:170-71.

[25]Albion Fellows Bacon, *Beauty for Ashes,* p. 13; p. 29.

[26]Bacon, *Beauty for Ashes.*   Bennett, *American Women,* pp. 117-37.   "Albion Fellows Bacon," *NAW*, 1:76-77.   "Albion Fellows Bacon," *WWW*, p. 64.

[27]Quoted in Bennett, *American Women,* p. 218.

[28]Bennett, *American Women,* pp. 1-45.   "Caroline Julia Bartlett Crane," *NAW*, 1:401-02. "Caroline Bartlett Crane," *WWW*, pp. 213-14.

[29]Flexner, *Century of Struggle*, p. 82.   Aileen S. Kraditor, *The Ideas of the Woman Suffrage Movement 1890-1920*, Chapter I.   See also *The History of Woman Suffrage.* Volumes I to III were edited by Elizabeth Cady Stanton, Susan Anthony, and Mathilda Joslyn Gage.   Volumes I and II were published in Rochester, New York, in 1881 and Volume III was published there also in 1896.   Susan B. Anthony and Ida Husted Harper edited Volume IV, which was published in Rochester in 1902.   The last two volumes, V and VI, were edited by Ida Husted Harper and published in New York in 1922.   For a recent interpretation of the early leaders for women's rights, see Hersh, "The Slavery of Sex."

[30]On the membership, see Kraditor, *Ideas,* p. 5.

[31]Flexner, *Century of Struggle*, pp. 221-225.

[32]*Ibid,* pp. 262-270.

[33] *Ibid,* pp. 272-275.

[34] *WWW,* p. 25.

[35] Elsie de Wolfe, *After All,* p. 140.

[36] Quoted in Flexner, *Century of Struggle,* p. 310.

[37] Mary Hallock Foote," *WWW,* p. 300.

[38] For other suffrage indicators, see Richard Jensen, "Family Career and Reform: Women Leaders of the Progressive Era," *The American Family in Social-Historical Perspective,* ed. Michael Gordon (New York: St. Martin's Press, 1973), pp. 267-80.

[39] "Catharine Gouger Waugh McCulloch," *NAW* 2:459-60.

[40] *Ibid.,* "Catherine Waugh McCulloch," *WWW,* p. 515.

[41] Lena Wooten Shackleford, *WWW,* p. 733.

[42] "Edith Mitchel Bradner," *WWW,* p. 122.

[43] Margaret Deland, "The Change in the Feminine Ideal," p. 299.

[44] "Gabrille DeVeaux Clements," *WWW,* p. 184. "Bessie Faunce Gill," *WWW,* p. 326.

CHAPTER VI

ACTIVITIES AND INTERESTS:
WOMEN'S CLUBS
AND OTHER TYPES OF FEMALE ASSOCIATIONS

More than any other single activity, women's clubs appealed to large numbers of prominent American women in the early twentieth century. From their inception in the late 1860's, membership in women's clubs mushroomed until by 1896 the General Federation of Women's Clubs could claim a following of 100,000 women. By 1912, the number was over a million.[1]

A.   Cultural Clubs

"Light Seekers" was the name given to the first woman's clubs because they were founded as study groups. In days when women were poorly educated, the club was viewed by middle class women as providing an opportunity for self-improvement. In fact, the early clubs came to be called the "'middle-aged woman's university' of the nineteenth century."[2]

Friends in Council, a group of women in Quincy, Illinois, met regularly since 1866, and the New England Woman's Club was founded in 1868. But the real mother of clubs was the Sorosis of New York, also founded in 1868. Much publicity attended its founding, which occurred as a protest against the exclusiveness of the New York Press Association. When Jennie June Croly, a noted journalist, was denied admission to the banquet held by the press association for Charles Dickens, she proceeded to found an organization of her own. The subsequent social fencing between the two organizations, Sorosis and the New York Press Association, drew national attention to this novelty, a woman's club.[3]

The early clubs were all literary in nature. An examination of Chicago's famous Fortnightly Club, founded in 1873, demonstrates how such clubs functioned. The Fortnightly met twice monthly, alternating afternoon meetings for members with open evening meetings. Members gave papers in the afternoon meetings on literary and historical topics. For example, in 1873 and 1874, the Fortnightly heard presentations on George Eliot's best seller *Middlemarch*, and the writings of Bret Harte, and deliberated for one whole afternoon on "Music, in Connection with Herbert Spencer's Essay on the Origin and Function of Music."

Occasionally, the club discussed a practical topic, such as the training of children. Men and women nonmembers addressed the group at evening meetings. The club prided itself on its scholarly seriousness. Although its numbers grew quickly, the Fortnightly maintained a socially exclusive membership policy.[4]

Less famous literary clubs continued to be founded and to prosper well into the twentieth century. The following exemplify the diversity of such clubs. The Shakespeare Society of Rockland, Maine, was founded in 1889. Its forty members studied three of Shakespeare's plays each winter, occasionally producing one of the plays. Alabama's first woman's club, the Thursday Literary Club of Selma, organized in 1890, had quite a different schedule of programs in its early years. They included "McCarthy's 'American Authors,' White's 'Eighteen Christian Centuries,' 'Foreign Cities,' and other topics." At the same time, the Women's Reading Club of Walla Walla, Washington, studied American and English authors and "parliamentary drills" during the year 1898.[5]

By 1914, literary clubs were still popular, although by then they had outlived their usefulness as a means of educating women. Naturally, women with careers in the arts showed the highest degree of literary interest, but women in the other occupational types also showed a high degree of literary predilections.

Art clubs were also popular as a means of self-education. Most of the clubs studied the history of art, especially that of classical Greece and Rome and modern Europe. In 1898, such disparate places as Oshkosh, Wisconsin, and Pueblo, Colorado, boasted art clubs. The Ruskin Art Club of Los Angeles took a unique tack by concentrating solely on the study of etching and engraving. The Arche Club of Chicago, formed in 1889, presents a rare instance of a cultural club which engaged in some practical work. It held an annual salon for the exhibition of the works of Chicago artists and sculptors, and some years awarded prizes to various artists. The Arche Club was even more rare in that it engaged in philanthropic work besides art study and art patronage.[6]

Twenty-nine percent (29%) of notable women in 1914 belonged to community art groups. Again, those with careers in the arts showed the highest degree of interest. There was little regional variance in relation to cultural activities.

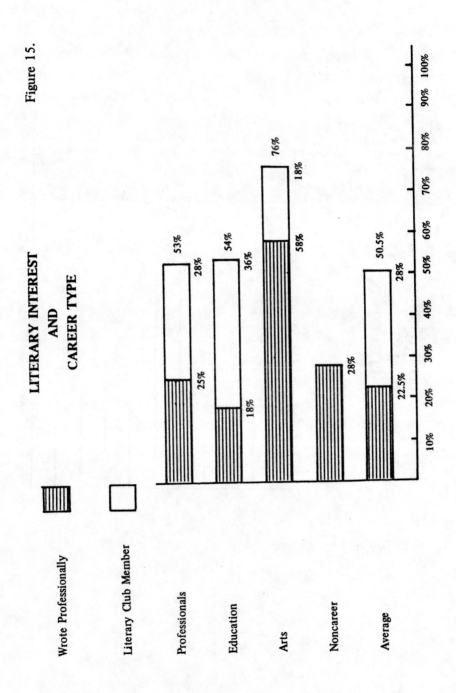

Figure 15.

LITERARY INTEREST
AND
CAREER TYPE

Wrote Professionally

Literary Club Member

Professionals

Education

Arts

Noncareer

Average

53%
28%
25%

54%
36%
18%

76%
18%
58%

28%

50.5%
28%
22.5%

10% 20% 30% 40% 50% 60% 70% 80% 90% 100%

Figure 16.

ART INTEREST
AND
CAREER TYPE

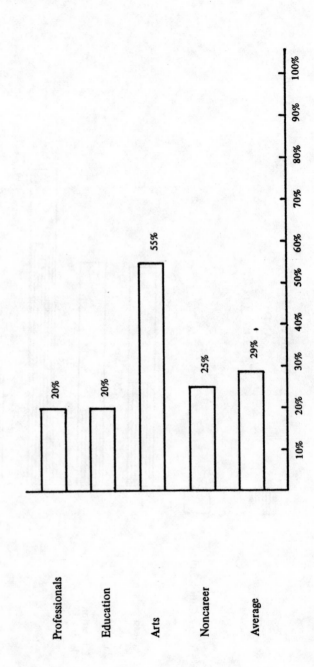

B.   The General Federation of Women's Clubs

After cultural clubs had begun to develop around the country, some members of Sorosis in New York decided that the clubs should band together in a national organization. Sorosis called a convention in 1889 which was attended by delegates from sixty-one clubs. From this convention sprang the General Federation of Women's Clubs.

The first constitution of the GFWC stated that member clubs must be primarily for literary, artistic, or scientific culture, not for political or philanthropic work. But only one year later, in 1891, Jennie June Croly called for the inclusion of reform work among club goals in a famous statement:

> ". . .The eagerness with which the women's clubs all over the country have taken up history, literature, and art studies, striving to make up for the absence of opportunity and the absorption in household cares of their young womanhood, has in it something almost pathetic. But this ground will soon have been covered. Is there not room in the clubs for outlook committees, whose business it should be to investigate township affairs, educational, sanitary, reformatory, and on lines of improvement, and report what is being done, might be done, or needs to be done, for decency and order in the jails, in the schools, in the streets, in the planting of trees, in the disposition of refuse, and the provision for light which is the best protection for life and property."[7]

In fact, almost from the beginning, women's clubs tended to branch out into general civic activity. Ellen M. Henrotin, elected president of the GFWC in 1894, initiated a study of the trend toward broader interests. A symposium which grew out of this inquiry included these thoughts from Mary E. Mumford, vice-president of the GFWC from 1894-1896:

> When the General Federation of Women's Clubs was first organized it was found that clubs in all parts of the country (though primarily intended for literary culture) had extended their studies to civic affairs. Many of them had also begun to concern themselves with the welfare of the communities to which they belonged, and the very first delegates' reports showed that practical results were already in evidence.
>
> The attention of the women seems to have been turned first toward the needs of children, and in many towns they brought to lagging school boards a knowledge of the newer thought in education. They advocated manual training (tool-work for boys, sewing and cooking

for girls), while their encouragement of kindergartens gave a valuable
impulse to that foundation principle of child training.[8]

Henrotin's administration was also noteworthy for defining the
relationship between state federations and the GFWC. Up to that time,
the General Federation had been an aggregation of local clubs, and the
idea of state federations seemed to threaten the integrity of the larger
body. By 1894, however, four states had already federated and many
others were in the process of doing so. Henrotin led the way in
welcoming this development as a means of strengthening the General
Federation. In her inaugural address at the second biennial convention,
held in Philadelphia in May 1884, Henrotin stated:

> . . .The impulse which has led to local centralization has been
> spontaneous and therefore points the lines of natural growth. The
> far West and the far South need a stronger stimulus than the
> biennial, that only the rare, privileged delegate can attend. Every
> permanent inspiration must be born from *within*. This it is which
> will make the cumulative momentum of the ideal federated force.
> The larger will give to the smaller, breadth; the smaller to the larger,
> intensity.[9]

The state federations almost immediately seized upon practical
work. In 1896, the state federation of Maine established kindergartens
and libraries in the public schools, while the federation of Michigan
elected to study household economics. Both the New York and Ohio
federations were also interested in educational questions and the
founding of public libraries, while the group in the District of Columbia
concentrated on reform laws affecting women and children in the
District.[10]

The General Federation amended its bylaws in 1896 to allow a
wider scope of interests for member clubs. The emphasis no longer lay
on literary, artistic, or scientific culture. The General Federation thus
came to encourage civic activity rather than self-education. There was,
however, no discussion of potentially explosive issues such as woman's
suffrage until the biennial convention of 1904. At that meeting, the
General Federation was prodded farther along the path of progressive
reform.[11]

Sarah Platt Decker, of Denver, Colorado, led part of the initial
discussion of woman's suffrage. Her presentation had such an impact
that she was elected the new president of the GFWC. Decker's
inaugural address was something of a bombshell. "Ladies," she began,
"you have chosen me your leader. Well, I have an important piece of
news to give you. Dante is dead. He has been dead for several

centuries, and I think it is time that we dropped the study of his Inferno and turned our attention to our own." She proceeded to describe the social and political problems which afflicted the globe, and she importuned the women to dispense with their cultural activities and to join the struggle for a better world. To prod the organization into action, Decker made a clean sweep of the committees, and appointed women more energetic in reform causes.[12]

The General Federation was too large and amorphous an organization to become a cohesive agent for reform, nevertheless, its influence should not be underestimated. Its very size and respectability lent prestige to reform work for women, at the same time attracting large numbers of women who would not otherwise have come into contact with civic activism. Most practical work was done on the local level by local groups, but the GFWC provided an encouraging atmosphere for them. Local groups knew that their compatriots in the General Federation were doing similar work across the country. The GFWC also lent itself to direct action in some cases. In one instance, it supported Julia Lathrop's work in the federal Children's Bureau by investigating the recording of births across the country for that agency.[13]

C.   Local Women's Clubs

The Chicago Woman's Club was one of the pioneer local clubs in the country both in its structure and in its emphasis on social activism. Organized in 1876 by twenty-one women, by 1883 it had begun to concentrate on practical work. The club was organized into six departments: reform, home, education, philanthropy, art and literature, and philosophy and science. Members were to belong to one department, although they could participate in the activities of other departments if they so desired. In 1892 about 60% of the membership belonged to the reform, philanthropy, and education departments.[14]

The club grew quickly. It more than tripled in size the first year of its existence, from 21 to 65, and ten years later, in 1886, it numbered about 200 members. By 1892, the number had grown to 566, and about 1900, club membership was limited to 1000. That limitation was raised to 1200 in 1911.[15]

The Chicago Woman's Club engaged in a wide variety of civic activities. Organized under its auspices were the Protective Agency of Women and Children, a legal aid society , the Physiological Institute, the Society of Physical Culture and Correct Dress, the Public Art Association, and the Chicago Political Equality League. It secured the appointment of women physicians in the Cook County Insane Asylum and in that in Kankakee for the care of female patients. It participated in direct relief work during the depression of 1893, providing employment and housing for destitute women. It supported a trial kindergarten in one of the public schools, and through subsequent efforts aided in the establishment of kindergartens throughout the public school system. It established a lodging house for women similar to those of the YWCA, and it sponsored a jail school for boys imprisoned for minor offenses. The club raised money to establish the Glenwood School, an industrial school for boys, after a bill for the proposed school was defeated in the Illinois legislature.[16]   Although the club never officially endorsed woman's suffrage, it definitely took a pro-suffrage stance. It not only helped to entertain Susan Anthony with the Illinois Woman's Suffrage League in 1888, but it sponsored the formation of the Political Equality League in 1894, which was to be headed by Woman's Club Members. At the same time, it used the myth of nonpartisanship to refuse to allow the Home Department to form an anti-suffrage group in 1888.[17]

One more unusual feature of the Chicago Woman's Club was the surprisingly liberal stance it took on the issue of race. Celia Parker Woolley introduced a resolution, passed in 1895, that women should not be excluded from membership on the basis of race or color. Through this resolution, Woolley established a membership for one black woman. She also helped to found the Frederick Douglass center in 1904, which worked to better living conditions for blacks, at the same time bringing middle class white people into contact with blacks.[18]

While the Chicago Woman's Club had considerable influence upon women's clubs across the country, it was unique in several respects. In size, it was much larger than most clubs. A club of several hundred members was considered large. One of more than 1000 members was definitely atypical--although in this case, the size of the club did correspond to the size of the city.

The character of its leadership also contributed to the distinctiveness of the Chicago Woman's Club. Dynamic professional women, such as the doctors Julia Holmes Smith, and Sarah Hackett Stevenson; the lawyers Myra Bradwell and Catherine Waugh McCulloch; educator Ella Flagg Young; social workers Jane Addams, Julia Lathrop, and Mary McDowell; coupled with reformers like Ellen Henrotin, Celia Parker Woolley, Lucy Flower and Frances Willard helped to stimulate the club toward extensive practical work and real social activism. By the same token, the very size and prestige of the club was of significant assistance to these reformers in their myriad causes.

The variety of local women's clubs which flourished in the late nineteenth and early twentieth centuries defy easy categorization and description. They ranged in size from 12 to 1200. Even small towns would boast two or three clubs, while metropolitan areas had hundreds. Most early clubs were cultural in nature. Women aspired to self-education through the meetings. By the late 1880's and early 1890's, many club women became more interested in doing practical community work. Clubs with small memberships met in each other's homes. Larger clubs rented quarters, and a few very large affluent clubs actually built their own clubhouses.

The trappings of club life were important. Almost every group had its motto, its insignia, its flower, its colors. The mottos illumine the aspirations and the spirit of those early groups. "Knowledge is power." "Wisdom, justice, and moderation." "Dare to be what you are, and learn to resign with a good grace all that you are not." "More light." "We believe; we achieve." "Self-culture is the basis of all culture." "No footsteps backward." "Neglect not the gift that is in thee." "And in these cities, there are not only men who pride themselves on learning, but women also."[19]

The clubs were named for Shakespeare and Browning, for the day of the week on which they met, for the century in which they were founded. The Chandler Thinking Club, the Boston Grammar School Club, the Ladies Library Association of Kalamazoo, the Woman's Press Club of Cincinnati, the Good Citizenship League of Long Island, the Industrial Club of Denver--all found their way into the GFWC. And nearly every city and village had one that was simply called the Woman's Club.

The way in which women's clubs developed in Skowhegan, Maine, illustrates how clubs spread within towns and from city to city. When Mrs. F. G. Keene visited Skowhegan in 1882, there were few women's clubs in Maine. Keene belonged to the Lynn Women's Club, of Lynn, Massachusetts, and she gave enthusiastic descriptions "of the work, of the broader outlook upon life, and the intellectual companionship" afforded the women of Lynn by their club. The women of Skowhegan became interested in the idea, and soon after Keene's visit founded the Skowhegan Woman's Club. The purpose of the club was purely literary, although it did help to found a kindergarten. The group had a membership limit of 60 which was eventually increased to 75.[20]

The Skowhegan Woman's Club was evidently composed of older women, because four years later, the young women of the town decided to form a group of their own. Thus, the Skowhegan Sorosis was formed with the intent of considering "questions relating to the moral, intellectual, and social improvement of women." That the programs were desultory and sophomoric apparently grieved some of the members, but the majority chose to value social fellowship above scholarly seriousness or any practical work. The membership began at 50, but was raised to 60 and then 75. Both the Woman's Club and Sorosis progressed from meeting in homes to meeting in the parlors of the public library, and often the two groups sponsored joint lectures.[21]

Ten years after the Skowhegan Sorosis was founded, the original Woman's Club spawned another organization. The Town Improvement Society had a membership of 45 women. It immediately tackled the litter problem in Skowhegan by placing waste receptacles about the town and in the Post Office. The group also caused a sewer to be repaired, and saw that the library grass was cut weekly throughout the summer rather than once or twice a year. In addition, the group studied the cultivation of flowers and the preservation of trees as well as the mode of municipal government, local property rights, and other topics related to current events.[22]

We can thus see how the club idea spread from one community in one state to another in a different state. And the founding of one woman's club in a town led to the founding of several more encompassing a variety of purposes. While the initial and primary impetus for the founding of the clubs in Skowhegan lay in a desire among women for feminine companionship and cultural stimulation, the idea of practical community work and education in current affairs soon surfaced and commanded a sizable following as well.

The Woman's Club of Cripple Creek, Colorado, illustrates how one club could become the central organization for women in a community, rivaling even the churches with its all encompassing nature. Having a charter membership of 35, the Woman's Club of Cripple Creek grew to 131 in the two months after it was founded in 1896. The club was composed of five departments: education, home, music, art and literature, and philanthropy. By 1898, the music department had a chorus which produced regular concerts. The philanthropy department had plans for a newsboy's club with night school. The education department, composed largely of teachers and school board members, sponsored a summer kindergarten. The art and literature department imported a young Denver artist, Charles Partridge Adams, to give an address. The pictures he brought with him formed the first art exhibition ever enjoyed by Cripple Creek. The report in Croly's *History of the Woman's Club Movement in America* included this evaluation of the group's worth: "Where there are no theatres, no lectures, and but little social life, a club like the Woman's Club is an infinite blessing."[23]

D.   Club Membership Among Prominent Women

By 1914, women's club membership and leadership was widespread among socially visible women. The vast majority were members

(77%), and almost half (49%) of all prominent women had held or were presently holding an office of some sort. Membership was highest among noncareer women (85%), and 54% of them were leaders in clubs. Women in the professions had a higher rate of leadership (57%), but a slightly lower rate (79%) for total membership than noncareer women. Women in education and women in the arts had similar rates in both categories. Seventy-one percent (71%) of the women in education were members of women's clubs, while 42% were leaders. For women in the arts, 70% were members and 39% were leaders. If one considers just the women's club leaders, 35% were noncareer women and 29% were in the professions, while only 19% were in education and 17% were in the arts.

Regarding regional variation, lifelong Southerners had the highest percentages both for total membership (83%) and for leadership (55%). Lifelong Midwesterners followed close behind with 82% for membership and 52% for leadership. When part Southerners and part Midwesterners were averaged in, the percentages dropped slightly. The rates for Easterners were below average, with 75% membership and 45% leadership. The rates for Westerners were below average for total membership with 70%, but average for leadership with 49%.

Since the West was more sparsely settled than other regions, it is understandable why the rate for membership in women's clubs should have been below average in the West. What is inexplicable is the variance between the East and the South and Midwest. The South had almost a 10% higher rate than the East both in terms of membership and leadership, and the Midwest had a 7% higher rate. And yet, the real birth of the women's club movement had taken place in the East. Nor could it be argued that women in the East had gone on to other activities by 1914. The club movement was stronger than ever at that time, and club membership was viewed as a basis for a wide variety of activities, whether social, cultural, or political. Prominent women in the East seem to have been peculiarly out of step with their sisters in other regions.

The clubs known as women's clubs--those embodied in the GFWC--were of supreme importance for middle class women in the late nineteenth and early twentieth centures. They offered intellectual stimulation through cultural studies. They offered regular female companionship to satisfy the social needs of women. They also managed to draw many more women into practical reform work than was done by specific reform groups like the Women's Trade Union League and the National Consumer's League. The latter groups were smaller and more cohesive, and therefore accomplished much regarding specific reforms. But the very size, respectability, and basic conservatism of women's

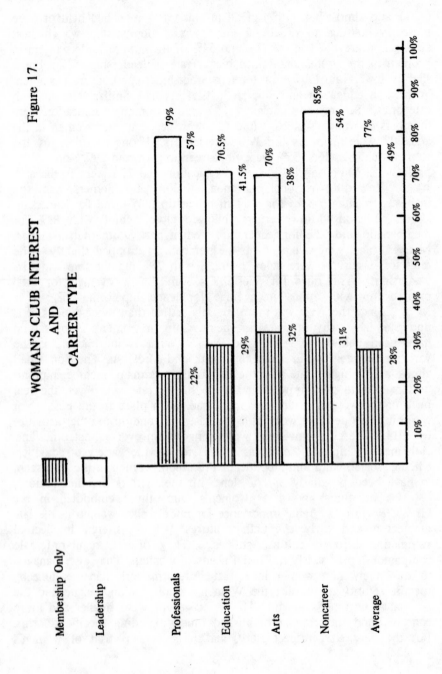

Figure 17.

WOMAN'S CLUB INTEREST
AND
CAREER TYPE

Membership Only

Leadership

Professionals 79% 57% 22%

Education 70.5% 41.5% 29%

Arts 70% 38% 32%

Noncareer 85% 54% 31%

Average 77% 49% 28%

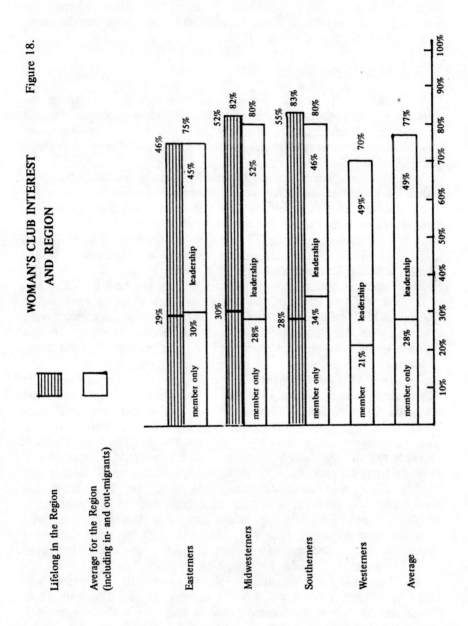

Figure 18.

WOMAN'S CLUB INTEREST
AND REGION

clubs, which made them unsuitable vehicles for radical reform, lent prestige to and provided a power base for individual reformers involved in a variety of reform causes.

E.   Alumnae Associations

Along with general women's clubs, a variety of organizations were founded to appeal to educational, occupational, and avocational interests. One such organization, the Association of Collegiate Alumnae, was formed to meet the social needs of women who were college graduates.

At a time when higher education was not only rare but fraught with innumerable obstacles for women, female graduates felt a need for companionship with their fellows who had shared a college experience. But socializing was not to be the only purpose of the ACA. The founders represented alumnae from eight colleges: Vassar, Boston University, Wellesley, Cornell, the University of Wisconsin, Smith, Oberlin and the University of Michigan. Their goal of furthering the cause of women's education in America was clear but how the ACA was to do that was not. In fact, the venerable Lucy Stone, a graduate of Oberlin in 1847, raised that very point at the organizational meeting held in January of 1882. Stone could see neither the necessity for the organization nor the means for accomplishing its purpose. But she failed to dampen the enthusiasm of the younger graduates.[24]

The ACA did provide a forum for studies concerning the education of women, and it did attempt to encourage high educational standards for colleges that admitted women. The restrictive admissions policy of the organization was ostensibly to promote the latter. A woman with a bachelor's degree was not eligible for membership in the ACA unless her alma mater was a member. Leaders in the ACA thought that pressure from alumnae eager to join the organizaton would force many schools to upgrade their standards.   In fact, the ACA itself was inconsistent and confused about its admissions policies. It continually sought a formula whereby applicant institutions could be uniformly examined, but no easy answer was ever found. At the same time, rifts developed among the membership of the ACA about the degree to which membership should be restricted.

The policy of restricted membership reflected the narrow and elitist nature of the organization which claimed to be national in scope. While the association represented alumnae from the Midwest and West also, the largest block of members lived in the East, reflecting the general settlement patterns of women college graduates.[25] It took the success of the independent Western Association of Collegiate Alumnae to push the organization to allow the affiliation of regional branches. Gradually, however, the group became more national in membership, although the headquarters remained in the East.

Another example of the elitism of the organization was the policy adopted by the ACA regarding postgraduate study for women in Europe. European universities began to open their doors to women pursuing advanced degrees during the 1880's and 1890's. American women responded in increasing numbers to such opportunities. Given the competition among American women, the ACA feared that unqualified applicants, i.e., women who had not attended colleges approved by the association, would damage the chances of better-trained women. The association voted in 1895 to establish a committee which would certify women who were applying for graduate work abroad. The association at the same time petitioned European universities to accept their certificate and, it was understood, reject those applicants who were not certified by the ACA. After six years, the ACA abandoned this effort in response to opposition from within the United States and from European universities.[26]

The regional alumnae associations, the Western Association of Collegiate Alumnae and the Southern Association of College Women, seemed to accomplish far more in the way of concrete, practical work than did the national association. The Western Association, founded in 1883, was comprised mainly of alumnae in the Chicago area. This energetic group sponsored such innovations as fellowships for graduate work and a job placement bureau for graduates interested in teaching. It also collated materials on graduate schools open to women, and even entered the political arena by pressing for the establishment of a reform school for girls in Illinois.[27]

The Southern Association, formed in 1903, was also noted for the practical work it accomplished in its region. Perhaps one of the most important contributions it made was spotlighting the backward state of women's education in the South. Elizabeth Avery Colton made several searching studies of the region's women's colleges. She found that in 1903 of more than 140 institutions calling themselves "college for women," only two of them offered four years of college work. Nine years later, the number had risen to four of 140. Colton continued to collect data and the association continued to publish and publicize her work for more than a decade.[28]

In addition, the Southern Association provided fellowships and sponsored college days in local high schools. During the latter, young women were acquainted with their opportunities for a higher education and were familiarized with college life in general. Entering the political arena, the group worked for laws concerning compulsory education for children in the South and promoted medical supervision for all school children.[29]

The ACA filled a definite need for women at the time it was formed. Women who had graduated from college in the decades after the Civil War felt isolated from other women their age and social status who had not attended college. Such women also felt disoriented and confused when they found little work waiting for them which was in accordance with their educations. The ACA provided companionship for these women not unlike that provided by alumni associations for men. It also offered some useful activities. At the same time, the restrictive admissions policy kept numerous other collegiate alumnae from enjoying the benefits they offered.

For the size of its membership, the ACA probably accomplished a minimum of practical work. But the local and regional alumnae organizations did much to promote not only women's higher education but also reforms on all educational levels.

In 1914, twenty-eight percent (28%) of prominent women claimed membership in an alumnae association. There was no relation between membership in an alumnae association and career type or region or birth. There was a direct relation between the amount of schooling a woman had and the likelihood that she would belong to an alumnae group. Women with little formal education had only a 4% membership rate, while those with some college experience had a 19% rate. In contrast, over half the women with college degrees belonged to alumnae associations. Those with bachelor's degrees had a 55% membership rate, while those who had done postgraduate work had a 51% rate.

Figure 19.

MEMBERSHIP IN ALUMNAE ASSOCIATIONS
AND
LEVEL OF EDUCATION

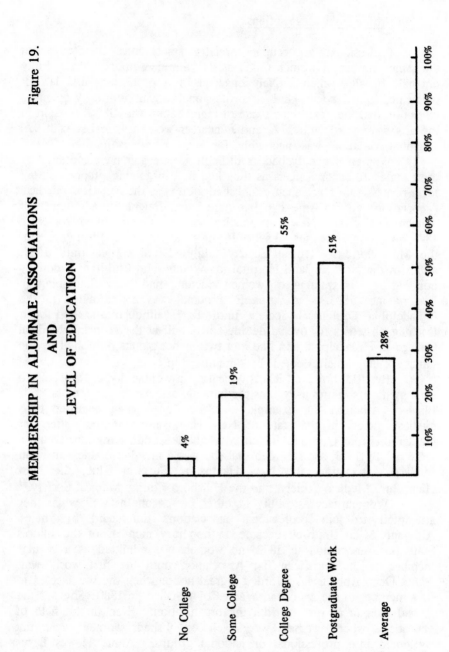

F.   Professional Associations

Professional, or occupation-related associations, attracted about the same number of women (30%) as did alumnae groups (28%). Fully one-half of all women actively engaged in a profession, like law or medicine, joined some kind of professional organization. Women in education had the next highest rate of membership with 38%. Women in the arts were third with 27%, and noncareer women were last with 9%. Regional variation was negligible for such membership.

Women generally had as difficult a time gaining acceptance by their male professional peers as they had had in gaining proper training for a profession. Thus, such established groups as the American Medical Association and the American Bar Association fought the admittance of women for decades. New York medical societies first admitted women in 1871, and soon thereafter, societies in the Chicago area did likewise. But the Massachusetts Medical Society admitted no women until 1884, although the New England Hospital for Women and Children, nationally honored for its training of women doctors, had been flourishing in Boston since 1863. Dr. Anna E. Broomal was not admitted to the Philadelphia Obstetrical Society until 1892, although she had been teaching obstetrics for over a decade and a half at the Woman's Medical College in Philadelphia and had had two of her papers published by the same society which denied her membership.[30]

By 1913, however, it was typical for a woman doctor to belong to local medical societies as well as the national association for doctors. Ella Blaylock Atherton, for example, was the first woman admitted to a medical society in the state of New Hampshire sometime after her graduation from Queen's University Medical School, Kingston, Ontario, in 1887. By 1913, she recorded that she was a member of the American Medical Association, the New Hampshire Surgical Club, the New Hampshire Medical Society, and the Hillsboro County Medical Society.[31]

Women faced hostility in other professions as well when they attempted to join professional associations dominated by males. Although Myra Bradwell became an honorary member of the Illinois State Bar Association in 1872, no woman was admitted as a regular member to the American Bar Association until the first world war. Agnes Dean Abbatt was afforded a great honor when she was elected to be a member of the American Water Color Society in 1880. She was the second woman allowed to join the organization. Even in the field of education, where women were well established, women were not welcomed into professional or national groups. Annie Howes Barus

stated in 1898:   "Even so representative a body as the National
Educational Association counted but few women among its members [in
1882]."[32]

In reaction to such exclusiveness, women formed their own
professional associations on the local, state, and even national level.
Clara Foltz organized the Portia Law Club in San Francisco in 1893, and
later a Women Lawyer's Club. Katherine Brownlee Sherwood became
the first president of the Ohio Newspaper Womens Association in 1902.[33]
In addition, other groups prospered ranging from women's ministerial
clubs to the League of American Pen Women. Such groups were an
important form of encouragement for women who felt isolated within
their occupations. These societies were typically confined to large cities
where there were sufficient numbers of professional women to become
members, but some groups, such as the Pacific Coast Woman's Press
Association, did attempt to draw women on a wider basis.

These professional associations for women functioned in various
ways. The Physicians' League of Buffalo, New York, met monthly to
discuss papers on medical topics, special cases, and new advances in the
field of medicine. The Lady Teachers' Association of Boston, founded in
1874, attempted to help needy teachers and promote the welfare of
Boston schools. In 1896, it became associated with a local hospital, so
that members could enter the hospital at the expense of the club. Thus
women's professional organizations offered both social exchange,
vocational encouragement, and aid for job-related problems.[34]

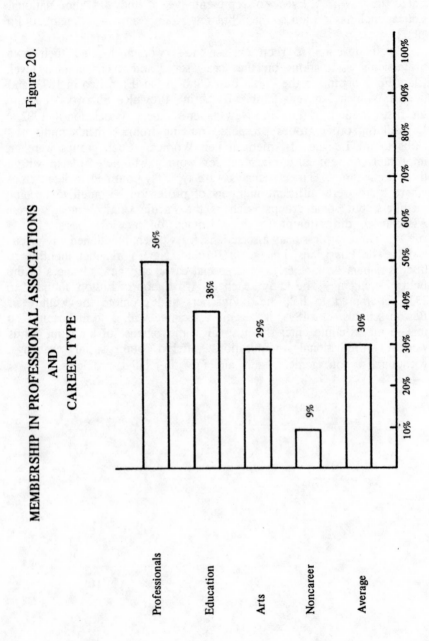

Figure 20.

MEMBERSHIP IN PROFESSIONAL ASSOCIATIONS
AND
CAREER TYPE

G.   Genealogical Interest

Patriotic or genealogical societies were another type of specialized woman's group that gained popularity in the late 19th century. One of the earliest was the Woman's Relief Corp, a female affiliate of the organization for Union veterans of the Civil War, the Grand Army of the Republic. Founded in 1883, the Woman's Relief Corp grew to a membership of 100,000 by the turn of the century. Its charitable work centered on obtaining aid for Union veterans and their families. The group also encouraged patriotic instruction in the nation's schools.[35]

The United Daughters of the Confederacy was the Southern counterpart of the Woman's Relief Corp. Local memorial and benevolent societies had flourished throughout the South in the decades after the Civil War, but it was not until 1894 that a group of women in Nashville founded a regional organization. As with other female patriotic societies, a male group, the United Confederate Veterans, had preceded the woman's society by some years. The United Daughters of the Confederacy sought to commemorate the Southern war effort through erecting monuments, plaques, and statues, establishing museums, and caring for historical sites. The group also aided Confederate veterans and their families. The UDC established strict membership regulations. The original constitution required that prospective members submit proof "that they are descendants of those who have honorably served in the army, or navy, of the Confederate States of America." Only a year later, in 1895, that membership concept was broadened to include the descendants of men who "served in the civil service of the Confederate States, or one of the Southern States; or, who gave personal service to the Confederate cause; or, those who wherever living, gave aid or comfort to the Confederate cause; or, those who wherever living, gave aid or comfort to the Confederate States during the war."[36] Meeting that requirement did not assure automatic membership in the organization, however; social standing was also important.

Although the official history of the UDC gives no membership figures, the organization did become very popular throughout the South. The *Woman's Who's Who* furnished proof in that almost half (48%) of all lifelong Southerners were members of patriotic societies, usually the UDC, or displayed an interest in their genealogy, compared with a 25% rate of interest for notable women in general. The unique history of the South fostered the high rate of interest in genealogy among its women. As losers in the Civil War, Southern women developed a deep-felt need to glorify secession and its consequences. They smarted under the assumption that theirs was the second-class region of the country, scorned and neglected by the dominant sections. What better way to support regional pride and individual self-respect than to memorialize the heroic leaders of the Lost Cause? Also indicative of these concerns was the exceptional interest of the UDC in school textbooks. It wanted to be sure that the "truth" regarding Southern history was taught in all the schools of the region. In addition, an organization such as the UDC was one way of perpetuating traditional social hierarchies and customs even after the improverishment wrought by the war had destroyed the economic base of the social elite.

The Daughters of the American Revolution became the most generally popular of the genealogical societies. Founded in 1890, it capitalized on the twin impulses of ancestor-hunting and patriotism which flourished at the time, but it promoted a national spirit lacking in the United Daughters of the Confederacy and the Woman's Relief Corp. The structure of the DAR was very hierarchical, with the national board of the organization dictating all policy to the local chapters.

The DAR absorbed itself in its own growth for the first decades of its existence. By limiting its members to direct lineal descendants of American patriots, the association appealed to a sense of snobbery and elitism among middle and upper class Americans at the turn of the century. It secured the utmost publicity, while emphasizing the blue-blooded nature of the organization, by choosing its first chief executives from among nationally prominent wives of high government officials. Mrs. Benjamin Harrison, the wife of the President, was the first president-general of the organization, and she was succeeded in office by Mrs. Adlai Stevenson, the wife of Grover Cleveland's Vice-President. In addition, the most popular feature of the DAR's annual congress was the reception given for it at the White House. At a time when native Anglo-Saxon Americans felt that American values were threatened by the hordes of immigrants pouring into the country, the DAR appeared as an attractive bastion for promoting those values. It was socially glamorous, and it solicited members on a nationwide basis. Its membership therefore grew quickly from 450 in 1891 to 80,000 in 1911. It soon outstripped the other patriotic organizations.[37]

Although the Daughters spent most of their time tracing lineages, they did valuable work of a practical nature in the preservation of historical papers, artifacts and sites. They anticipated restoration projects such as that in Williamsburg by nearly half a century. Nor was the organization immune to the Progressive reform movement which flourished in the first decades of the twentieth century. Emily Nelson Ritchie McLean, elected president-general of the DAR in 1905, reflected the desires of a large segment of the membership when she guided the society toward greater activity in contemporary affairs. The DAR began to take an active interest in legislation pending before Congress, especially that regarding child-labor laws and conservation measures. Standing committees dealing with reform causes were established, and Gifford Pinchot, Chief Forester under Theodore Roosevelt and ardent conservationist, was the keynote speaker for the DAR congress of 1909.[38]

McClean's successor, Julia Green Scott, continued the progressive policies of her predecessor. She helped to channel the DAR into the peace movement, and even urged the Daughters to join the Consumer's League in its war on unfair labor practices. When Julia Lathrop was appointed director of the newly-created Children's Bureau of the Department of Commerce, Scott highlighted the event by proclaiming: "No amount of eloquent verbal appreciation of heroic ancestors will absolve this generation of its difficult task of working out ethical and humane solutions for all the pressing economic and social problems of our times." This reform spirit continued to move the Daughters until the climate of the country changed after World War I.[39]

One-quarter of all prominent women in 1914 belonged to a patriotic society or mentioned an interest in genealogy. Career type was related to such interests. Women with careers in the arts displayed a greater interest in their ancestors than did women in other professions. Over one-third (34.8%) of such women either mentioned an illustrious forebear or belonged to a society like the DAR or the Colonial Dames, while over one-fourth (28.9%) of the non-career women showed such interest. Women in education and women in professions had the least interest in genealogy.

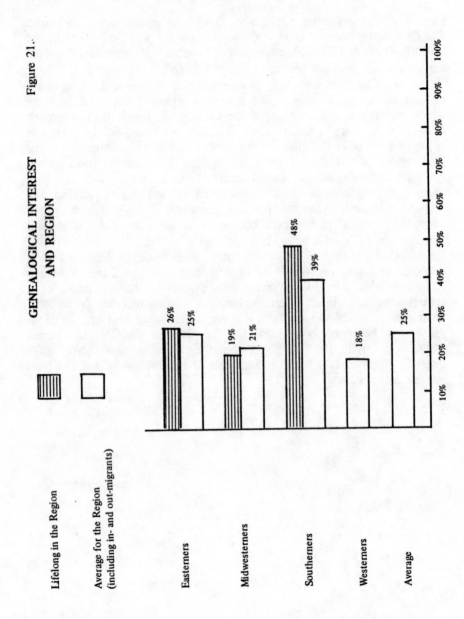

Figure 21.

GENEALOGICAL INTEREST AND REGION

Lifelong in the Region

Average for the Region
(including in- and out-migrants)

Easterners 26% 25%

Midwesterners 19% 21%

Southerners 48% 39%

Westerners 18%

Average 25%

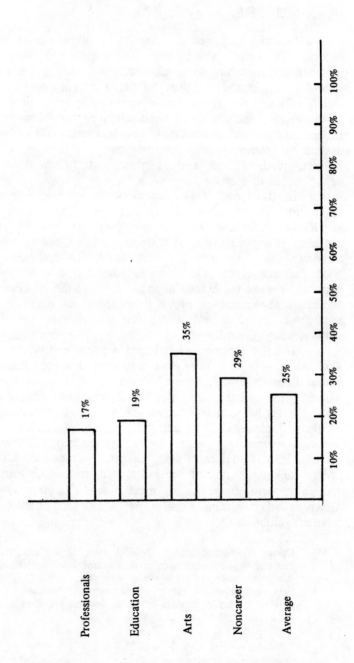

Figure 22.

GENEALOGICAL INTEREST
AND
CAREER TYPE

H.   Conclusion

Whether they were reading British authors or seeking American ancestors, the women who belonged to the clubs discussed in this chapter sought companionship above all else.   The various types of clubs that were founded in the last third of the nineteenth century illustrate the variety of interests that eminent women had in common with each other. In the literary and art clubs, women looked for fellowship in learning. In the alumnae societies, women who had enjoyed a college experience desired the companionship of their peers.   Likewise, women doctors, lawyers, teachers and authors wanted to know their compatriots struggling in the same profession.

In part, such organizations were a negative reaction to the nineteenth century ideal of separate spheres for men and women. Previously, men had had a monopoly on fraternal societies and professional organizations.   It is understandable that women would want to copy some of the activities from which they had been excluded.   A good example is the Daughters of the American Revolution, which patterned themselves exactly after the Sons of the American Revolution. Women also wanted to prove their ability to organize a society, to administer its finances, and even to master the intricacies of parliamentary procedure.

But the groups also reflected a positive drive to be with other women. In striving to overcome isolation within their homes or isolation within their professions, these women reached out to one another as women. In so doing, they developed supportive female networks that distinctly furthered the progress of women in breaking out of the confines of domestic duties and entering into public life. In 1916 Edith Wharton successfully satirized the dilettantism of women's cultural societies in a famous short story "Xingu." (It began with the sentence, "Mrs. Ballinger is one of the ladies who pursue Culture in bands, as though it were dangerous to meet alone.")[40]   But another novelist, Gertrude Atherton, sensed the deeper significance of the development of women's clubs.

> During my married years [1876-1887] when life was more tranquil-- and dull--I rarely heard women discuss anything but personalities, a fashionable novel, or some actress who was 'the rage.' They may have been dependent for happiness upon their husbands, but they took no interest in business or the professions, and lived their days in a small world of their own.
>
> **
>
> We all know the names of the great women who founded the political revolution of their sex, but who was the unsung

benefactress in whose aspiring mind was born the idea of the
Literary Club?. . .At all events there came a time when those clubs
were springing up all over the land, and women by the hundreds
were discussing something besides dress, children, servants, and
gossip. Their gropings were feeble at first, and they were the
subject of much good-natured ridicule, but they had begun definitely
to climb up from the pit of inconsequence.

**

Now it stands to reason that when women began to respect their
own minds and the minds of others of their sex associated with
them in a common interest--self-improvement--they had taken a long
swing upward and personalities had ceased to be the major interest
of their leisure hours.[41]

More than any other organization, the General Federation of Women's
Clubs--with its amorphous, grass roots, all-encompassing nature--
embodied the positive force in women's organizations. But even such
narrow groups as patriotic societies and alumnae associations enabled
women to emerge from their homes and establish valuable contacts with
each other.

NOTES

[1]Croly, *Woman's Club Movement*, p. 169. William L. O'Neill, *Everyone Was Brave*, p. 84.

[2]Beadle, *Fortnightly*, p. 50.

[3]Croly, *Woman's Club Movement*, pp. 15-23.

[4]Beadle, *Fortnightly*, pp. 20; 50.

[5]Croly, *Woman's Club Movement*, p. 569; pp. 232, 233; p. 1143.

[6]*Ibid.*, p. 1169, p. 287, p. 246, p. 377.

[7]*Ibid.*, p. 112.

[8]*Ibid.*, pp. 154-155.

[9]*Ibid.*, p. 148.

[10]*Ibid.*, p. 167.

[11]Mary L. Ely and Eve Chappell, *Women in Two Worlds* (New York: American Association for Adult Education, 1938), p. 129.

[12]Rheta Childe Dorr, *A Woman of Fifty*, pp. 118-120.

[13]Mary Ritter Beard, *Woman's Work in Municipalities* (New York: D. Appleton and Company, 1916), p. 57.

[14]Croly, *Woman's Club Movement*, pp. 62-63. Dorothy Edwards Powers, "Chicago Woman's Club" (Master's Thesis, University of Chicago, 1939), p. 80; p. 75.

[15]Powers, "Chicago Woman's Club," pp. 92-93.

[16]Croly, *Woman's Club Movement*, pp. 66-69. Powers, "Chicago Woman's Club," pp. 119-120; 122.

[17]Powers, "Chicago Woman's Club," p. 129.

[18]*Ibid.*, pp. 300-01.

[19]Croly, *Woman's Club Movement*, p. 292, p. 364, p. 701, p. 1008, p. 993, p. 788, p. 784, p. 739.

[20]Croly, *Woman's Club Movement*, pp. 546-47.

[21]*Ibid.*, pp. 547-549.

[22]Croly, *Woman's Club Movement*, pp. 549-550.

[23]*Ibid.*, pp. 296-98.

[24]Marion Talbot and Lois K. M. Rosenberry, *The History of the American Association of University Women, 1881-1931* (Boston: Houghton Mifflin Company, 1931), pp. 3-12.

[25]*Ibid.*, p. 40.

[26]*Ibid.*, pp. 149-152.

[27]*Ibid.*, pp. 40-45.

[28]*Ibid.*, p. 48. E. A. Colton, "Report of Committee on Standards of Colleges," Southern Association of College Women, *Proceedings*, Bulletin II (1912), pp. 26-27. The four schools that did offer four years of college work in 1912 were Agnes Scott, Goucher, Randolph-Macon, and Sophie Newcomb.

[29]Southern Association of College Women, *Proceedings*, Bulletin II (1912), pp. 50-51.

[30]"Introduction," *NAW*, 1:xxx.   "Anna Elizabeth Broomall," *NAW*, 1:246-47.

[31]"Ella Blaylock Atherton," *WWW*, pp. 58.

[32]"Myra Colby Bradwell," *NAW*, 1:225.   Dorothy Thomas, *Women Lawyers in the United States*, p. ix. "Agnes Dean Abbatt," *WOC*, p. 1. Annie Howes Barus, "The College Woman's Opportunity in Cooperative Work," *Publications of the Association of Collegiate Alumnae*, III (December 1898), p. 79.

[33]"Clara Shortridge Foltz," *NAW*, 1:642.   "Katherine Margaret Brownlee Sherwood," *NAW*, 3:282.

[34]Croly, *Woman's Club Movement*, pp. 895-96; p. 634.

[35]"Katherine Margaret Brownlee Sherwood," *NAW*, 3:282.

[36]Mary B. Poppenheim, et. al., *The History of the United Daughters of the Confederacy* (Richmond: Garrett and Massie, 1938), p. 11; p. 22.

[37]Margaret Gibbs, *The DAR* (New York: Holt, Rinehart and Winston, 1969), pp. 58-61. On the founding of the DAR, see also Flora Adams Darling, *Founding and Organization of the Daughters of the American Revolution and Daughters of the*

Revolution. (Philadelphia: Independence Publishing Company, 1901.) Darling gives her side on the founding in contradiction to the accounts given in official DAR literature.

[38]Gibbs, *DAR*, pp. 77-79.

[39]*Ibid.*, pp. 80-83.

[40]Edith Wharton, *Xingu and Other Stories* (New York: Charles Scribner's Sons, 1916), p. 3.

[41]Gertrude Atherton, *Can Women Be Gentlemen?*, pp. 40-41.

CONCLUSION

The prominent women of 1914 were indeed uncommon in comparison with previous generations of American womanhood. In fact, a book such as the *Woman's Who's Who* would have been an impossibility in their mother's day. In mid-nineteenth century America, prominence for women would have been almost solely a local matter, except for the wives of the nation's political leaders. And even on the local level, social visibility would have rested upon the social standing of their families, which in turn depended largely on the professions of the husbands and fathers. By 1914, many women had surpassed locality to become known on the regional and even national levels. More important, their fame was not simply a vague reflection of the accomplishments of the males in their lives. These women attained status through their own accomplishments.

Born shortly after mid-century, they entered a milieu in which the traditional role of women was undergoing only gradual modification. Women remained devoted to traditional duties. Few schools in the country offered a woman the opportunity for higher education. Few career opportunities were open to women other than as teachers in elementary schools. Few social organizations other than local mission societies accepted women members.

But the seeds of change planted here and there decades earlier began to blossom after the Civil War. Women's colleges were founded and state universities became coeducational. Increasing educational opportunities stimulated greater career openings. Even the staid male professions of medicine, law, and the ministry began to falter before the assaults of determined females. Women also began banding together. They founded literary clubs. They developed their local mission societies into regional and national organizations, and even took administrative control themselves rather than continuing to turn their offerings and collections over to men for disbursement. Of special importance was the national popularity achieved by the Woman's Christian Temperance Union, a female organization that leaped the chasm from religious fervor to political agitation.

These currents caught up and swept along many of the young middle class girls growing to maturity in the postwar decades. These girls seized the new educational opportunities and fought to broaden them as well. The result was that the average prominent woman of 1914 was well educated. The majority (64%) had some schooling beyond the high school level, and a large number (44%) had actually earned bachelors' degrees.

Pursuit of a career seemed the natural consequence of obtaining a good education. More than two-thirds (68%) of the prominent women either entered a profession or committed themselves to a cause that became their life's work. The choice of occupation was of utmost importance; more than any other variable, career type determined the general shape of a prominent woman's adult years. Career type for a woman signified a certain level of education. It meant membership in specific organizations and not others. It meant the expenditure of time for some activities and not others. It influenced political views on the suffrage question. It even had repercussions for marriage--some career types had higher marriage rates and higher divorce rates than others.

Given the centrality of a chosen career in influencing the lives of prominent women, the variations among the four major career types are highly instructive. (See Figures 2, 3, and 4 for the graphs comparing the career types.) Women in the professions were very well-educated, and had the highest percentage membership (50%) in professional or national associations. They frequently gave lectures and published articles or books either on technical subjects or on topics of social interest. These professionals lived predominantly in large cities but were geographically mobile. They had the second lowest marriage rate (57%) and the second highest divorce rate (16%). Professional women were also the most active of any group in humanitarian work, reform movement, and as leaders in women's clubs. They showed less interest in purely cultural activities. In comparison with other prominent women, the professionals were highly politically aware and energetic in political causes. They strongly favored suffrage and agitated for it.

Women with careers in education were quite different from those in other professions. First, more of them chose to remain single. Only 40% married, and only one-quarter had children. Women with careers in education had the best formal education of any group, though professional women equaled them in attendance at graduate or professional schools. Female educators did belong to career-related professional organizations, though not to the extent of women in the professions. They joined alumnae groups in greater numbers (43% did so) than other prominent women. They failed to publish as much as women in the arts or even as much as did professional women, even though professional scholars were included in their ranks. Women in education were low on community cultural interests, although they did belong to literary clubs and societies in larger numbers than women in other fields. Although half their number (50%) engaged in humanitarian activities, women in education equaled women in the arts as having the least interest in such causes. They exhibited the least interest (43.5%) in reform work. While most women in education (70.5%) belonged to women's clubs, they failed to equal the membership rates of women in the professions (79%) or noncareer women (85%). Nor did as many of them accept leadership positions in these clubs as did the latter two groups. A majority of women in education favored woman suffrage, but few worked for it. Only 19% were suffragists compared to almost 40% for professional women. Women in education were non-urban, but they were highly geographically mobile. The vast majority were neither born in large cities nor did they live in large cities in 1914. They moved from place to place often, and frequently changed states, although they did not move outside their home region as much as did women in the professions.

Why did women educators, with their good educations, have a lower political consciousness than women in the professions? And why did they fail to involve themselves in the wide spectrum of activities that interested most middle class women of this period? Perhaps because of its manifold opportunities for women, the teaching profession seems to have been a self-contained, inward-directed occupation. Teaching was so eminently respectable for women by this time, that they did not have to face the obstacles in training nor the difficulties of becoming established that women interested in more traditionally male professions experienced. Hence, women in education did not feel the need to reform society. By contrast, women who attempted careers in medicine, law, journalism, business, or the ministry had little option but to change society first. In addition, maintaining a low political profile was probably advisable in education for maintaining job security. Moreover, teaching careers brought women into close contact with numerous female colleagues, thus they felt less need to join the popular women's clubs.

Women with careers in the arts were different from both women in the professions and those in education. Women in the arts did not acquire the years of formal education of women in the other two career types. In fact, the majority of women in the arts had no advanced education beyond technical artistic training, such as piano lessons or art school. Two-thirds (68%) of the women in the arts were married and 38% had children. This gives them the second highest marriage rate, second only to noncareer women with a rate of 94%. They also had the highest divorce rate (28%). Their pattern of outside activities followed that of women in education. Arts women were low on humanitarian interests and on women's club leadership; they lacked political consciousness nor were they as active in reform causes. Less than half of them favored woman suffrage. However, they displayed the highest degree of interest in genealogy (35%) and in community arts (55%). They tended to live in large cities, as did women in the professions, but they were not as geographically mobile as women in the other two career types.

Perhaps women in the arts, like teachers, were not interested in reform work because they did not face great difficulties in training and in pursuit of a profession. Writing novels or poems, singing, or teaching piano lessons were all considered respectable endeavors for women. Thus, women in the arts failed to develop the sense of dissatisfaction with society which characterized most women doctors or lawyers. This would also explain their lack of interest in the suffrage question. Women in the arts saw no need to protect their rights and pursue new reforms through the ballot.

More puzzling was their relatively lower interest in humanitarian causes and in women's clubs. These women did pursue certain specific interests such as genealogy and community arts, but failed to join in the general community women's groups to the extent of women in the professions and noncareer women. The plea of involvement in their career work would not be a valid excuse for their nonactivity, since women in the professions had a high degree of activism while maintaining demanding careers. Artistic pursuits, however, often required almost total self-absorption. Such ego-involvement could have precluded community interests in the same way that it probably occasioned the high divorce rate among this group. Another indication of that ego-centrism was their unusually high interest in genealogy.

The noncareer women had their own characteristics distinct from women in education, the arts, or the professions. While these women had the highest marriage rate (94%), they had a low divorce rate (7%). Both of those figures fit the national average of 90% and 6-8% respectively. Over 73% of these women had children.

Noncareer women were the most poorly educated. They had neither advanced formal education, as did women in the professions and in education, nor did they have the technical training of women in the arts. Yet, they consistently displayed more interest in general women's activities--women's clubs, church groups, humanitarian endeavors--than did women in education or the arts. They could not compare, however, in social and political activism with women in the professions. As with women in the arts, less than a majority of noncareer women favored woman suffrage. Noncareer women were the most interested and active, though, in religious groups. The socially visible women without careers generally lived in large cities and were less mobile than other prominent women.

Husbands often performed key roles in the development of their wives careers. Supportive husbands not only patronized extant professions but often encouraged the pursuit of a vocation in wives who had no such ambitions. Common interests led to common occupations. Husbands and wives met in law school, or lawyer husbands induced their wives to join in their work. But supportive husbands were not a prerequisite for married women to follow professional inclinations or avocational interests. Relatively high divorce rates indicate an increasing willingness on the part of women to develop their own potential in spite of indifferent or hostile husbands. In this respect, supportive female societies may have been instrumental in sustaining women who had to overcome domestic difficulties to pursue their interests.

Nevertheless, self-reliance and independence were two noticeable qualities of the eminent women in the Progressive Era. Widowed and divorced women especially exhibited such characteristics when they withstood severe privations rather than relying upon charity from friends and relatives. Newer job opportunities for women afforded such women the option to be self-sufficient--an option which few of their mothers had--and the women were quick to seize upon it.

The purposefully low birth rate of the women provides another indication of their strong determination to control their lives. They did not want to be trapped by unrestrained childbearing, and they were willing to use whatever means was necessary--whether contraceptive devices or self-denial--to limit their offspring to two or less children. Their success in this endeavor helped to free the married women to engage in the wide variety of activities which made them eminent.

The women did not essentially challenge the institutions of marriage and the family. Nor did they dispute the importance of marriage and motherhood in a woman's life. But they succeeded in developing an equality in the marital state that has not typically characterized the marriages of their mothers. This equality encompassed pursuit of their own careers, activities, and interests. It meant that domestic chores, including childcare, evolved to household help. Even their sexual relationships were affected by a desire for mutuality. Thus, a determination to control their own lives and develop their own capabilities--whether inside or outside of marriage--was a hallmark of the notable women in the early twentieth century.

What happened to the women after 1914? Does the analysis of middle class women according to career types remain valid for the rest of their lives? Since the median age of the women was 50 in 1914, most had reached the apex of their careers by that time, and they continued with the same careers and activities until their deaths. The advent of the war in Europe, however, did bring a heightened concern for peace and peace-keeping mechanisms among many women who had been active in the Progressive reform movement. Jane Addams, for example, had published a book entitled *Newer Ideals of Peace* as early as 1907, and after 1914 she devoted her efforts to ending the war, while maintaining only a muted interest in Hull House. The ratification of the Nineteenth Amendment after the war encouraged others, such as Carrie Chapman Catt, to widen their field of endeavor by devoting themselves to the international peace movement of the 1920's. But the typologies remained the same. Those women interested in reform discovered new causes, but those who had avoided the old movements remained impervious to the new.

A few younger women did develop their primary identities after the *Woman's Who's Who* was published. Frances Perkins, for example, achieved her greatest fame in the years of the New Deal. But even her later efforts were a logical extension of her Progressive reform interests.

With the end of the suffrage movement in 1920 and the decline of progressivism throughout the 1920's, women lost their most likely avenues to political prominence. Women could still command respect for accomplishments in professions and the arts, and women's clubs still flourished--but national concerns had changed. The place and status of women was no longer a central issue even for women. The role of women in society had been a vital concern in the Progressive Era in part because society in general was undergoing rapid structural changes. But perhaps the reformers had done their work too well. Women had succeeded in making in-roads into a wide variety of professions, and they had succeeded in bringing the legal status of women into accord with the practices of society by 1920. At any rate, people had grown tired of crusades; and so the questions that were still unresolved about the role of women in American society lay dormant for half a century. When social reform issues again captured the nation's attention in the 1960's, women responded as had their forebears in the Progressive Era. They refocused concern upon the status of women in American society. Consequently, widespread interest has again been directed to the lives of individual women and their accomplishments in the professions, the arts, and the new woman's movement.

CHAPTER V

ACTIVITIES AND INTERESTS: RELIGIOUS AND POLITICAL

From a blossoming after the Civil War, women's public activities had grown to cover a wide spectrum by 1913. Alumnae associations, genealogical societies, women's clubs, professional groups--all claimed membership by women that numbered into the millions. Two of the most important kinds of activities in which women were involved were religious and political in nature. It is on these two kinds of activities among women that this chapter will focus. But first an overview of the history of women's social activities will provide the proper background to examine religious and political activism among American women in the early twentieth century.

A.   The Development of Women's Organizations

Relatives and neighbors comprised the basic elements in women's social lives in the nineteenth century. In days when the normal form of transportation was walking, and before the telephone connected distant parts of cities, women naturally turned to those who lived around them for social exchange.

The basic institution where neighbors and relatives could meet regularly was the local church. It provided a time and a place for weekly social occasions; it provided excuses for projects outside of the regular services. Church sewing circles, prayer meetings, and charitable aid societies became the earliest forms of women's public organizations. And they remained in force into the twentieth century.

Family, neighbors, church--these dominated the social lives of farm and working class women throughout the nineteenth century, although the Grange and Populists reached certain numbers of farm women late in the century. While these three remained important to middle and even upper class women, the circle of their associations and activities broadened throughout the century.

Entertaining was a time-honored means of social contact. Wives met their husband's business and political associates in this way. For women of the upper classes, entertaining their own female friends became a regular formal function toward the end of the century. Women chose certain days of the week when they would be at home to receive callers. In Chicago, for example, women who lived on the north side of the city in the 1880's were at home to their friends on Mondays, and women on the south side were at home on Tuesdays. Refined women were expected to get through their lists once a year. May Wright

Sewall, the famous woman's club leader of Indianapolis, held weekly teas on Wednesday. Two working New Yorkers, Elsie de Wolfe and Elizabeth Marbury, had to have their guests on Sundays. But this suited their aspirations to a more European-type salon, since men could attend then also.[1]

While formal public women's organizations can be traced back to church groups founded early in the nineteenth century, the real budding of associations among women came after the Civil War. The war itself forced thousands of women into activities outside the home. Women were eager to do hospital and relief work. In the North, two citizens' organizations, the Sanitary Commission and the Christian Commission, channeled the efforts of countless women into aid for the army's medical care. In addition, many soldiers' wives were forced upon their own resources in supporting themselves and their families. Thus, war-related exigencies served to undermine traditional notions about women's proper sphere of activities.[2]

In the decades after the war, the increasing industrialization of the American economy produced a domestic revolution in American households. The development of canning factories, the commercial production of ice, the popularization of the sewing machine, besides the increasing availability of ready-made mens' and boys' clothing, the improvement of furnaces, stoves and washtubs helped to reduce the extent and speed the process of household chores. Better city services, such as water and sewage systems, animal control, and the introduction of gas lighting, also aided home life.[3] In addition, the large numbers of immigrants made domestic help readily available. These factors provided increased amounts of leisure time to women in the middle and upper classes. To fill that leisure time, women sought advanced educations, pursued careers, formed organizations, and in general, began to take an active part in public affairs in America.

Of course, having the leisure time was not in itself a sufficient motive for the growing endeavors of American womanhood. New interests had been quickened among women by the opening up of higher education and professional careers to their sex. Women became aware of the many ways in which they might have an effect upon their society. And once a spirit of reform pervaded the land, each reform project spawned many others. Thus, a growing sense of the possible, an accumulation of experience, and the formulation of networks of cooperating friends helped to foster the multiplicity of women's organizations that arose in the later decades of the century.

These same kinds of factors help to account for the large numbers of men's organizations which were also founded during these years. While many men's groups preceded comparable women's groups by a few years, the impulse to organize was virtually simultaneous.

The relationship between men's organizations and women's organizations was varied. In some cases, women's auxiliaries were directly attached to male groups. Such was the case for the Grand Army of the Republic, an organization for Union veterans, with its Woman's Relief Corp affixed to it. Some chapters of the Young Men's Christian Association also had auxiliaries. In other cases, separate women's organizations were founded on male models. When the Sons of the Revolution refused to allow female affiliates, the Daughters of the American Revolution was founded as an independent group. Likewise, the Young Women's Christian Association had no formal ties to the Young Men's Christian Association. There also developed powerful women's groups for which there were no comparable male organizations. Some examples are the Association of Collegiate Alumnae, the Woman's Christian Temperance Union, the General Federation of Women's Clubs, and the National American Woman Suffrage Association.

There were also groups which were open to both men and women. In such organizations, men generally retained the leadership positions. The Grange and the Populists in the rural Midwest and West were two such groups. YMCA student associations which were founded on coeducational campuses were often open to both male and female students. In cities, charity organizations and civic improvement societies came to be characterized by joint efforts among the sexes.

Many prominent women also enjoyed forms of recreation which were not necessarily social in nature. These ranged from such sedentary activities as gardening to vigorous athletic activities like horseback riding and mountain climbing. Even driving an automobile was considered a rather daring recreation for those days. In 1913, 16.5% of the prominent women mentioned their interest in sedentary kinds of activities, while 12.4% declared an interest in athletic types of pursuits. Another 4.8% of the women had an interest in both forms of recreation. Over one-quarter (26.5%) of the women were outdoor enthusiasts, which included both sedentary and athletic kinds of activities. Although Western women were more inclined toward athletics than their compatriots in other regions, there was no real correlation between region and recreational preferences. Nor were there correlations between the latter variables and occupation type, reform interest, or suffrage opinion. Thus, recreation was nonideological, noncontroversial, and not tied to activism in other areas.

B.   Religious Activism

As for women's formal public activities, religious activism was the earliest way for a woman to join in organized endeavors with other women. It is fairly easy to trace the beginnings of women's political activity to the group of women who championed the cause of anti-slavery and began the campaign for women's rights in America. It is less easy to pinpoint the women or groups of women who began public activity among their sex in the field of religion. Every author who writes on the topic has his or her favorite group which was the earliest woman's organization in the country. Obviously informal groups which met for prayer meetings or sewing circles were regular features of many Protestant churches since the end of the eighteenth century. But these groups came and went leaving no record and no impact but for precedence. Jennie June Croly, in her *History of the Woman's Club Movement in America*, mentioned "cent" societies which were founded around 1801 and 1804. A candidate for the first woman's organization which had some longevity was a little group in Baldwinsville, New York, the Female Charitable Society, which was founded in 1807 and still extant in 1898.[4]

Croly also noted the Woman's Auxiliaries to the Board of Foreign Missions, which were also founded early in the century. These auxiliaries grew to over 680 societies by 1839, but they were nearly extinct by 1860. They left an impact though, for in the mid-1860's, similar groups were established in almost every Protestant denomination. These groups took the name of Woman's Auxiliary to the American Board of Home and Foreign Missions.[5]

About the same time, in 1864, an independent union of women missionary workers was formed in New York. Unaffiliated with any particular denomination, it managed its own affairs, raised its own funds, and sent out its own missionaries, including both men and women. Croly stated that the existence of the missionary union was a source of strength to the women's auxiliaries, "stimulating them to independent action, and especially to the demand for a voice in the disposal of the large sums they raise and turn over into the treasury of the American Board."[6]

The Methodists led the way in the organization of women for evangelical and charitable work independent of male control. The denomination established a central board, the Woman's Home Missionary Society, in the late nineteenth century to disburse the funds raised in local parishes. At the same time, the job of deaconess was introduced as a means for women to work full time in evangelical social service.[7] The dispute in the Methodist Church over voting rights for women, which occurred at the end of the century, also illustrates the concern in the denomination about the status of women.

C.   Denominational Preference

While religious groups were the oldest kinds of female organizations, church membership itself was an even older public affiliation of women. The local churches had been the social heart of most American communities throughout the nineteenth century, and church membership was still strong in the early decades of the twentieth century. Almost three-quarters (74.6%) of the prominent women in 1913 declared a religious affiliation. Of those that did, 74.2% belonged to Protestant churches of high prestige, i.e., Episcopalian, Presbyterian, Congregational, Quaker, or Unitarian churches. Another 18.5% of the women belonged to Protestant churches of lesser prestige, which included the Methodists, Baptists, Lutherans, Christian churches, and the Disciples of Christ. Only 7.1% were affiliated with churches outside of the major Protestant denominations or declared themselves to be agnostic.

In part, these figures represent a bias in the sample. Roman Catholic nuns who ran schools were certainly important in their communities, yet few found their way into the Woman's Who's Who. The Catholic and Jewish women who were included, 3% of the total in the book, had generally found acceptance among the socially prominent Protestant women through women's club work and general civic activity, although they may have been highly active in work for their own denomination as well. A good example is Hannah Greenebaum Solomon who founded the National Council of Jewish Women and did important reform work with Jewish immigrants in Chicago, but who was also the first Jewish woman to become a member of the Chicago Woman's Club. Besides her membership in the latter, Solomon's aid in founding the Illinois Federation of Woman's Clubs and the Council of Women of the United States also assisted her entrance into the Woman's Who's Who.[8] So although the Woman's Who's Who does not give a fair representation of prominent Jewish and Catholic women, it can safely be stated that the overwhelming majority of women who were socially prominent in 1914 were Protestant in religious affiliation or origin.

There was no relation between denominational preference and career type except for the small percentage of women who were non-Protestant. Of the women who were Catholic or Jewish in faith, a smaller portion were in education than in any other career type. This again would indicate that Catholic school administrators were under-represented in the book. Roughly half of the non-Protestant group were agnostic, socialist, or indicated a rare sect. These women had a strange distribution over career types. Seventy percent (70.0%) were in the professions, none were in education, fifteen percent (15.0%) were in the arts, and fifteen percent (15.0%) were noncareer women. By the same token, professional women had a higher percentage (8.3%) who indicated a rare sect or declared themselves to be agnostic than any other career type, the next closest being women in the arts with three percent (2.9%). If one adds the percentage who were Catholic or Jewish, one discovers that almost twelve percent (11.9%) of the professional women who gave a religious preference were non-Protestant. Women in the arts, however, had the highest percentage that were Catholic or Jewish (7.6%), so that 10.5% of the women in the arts were non-Protestant.   Women in professions and women in the arts therefore had a significantly higher proportion of women who were non-Protestant than the other two career types.   (See Figure 5.)

Both the professions and the arts could be said to promote a certain amount of nonconformity.   Women who chose professional careers had to overcome a great many obstacles regarding training and establishing themselves. It would not be surprising for them to reject orthodoxy in religion, equating it with the conservative view of women which they were struggling to overcome. Careers in the fine arts, such as acting or singing, helped some women with less acceptable backgrounds to become prominent and acceptable to the Protestant majority. In the latter cases, the artistic career made nonconformity in religion acceptable, whereas with professional women, pursuance of the career produced nonconformity in religion.

Almost one-third (30.4%) of all prominent women took an active part in religious work, or of the women who gave a denominational preference, 41.8% did church work. The women most likely to be involved in religious activity were the women without careers (35.7%) followed by women in the professions (32.7%). One-fourth of the women in education (25.4%) and in the arts (24.6%) indicated an interest in religious work.   (See figure 6.)

The thirty percent figure of prominent women who were religiously active is probably low compared with the national average for middle class women.   Since church work was the earliest kind of association for women and the one which remained the most eminently respectable, the majority of middle class women most likely belonged to some kind of ladies' organization connected with their church. Prominent women tended to have careers and were engaged in a myriad of professional, social, and reform activities. They had left church work behind.

From a regional perspective, the South was the one area which manifested a real difference from the average for prominent women. Of the women who were both born in the South and still lived in the South in 1913, 43.6% were active in religious work. This is not surprising given the geography and culture of the region.   The South was still predominantly rural; the lack of large cities meant an equal lack of the

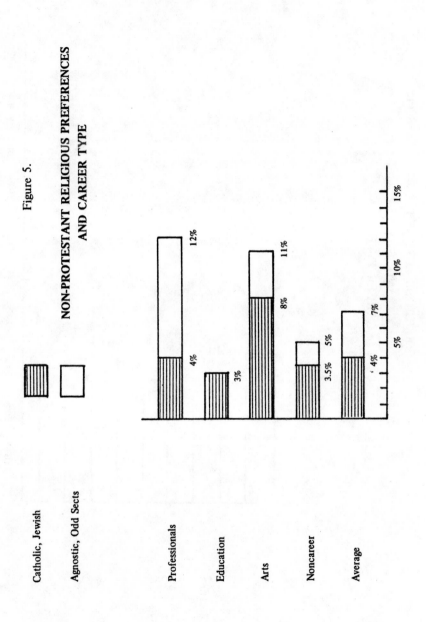

Figure 5.

NON-PROTESTANT RELIGIOUS PREFERENCES
AND CAREER TYPE

Catholic, Jewish

Agnostic, Odd Sects

Professionals — 12%, 4%

Education — 3%

Arts — 11%, 8%

Noncareer — 5%, 3.5%

Average — 7%, 4%

15%   10%   5%

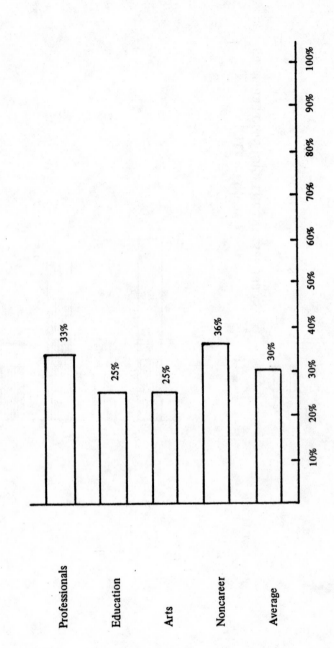

Figure 6.

RELIGIOUS ACTIVISM
AND
CAREER TYPE

Professionals — 33%
Education — 25%
Arts — 25%
Noncareer — 36%
Average — 30%

BIBLIOGRAPHY

An asterisk (*) by a name denotes a woman found in the *Woman's Who's Who of America, 1914-1915.*

*Abbott, Edith. "One Hundred Years after Seneca Falls 1848-1948," *Social Service Review,* 22 (June 1948), p. 254.

*Adams, Elizabeth K. *Women Professional Workers.* New York: The Macmillan Company, 1921.

Adams, Marie. *Ellen Clara Sabin: A Life Sketch.* Madison: University of Wisconsin Press, 1937.

*Addams, Jane. *Twenty Years at Hull-House.* New York: The Macmillan Company, 1910.

*Alden, Isabella M. *Memories of Yesterdays.* Philadelphia: J. B. Lippincott Company, 1931.

Alsop, Gulielma Fell. *History of the Woman's Medical College, Philadelphia, Pennsylvania 1850-1950.* Philadelphia: J. B. Lippincott Company, 1950.

Anderson, Harriet. "Woman." *The Atlantic Monthly,* 110 (August 1912), pp. 177-83.

*Andrews, Eliza Frances. *The War-Time Journal of a Georgia Girl, 1864-1865.* New York: D. Appleton & Co., 1908.

*Andrews, Irene Osgood. *The Relation of Irregular Employment to the Living Wage for Women.* New York: New York State Factory Investigating Commission, 1915.

Annual Catalogue of Milwaukee and Downer Colleges, 1896-1897. Milwaukee: Milwaukee-Downer College, 1896.

*Atherton, Gertrude. *Adventures of a Novelist.* New York: Liveright, 1932.

————. *Can Women be Gentlemen?* Boston: Houghton Mifflin Company, 1938.

————. *Julia France and Her Times.* London: John Murray, 1912.

*Austin, Mary Hunter. *Earth Horizon.* New York: Houghton Mifflin Company, 1932.

————. *A Woman of Genius.* Boston: Houghton Mifflin Company, 1917.

*Bacon, Albion Fellows. *Beauty for Ashes.* New York: Dodd, Mead and Company, 1914.

*Bailey, Hannah Johnson. *Reminiscences of a Christian Life.* Winthrop Centre, Maine: Banner Book and Job Print, 1889.

*Baker, Sara Josephine. *Child Hygiene.* New York: Harper & Brothers, Publishers, 1925.

_____. *Fighting for Life.* New York: The Macmillan Company, 1939.

Bane, Lita. *The Story of *Isabel Bevier.* Peoria: Chas A. Bennett Co., 1955.

*Banks, Elizabeth L. *The Autobiography of a "Newspaper Girl."* New York: Dodd, Mead, 1902.

*Barr, Amelia E. *All the Days of My Life.* New York: D. Appleton and Company, 1913.

_____. "Discontented Women." *North American Review,* 162 (1896), pp. 201-09.

*Barrows, Isabel C. *A Sunny Life.* Boston: Little, Brown, and Company, 1913.

*Barrymore, Ethel. *Memories.* New York: Harper & Brothers, 1955.

Barus, Annie Howes. "The College Woman's Opportunity in Cooperative Work." *Publications of the Association of Collegiate Alumnae,* 3 (December 1898), pp. 78-82.

Beadle, Muriel, and the Centennial History Committee. *The Fortnightly of Chicago: The City and Its Women: 1873-1973.* Chicago: Henry Regency Company, 1973.

*Beard, Mary R., ed. *America Through Women's Eyes.* New York: The Macmillan Company, 1933.

_____. *A Changing Political Economy as It Affects Women.* Washington: American Association of University of Women, 1934.

_____. *On Understanding Women.* New York: Longmans, Green and Co., 1931.

_____. *Woman as Force in History.* New York: The Macmillan Company, 1946.

_____. *Woman's Work in Municipalities.* New York: D. Appleton and Company, 1915.

*Beaux, Cecilia. *Background with Figures.* Boston: Houghton Mifflin Company, 1930.

*Belmont, Mrs. O. H. P. "Women as Dictators," *Ladies Home Journal,* 39 (September 1922), pp. 7, 43.

Bennett, Helen Christine. *American Women in Civic Work.* New York: Dodd, Mead and Company, 1915.

Bennett, Helen M. *Women and Work.* New York: Appleton & Company, 1917.

Birney, Mrs. Theodore. "The Twentieth-Century Girl: What We Expect of Her." *Harper's Bazar,* 33 (May 26, 1900), pp. 224-27.

The Birth Control Review, 1 (1917-1919).

*Bisland, Elizabeth. "The Modern Woman and Marriage." *North American Review*, 160 (June 1895), pp. 753-55.

*Bissell, Mary Taylor. *Household Hygiene*. New York: N.D.C. Hodges, Publisher, 1890.

*Blake, Lillie Devereux. *A Daring Experiment*. New York: Lovell, Coryell & Company, 1892.

_____. *Fettered for Life*. New York: Sheldon & Company, 1874.

*Blankenburg, Lucretia. *The Blankenburgs of Philadelphia*. Philadelphia: The John C. Winston Company, 1928.

*Blatch, Harriot Stanton. *Challenging Years*. New York: G. P. Putnam's Sons, 1940.

*Bolton, Sarah K. *Sarah K. Bolton*. Boston: Thomas Todd Company, 1923.

*Bond, Carrie Jacobs. *The Roads of Melody*. New York: D. Appleton and Company, 1927.

Boyesen, Hjalmar Hjorth. "The Matrimonial Puzzle." *North American Review*, 160 (February 1895), pp. 203-209.

*Breckinridge, Sophonisba P. *Women in the Twentieth Century*. New York: McGraw-Hill Book Company, 1933.

*Buell, Jennie. *The Grange Master and the Grange Lecturer*. New York: Harcourt, Brace and Company, 1921.

_____. *One Woman's Work for Farm Women*. Boston: Whitcomb & Barrows, 1908.

*Burnett, Frances Hodgson. *Little Lord Fauntleroy*. New York: C. Scribner's Sons, 1886.

Burnett, Vivian. *The Romantick Lady*. New York: Charles Scribner's Sons, 1927.

Burnham, John C. "The Progressive Era Revolution in American Attitudes Toward Sex." *Journal of American History*, 59 (March 1973), pp. 885-908.

Burton, Margaret. *Mabel Cratty: Leader in the Art of Leadership*. New York: The Woman's Press, 1929.

Cabot, Ellas Lyman; *Fannie Fern Andrews; Fanny E. Coe; Mabel Hill; and Mary McSkimmon. *A Course in Citizenship*. Boston: Houghton Mifflin Company, 1914.

*Campbell, Helen Stuart. *Darkness and Daylight*. Hartford: The Hartford Publishing Company, 1895.

Child, Lydia Maria. *The Mother's Book*. Glasgow: R. Griffin & Co., 1832.

Clarke, Edward Hammond. *Sex in Education*. Boston: J. R. Osgood and Company, 1873.

Cole, Margaret. "The Woman's Vote: What Has It Achieved?" *Political Quarterly*, 33 (January 1962), pp. 74-83.

*Colton, Elizabeth Avery. "Report of Committee on Standards of Colleges." *Proceedings*. Southern Association of College Women, Bulletin, 2 (1912), pp. 25-29.

*Commander, Lydia Kingsmill. *The American Idea*. New York: A. S. Barnes & Company, 1907.

*Comstock, Anna Botsford. *The Comstocks of Cornell*. Ithaca: Cornell University Press, 1953.

Conway, Jill K. "Perspectives on the History of Women's Education in the United States." *History of Education Quarterly*, 14 (Spring 1974), pp. 1-12.

*Corbin, Caroline Fairfield. *A Woman's Secret*. Chicago: Central Publishing House, 1867.

Cott, Nancy F. *Root of Bitterness: Documents of the Social History of American Women*. New York: E. P. Dutton & Co., 1972.

Croly, Jane Cunningham. *The History of the Woman's Club Movement in America*. New York: Henry G. Allen & Co., 1898.

Curti, Merle Eugene, and Vernon Carstensen. *The University of Wisconsin, a History, 1848-1925*. Madison: University of Wisconsin Press, 1949.

Darling, Flora Adams. *Founding and Organization of the Daughters of the American Revolution and Daughters of the Revolution*. Philadelphia: Independence Publishing Company, 1901.

Davis, Allen F. *American Heroine: The Life and Legend of Jane Addams* (New York: Oxford University Press, 1973).

_____. *Spearheads for Reform*. New York: Oxford University Press, 1967.

*Davis, Katherine Bement. *Factors in the Sex Life of Twenty-Two Hundred Women*. New York: Harper & Brothers, Publishers, 1929.

Davis, Rebecca Harding; Rose Terry Cooke; *Marion Harland; Catherine Owen; and *Amelia E. Barr. "Are Women to Blame?" *North American Review*, 148 (May 1889), pp. 622-42.

Degler, Carl N. "What Ought to Be and What Was: Women's Sexuality in the Nineteenth Century." *The American Historical Review*, 79 (December, 1974), pp. 1467-90.

*Deland, Margaret. "The Change in the Feminine Ideal." *The Atlantic Monthly*, 105 (March 1910), pp. 289-302.

*De Wolfe, Elsie. *After All.* New York: Harper & Brothers, 1935.

*Dorr, Rheta Childe. *A Woman of Fifty.* New York: Funk & Wagnalls Company, 1924.

Douglas, Emily Taft. *Margaret Sanger: Pioneer of the Future.* New York: Holt, Rinehart and Winston, 1970.

Dublin, Louis I. "Birth Control." *Social Hygiene*, 6 (January 1920), pp. 6-16.

*Duniway, Abigail Scott. *Pathbreaking.* Portland: James, Kerns & Abbott Co., 1914.

Ely, Mary L., and Eve Chappell. *Women in Two Worlds.* New York: American Association for Adult Education, 1938. George Grady Press, 1938.

Engelmann, George J. "Education Not the Cause of Race Decline." *Popular Science Monthly*, 63 (June 1903), pp. 172-84.

Flexner, Eleanor. *Century of Struggle.* Cambridge: Harvard University Press, 1959.

*Fisher, Dorothy Canfield. *The Home-Maker.* New York: Grosset & Dunlap Publishers, 1924.

_____. *A Montessori Mother.* New York: Henry Holt and Company, 1912.

*Fisk, May Isabel. *The Eternal Feminine.* New York: Harper & Brothers Publishers, 1911.

*Foote, Harry Hallock. *Edith Bonham.* Boston: Houghton Mifflin Company, 1917.

Fryer, Peter. *The Birth Controllers.* London: Secker & Warburg, 1965.

Gaffney, Fannie Humpheys. "The Club Woman of Today." *Harper's Bazar*, (May 5, 1900), pp. 36-39.

*Gardener, Helen Hamilton. *Facts and Fictions of Life.* Boston: Arena Publishing Company, 1895.

_____. *Is This Your Son, My Lord?* Boston: Arena Publishing Company, 1892.

*Gates, Eleanor. *Apron-Strings.* New York: Grosset & Dunlap, 1917.

_____. *Biography of a Prairie Girl.* New York: Grosset & Dunlap, 1902.

*Gestefeld, Ursula N. *The Woman Who Dares.* New York: Lovell, Gestefeld & Company, 1892.

Gibbs, Margaret. *The DAR.* New York: Holt, Rinehart and Winston, 1969.

*Gilder, Jeannette L. *The Autobiography of a Tomboy.* New York: Doubleday, Page & Company, 1900.

*Gilman, Charlotte Perkins. *The Living of Charlotte Perkins Gilman.* New York: D. Appleton-Century, 1935.

_____. *The Man-Made World.* New York: Charlton Company, 1911.

_____. *Women and Economics.* Boston: Small, Maynard & Company, 1900.

_____. "Woman, the Enigma." *Harper's Bazar,* 42 (December 1908), pp. 1193-97.

Ginzberg, Eli, and Alice M. Yohalem. *Educated American Women: Self-Portraits.* New York: Columbia University Press, 1966.

*Glasgow, Ellen. *Life and Gabriella.* London: John Murray, 1921.

_____. *Phases of an Inferior Planet.* New York: Harper & Brothers Publishers, 1898.

Gordon, Linda. "Voluntary Motherhood: The Beginnings of Feminist Birth Control Ideas in the United States." *Clio's Consciousness Raised: New Perspectives on the History of Women.* Edited by Mary Hartman and Lois W. Banner. New York: Harper & Row, Publishers, 1974, pp. 54-71.

*Guerber, Helene Adeline. *Yourself.* New York: Dodd, Mead & Company, 1902.

Gusfield, Joseph R. "Social Structure and Moral Reform: A Study of the Woman's Christian Temperance Union." *American Journal of Sociology,* 61 (November 1955), pp. 221-32.

Hall, G. Stanley. *Adolescence.* 2 vols. New York: D. Appleton and Company, 1908.

Hammond, William. "Woman in Politics." *North American Review,* 137 (August 1883), pp. 137-46.

*Harbert, Lizzie Boynton. *Out of Her Sphere.* Des Moines: Mills & Co., 1871.

Harrison, Mrs. Burton. "Home Life as a Profession." *Harper's Bazar,* 33 (May 19, 1900), pp. 148-50.

Hart, Lavinia. "When Woman's Ideals Fall." *Cosmopolitan, 33* (1902), pp. 695-99.

_____. "Women as College Presidents." *Cosmopolitan,* 33 (1902), pp. 72-79.

Hathaway, Grace. *Fate Rides a Tortoise: A Biography of *Ellen Spencer Mussey.* Chicago: The John C. Winston Company, 1937.

*Hawthorne, Hildegarde. *Women and Other Women.* New York: Duffield & Company, 1908.

Hays, Elinor Rice. *Those Extraordinary Blackwells.* New York: Harcourt, Brace & World, 1967.

Hersh, Blanche Glassman. "'The Slavery of Sex:' Feminist-Abolitionists in Nineteenth Century America."   Ph.D. Dissertation, University of Illinois, Chicago, 1975.

*Hewitt, Emma Churchman. *Queen of Home.*   Philadelphia: Miller Megee, 1888.

*Holley, Marietta. *Josiah Allen on the Woman Question.* New York: Fleming H. Revell Company, 1914.

Hopkins, C. Howard.   *History of the Y.M.C.A. in North America.*   New York: Association Press, 1951.

*Hurd-Mead, Kate Campbell. *A History of Women in Medicine.* Haddam, Connecticut: The Haddam Press, 1938.

_____. *Medical Women of America.*   New York: Proben Press, 1933.

Jacobi, Mary Putnam. "Status and Future of the Woman Suffrage Movement." *Forum,* 18 (1895), pp. 406-14.

James, Edward T.; Janet Wilson James; and Paul S. Boyer, eds. *Notable American Women, 1607-1950: A Biographical Dictionary.* 3 vols. Cambridge: Harvard University, Belknap Press, 1971.

Jeger, Lena. "The Women's Vote: Has It Made Any Difference?" *New Statesman,* 75 (February 16, 1968), pp. 198-99.

Jeffrey, Kirk. "Family History: The Middle-Class American Family in the Urban Context, 1830-1870."   Ph.D. Dissertation, Stanford University, 1972.

_____. "Marriage, Career, and Feminine Ideology in Nineteenth-Century America: Reconstructing the Marital Experience of Lydia Maria Child, 1828-1874." *Feminist Studies,* 2 (1975), pp. 113-30.

Jensen, Richard. "Family, Career, and Reform: Women Leaders of the Progressive Era." *The American Family in Social-Historical Perspective.* Edited by Michael Gordon. New York: St. Martin's Press, 1973, pp. 267-80.

*Johnston, Mary. "The Woman's War." *The Atlantic Monthly,* 105 (April 1910), pp. 559-70.

Jordan, David Starr. "The Outlook for College Women." *Harper's Bazar,* 33 (May 5, 1900), pp. 44-45.

*Kelly, Florence Finch. *Flowing Stream.* New York: E. P. Dutton & Co., 1939.

Kennedy, David M. *Birth Control in America.* New Haven: Yale University Press, 1970.

Key, Ellen. "Motherliness." *The Atlantic Monthly,* 110 (October 1912), pp. 562-570.

Kieckhefer, Grace Norton. *The History of Milwaukee-Downer College, 1851-1951.*

Knobe, Bertha Damaris. "Mrs. May Wright Sewall: Leader of 5,000,000 Women." *Harper's Bazar,* 33 (June 2, 1900), pp. 278-81.

Kraditor, Aileen S. *The Ideas of the Woman Suffrage Movement.* New York: Columbia University Press, 1965.

Lasch, Christopher. *The New Radicalism in America.* New York: Alfred A. Knopf, 1965.

*Laughlin, Clara E. *The Evolution of a Girl's Ideal.* Chicago: Fleming H. Revell Company, 1902.

_____. *The Keys of Heaven.* New York: George H. Doran Company, 1918.

Lemons, J. Stanley. *The Woman Citizen: Social Feminism in the 1920's.* Urbana: University of Illinois Press, 1973.

Leonard, John William, ed. *Men of America.* New York: L. R. Hamersly & Company, 1908.

_____. *Who's Who in America, 1901-1902.* Chicago: A. N. Marquis & Company, 1901.

_____. *Woman's Who's Who of America, 1914-1915.* New York: American Commonwealth Company, 1914.

Lopata, Helena Z. "The Life Cycle of the Social Role of Housewife." *Sociology and Social Research,* 51 (October 1966), pp. 5-22.

*Lowry, Edith B. *Herself: Talks with Women Concerning Themselves.* Chicago: Forbes & Company, 1913.

_____, and Richard J. Lambert. *Himself: Talks with Men Concerning Themselves.* Chicago: Forbes and Company, 1913.

Mann, Dorothea Lawrence. *Katherine Lee Bates.* Reprinted from Boston Evening Transcript, 1931.

Marcus, Steven. *The Other Victorians.* New York: Basic Books, 1964.

Martin, John, and Prestonia Mann Martin. *Feminism.* New York: Dodd, Mead and Company, 1916.

Massey, Mary Elizabeth. *Bonnet Brigades.* New York: Alfred A. Knopf, 1966.

"Matrimony--Our Most Neglected Profession" *McClures,* 38 (April 1912), pp. 625-35.

McGovern, James K. "The American Woman's Pre-World War I Freedom in Manners and Morals." *Journal of American History*, 55 (September 1968), pp. 315-33.

McManis, John T. *Ella Flagg Young and a Half-Century of the Chicago Public Schools.* Chicago: A. C. McClurg, 1916.

Mead, Margaret, and Frances Balgley Kaplan, ed. *American Women: The Report of the President's Commission on the Status of Women and Other Publications of the Commission.* New York: Charles Scribner's Sons, 1965.

Mead, Margaret. *Blackberry Winter.* New York: Morrow, 1972.

Meehan, Jeannette Porter. *The Lady of the Limberlost.* Garden City, New York: Doubleday, Doran & Company, 1928.

Meikle, Wilma. *Towards a Sane Feminism.* New York: Robert M. McBride & Company, 1917.

Mencken, H. L. *In Defense of Women.* New York: Alfred A. Knopf, 1918.

Merrill, Margaret Manton. "Sorosis." *Cosmopolitan*, 15 (1893), 153-58.

*Meyer, Annie Nathan, ed. *Woman's Work in America.* New York: Henry Holt and Company, 1891.

Moore, Joan W. "Patterns of Women's Participation in Voluntary Associations." *American Journal of Sociology*, 66 (May 1961), pp. 592-98.

Morrison, Anne Hendry. *Women and Their Careers.* New York: National Federation of Business and Professional Women's Clubs, 1934.

Nearing, Scott and *Nellie M. S. Nearing. *Women and Social Progress.* New York: The Macmillan Company, 1912.

O'Neill, William L. *Divorce in the Progressive Era.* New Haven: Yale University Press, 1967.

_____. *Everyone Was Brave.* Chicago: Quadrangle Books, 1969.

Palmer, George Herbert. *The Life of *Alice Freeman Palmer.* Boston: Houghton Mifflin Company, 1908.

Paterfamilias. "'Race Suicide' and Common Sense." *North American Review*, 176 (June 1903), pp. 892-900.

*Patrick, Mary Mills. *Sappho and the Island of Lesbos.* London: Methuen & Co., 1912.

_____. *Under Five Sultans.* London: Williams and Norgate, 1930.

Pearce, T. M.   *Mary Hunter Austin.   New York: Twayne Publishers, 1965.

Peck, Mary Gray.   *Carrie Chapman Catt.   New York: The H. W. Wilson Company, 1944.

Poppenheim, Mary B.; Maude Blake Merchant; May M. Faris McKinney; Rassie Hoskins White; Eloise Welch Wright; Anne Bachman Hyde; Susie Stuart Campbell; Charlotte Osborne Woodbury; and Ruth Jennings Lawton.   The History of the United Daughters of the Confederacy.   Richmond: Garrett and Massie, 1938.

*Putnam, Emily James.   The Lady.   G. P. Putnam's Sons, 1910.

Pyke, Rafford.   "The Woman's Side."   Cosmopolitan, 33 (1902), pp. 323-28.

"The Question of the Birth-Rate."   The Nation, 76 (June 11, 1903), pp. 468-69.

Riegel, Robert E.   "The Split of the Feminist Movement in 1869."   The Mississippi Valley Historical Review, 49, (December 1962), pp. 485-96.

*Roach, Abby Meguire.   Some Successful Marriages.   New York: Harper & Brothers Publishers, 1906.

Rogers, Anna A.   "Why American Marriages Fail."   The Atlantic Monthly, 100 (September 1907), pp. 289-98.

Ross, Aileen D.   "Control and Leadership in Women's Groups: An Analysis of Philanthropic Money-Raising Activity."   Social Forces, 37 (December 1958), pp. 124-31.

Ryan, Mary.   "American Society and the Cult of Domesticity. 1830-1860.'   Ph.D. Dissertation, University of California, Santa Barbara, 1971.

Sanger, Margaret.   Margaret Sanger: An Autobiography.   New York: W. W. Norton & Company, 1938.

Scott, Anne Firor.   The Southern Lady: From Pedestal to Politics, 1830-1930.   Chicago: The University of Chicago Press, 1970.

Scott, Joan W., and Louise A. Tilly.   "Women's Work and the Family in Nineteenth-Century Europe."   Comparative Studies in Society and History, 17 (January 1975), pp. 36-64.

*Scudder, Janet.   Modeling My Life.   New York: Harcourt, Brace and Company, 1925.

*Scudder, Vida.   On Journey.   New York: E. P. Dutton & Co., 1937.

*Shaw, Anna Howard.   The Story of a Pioneer.   New York: Harper & Brothers Publishers, 1915.

*Shaw, Mary.   "My 'Immoral' Play: The Story of the First American Production of 'Mrs. Warren's Profession.'"   McClures, 38 (April 1912), pp. 684-94.

Sicherman, Barbara. "Review Essay: American History." *Signs*, 1 (Winter 1975), pp. 461-85.

Sims, Mary S. *The Natural History of a Social Institution--The Young Women's Christian Association.* New York: The Woman's Press, 1936.

Sinclair, Andrew. *The Better Half.* New York: Harper & Row, 1965.

Sklar, Kathryn Kish. *Catherine Beecher.* New Haven: Yale University Press, 1973.

Skolnick, Arlene S., and Jerome H. Skolnick. *Family in Transition: Rethinking Marriage, Sexuality , Child Rearing and Family Organization.* Boston: Little, Brown and Company, 1971.

Smith, Daniel Scott. "Family Limitation, Sexual Control, and Domestic Feminism." *Clio's Consciousness Raised: New Perspectives on the History of Women.* Edited by Mary Hartman and Lois W. Banner. New York: Harper & Row, Publishers, 1974, pp. 119-36.

_____, and Michael S. Hindus. "Premarital Pregnancy in America, 1640-1971: An Overview and Interpretation." *Journal of Interdisciplinary History,* 5 (Spring, 1975), pp. 537-70.

Smith, Page. *Daughters of the Promised Land.* Boston: Little, Brown and Company, 1970.

Smith-Rosenberg, Carroll. "The Female World of Love and Ritual: Relations between Women in Nineteenth-Century America." *Signs*, 1 (Autumn 1975), pp. 1-29.

Sochen, June. *The New Woman.* New York: Quadrangle Books. 1972.

*Spencer, Anna Garlin. *The Family and Its Members.* Philadelphia; J. B. Lippincott Company, 1923.

_____. *Woman's Share in Social Culture.* Philadelphia: J. B. Lippincott Company, 1912.

*Stephens, Kate. *American Thumb-Prints.* Philadelphia: J. B. Lippincott Company, 1905.

_____. *Workfellows in Social Progression.* New York: Sturgis & Walton Company, 1916.

*Talbot, Marion, and Lois K. M. Rosenberry. *The History of the American Association of University Women 1881-1931.* Boston: Houghton Mifflin Company, 1931.

_____. *More Than Lore.* Chicago: The University of Chicago Press, 1936.

*Tarbell, Ida M. *The Business of Being a Woman.* New York: The Macmillan Company, 1912.

*Trask, Katrina. "Motherhood and Citizenship: Woman's Wisest Policy." *Forum*, 18 (1895), pp. 609-15.

Taylor, A. Elizabeth. "The Woman Suffrage Movement in Texas." *Journal of Southern History*, 17 (May 1951), pp. 194-215.

Taylor, William R., and Christopher Lasch. "Two 'Kindred Spirits': Sorority and Family in New England, 1839-1846." *New England Quarterly*, 36 (March 1963), pp. 23-41.

Thomas, Dorothy. *Women Lawyers in the United States.* New York: The Scarecrow Press, 1957.

Thorndike, Edward L. "The Decrease in the Size of American Families." *Popular Science Monthly*, 63 (May 1903), pp. 64-70.

Uhlenberg, Peter R. "A Study of Cohort Life Cycles: Cohorts of Native Born Massachusetts Women, 1830-1920." *Population Studies*, 23 (November 1969), pp. 407-20.

*Van Vorst, Bessie. *The Issues of Life.* New York: Doubleday, Page & Company, 1904.

Veblen, Thorstein. *Theory of the Leisure Class.* New York: The Macmillan Company, 1915.

*Wald, Lillian. *The House on Henry Street.* New York: Henry Holt and Company, 1915.

Wein, Roberta. "Women's Colleges and Domesticity, 1875-1918." *History of Education Quarterly*, 14 (Spring 1974), pp. 31-47.

Welter, Barbara. "The Cult of True Womanhood: 1820-1860." *American Quarterly*, 18 (Summer 1966), pp. 151-74.

Westoff, Charles F., and Raymond H. Potvin. "Higher Education, Religion, and Women's Family-Size Orientations." *American Sociological Review*, 31 (August 1966), pp. 489-96.

*Wharton, Edith. *The Descent of Man and Other Stories.* New York: C. Scribner's Sons, 1904.

_____. *Ethan Frome.* New York: Charles Scribner's Sons, 1911.

_____. *Xingu and Other Stories.* New York: Charles Scribner's Sons, 1916.

Wiebe, Robert H. *The Search for Order 1877-1920.* New York: Hill and Wang, 1967.

Willard, Frances E., and Mary A. Livermore. *A Woman of the Century.* Buffalo: Charles Wells Moulton, 1893.

Wilson, Elizabeth. *Fifty Years of Association Work among Young Women: 1866-1916.* New York: National Board of the Young Women's Christian Association, 1916.

*Winslow, Helen M.   *A Woman for Mayor.* Chicago: Reilly & Britton Co., 1909.

Women's Medical Association of New York City, ed.   *Mary Putnam Jacobi, M.D.: Pathfinder in Medicine.*   New York: G. P. Putnam's Sons, 1925.

Woody, Thomas.   *A History of Women's Education in the United States.* 2 vols. New York: The Science Press, 1929.

*Yarros, Rachelle S.   *Modern Woman and Sex.* New York: The Vanguard Press, 1933.

Young, Elva Hulburd.   "The Law as a Profession for Women."   *Publications of the Association of Collegiate Alumnae,* 3 (February 1902), pp. 15-23.

APPENDIX A

Richard Jensen and Barbara Campbell, "How to Handle a Liberated Woman," *Historical Methods Newsletter,* 5 (June 1972), pp. 109-13.

Reprinted by permission of the Department of History, University of Pittsburgh.

How to Handle a Liberated Woman

Richard Jensen and Barbara Campbell
Department of History
University of Illinois at Chicago Circle

Quantitatively, of course!

The historiography of prominent American women has been dominated thus far by policy-oriented studies of reform movements on the one hand and biographies on the other. There is a strong tendency in such studies to allow biases such as male criteria for success or current ideological concerns to distort the examination of womens' roles. This paper describes the quantitative analysis of a large number of active women according to the standards of importance they established for themselves.

Using 9,000 autobiographical questionnaires returned in 1913 to a pioneer editor of who's who directories by nationally or locally prominent women, we have set up 40 variables to reconstitute the distribution of their life-cycle, environmental, career, activity, and attitudinal characteristics.[1] The data (for a random sample of n = 879) has been coded and is being used to generate multivariate contingency tables with the SPSS computer programs. The patterns which we will find buried in the output (after controlling for age, region and the like) will provide new information about the relationships and distributions of the characteristics, making possible a realistic study of the actual behavior of women. We will be able to tell who became an author and who became a teacher; who remained single, and who married, when and with how many children. We will even be able to tell what type of woman became a suffrage activist, and what types favored, ignored or rejected the vote.

The hardest tasks were to devise a valid coding scheme to fulfill these objectives and to code our sample accurately. The questionnaires sent out by the editor did not, of course, ask exactly the same questions we wanted to answer. It was thus necessary to set up an interpretive

coding scheme which would capture the essence of the patterns we were
seeking with a minimum of sensitivity to erroneous or (a more serious
problem) incomplete reports. We used various other compilations, such
as *Who's Who in America* and *Notable American Women* to fill in gaps
where possible.

Our coding scheme is designed for statistical interpretation rather
than data storage. We used categorical variables throughout, to simplify
the statistical analysis and to minimize error. Someone asking different
questions would code the data differently and might be frustrated by our
scheme. The easy access to the source, however, should make it simple
for anyone to add additional codes to ours.[2]

For the most part, the codes are straightforward. The number of
categories was deliberately kept small, partly in order to prevent the
nuisance of inadequate sub-samples and partly because we were not
always confident about making fine distinctions. For example, we
hesitated to break down the occupational subcode "writers and authors,
except salaried journalists," since we could not tell poets from novelists
on the basis of titles. Age was troublesome, since one-third of our
sample did not report it. Five-sixths of these cases were estimated by
year, or at least by decade of birth, on the basis of other dates provided
in the entry. For example, we assigned 22 as the age of graduation from
college and assumed women were married in their mid-20's. Since we
will be grouping ages by decades, the coding reliability should be very
high. One happy item included by the editor was attitude toward
woman suffrage (variable 39 [see p. 112]). We used a detailed code for
this variable and plan to analyze it carefully. We probably will
supplement the basic sample with the names of all women who actively
opposed suffrage, since this interesting subgroup is almost wholly
unknown.

The occupational code (variable 16) required much trial and
error, and we are still not completely satisfied. The four main (first
digit) categories (professions, education, arts, and society/clubs) seem to
be both comprehensive and historically meaningful. Thus far the
subcodes have encompassed everyone and the general codes (i.e., 10, 20,
30 or 40) have been used rarely. The grouping of government with
social work (code 13) or agitator with lawyer (code 17) simply pairs
career types that almost always went together for the women of 1913.
Librarians (code 25) could have been grouped with professionals but
seem to have resembled college teachers more; indeed, many were
college librarians at one time or another. The line between society
women (code 41) and clubwomen (code 42) is an attempt to differentiate
upper-class and middle-class women. To determine class we relied
chiefly on indicators of private schooling, religion, listing in the *Social
Register*, and membership in groups like the DAR, and the criteria for

upper-class were more stringent in large cities than in small towns.[3] For about half the women, we coded a secondary career activity (variable 17). Most often this was a society/club code, though some women engaged in completely distinct careers at different times, or even at the same time. Lottie Park of Los Angeles, for instance, was a physician (code 15), lawyer (17), social worker (15), clubwoman (42), poet (34) and suffragette (17). Our two occupational variables could not cope with these rare instances, though we did capture most of these characteristics with our activity codes.

Not every woman fully reported her memberships and activities- in one case, a woman even neglected to mention her six children. To cope with this variability in the data, we used a series of dichotomous codes (variables 20, 25, 43 and 51, for example) and interpreted them rather generously. Unless there was a systematic bias for certain types of women not to respond as fully as others, multivariate statistical methods should generate reasonably valid clusters of these activities and interests for the various types of women.

NOTES

[1]John William Leonard, *Woman's Who's Who in America* (New York, 1914) was the basic source; we arbitrarily excluded several hundred Canadian women. Leonard was the first editor of *Who's Who in America* and continued his high editorial standards in this book. For comparable men and the statistical techniques to be used, see Richard Jensen, "Quantitative Collective Biography: An Application to Metropolitan Elites," in Robert Swierenga, ed., *Quantification in American History* (New York, 1970), 389-405.

[2]Our coding scheme is by no means perfect. It was devised before we appreciated how easy it is to recode our SPSS. We should have coded the exact number of children (variable 2), precise denomination (22), exact third party (24), and, perhaps, state (7, 10). It is easy but very expensive to add variables to an SPSS file. Unfortunately, it is quite difficult to correct coding or keypunching errors through SPSS.

[3]Richard Coleman and Bernice Neugarten, *Social Status in the City* (San Francisco, 1971) has the best differentiation of the social status of American women.

GROUP	VARIABLE NUMBER	VARIABLE NAME	CODE (with the percentage for each value where 100% = 879 cases)
Identification	0		page and entry number
Life	1	Marital Status	0 = single (32.3) 1 = married (60.8) 2 = widow, divorced, or remarried (6.9)
Cycle	2	Number Children	0 = married but none (22.8) 1 = 1(14.6) 2 = 2(11.3) 3 = 3 or 4(14.9) 4 = 5(4.2) 5 = unmarried (32.3)
	3	Age (reliability)	0 = unknown (5.8) 1 = given (66.6) 2 = estimated (27.6)
	4	Age	0 = unknown (5.8) 1 = born after 1880 (12.5) 2 = b. 1870-79 (28.9) 3 = b. 1860-69 (26.8) 4 = b. 1850-59 (16.7) 5 = b. before 1850 (9.2)
	5	Age (detail)	last 2 digits of year of birth
	6	Age First Marriage	0 = unmarried (32.4) 1 = married but unknown (15.8) 2 = 20 and under (6.6) 3 = 21-25 (22.1) 4 = 26-30 (14.3) 5 = 31+ (8.9)
	11	Mobility: Number of Places Lived or Mentioned	1 = 1(8.4) 2 = 2 or 3(49.5) 3 = 4-7(35.8) 4 = 8+ (6.3)
	12	Lifetime Mobility	1 = stayed in homestate (23.7) 2 = strayed beyond homestate, now returned (19.6) 3 = changed status inside region (21.8) 4 = changed regions or countries (34.9)
Environmental	7	Region of Birth	1 = Northeast (47.7) 2 = Midwest incl. Missouri (32.3) 3 = South incl. Border (12.6) 4 = West (2.5) 5 = Foreign (4.2) 0 = ?, other U.S. (0.7)
	8	Population of Birthplace	1 = under 3000 (43.4) 2 = 3000-20,000 (18.8) 3 = over 20,000 (34.9) 4 = foreign (3.0)
	9	Population of Current Home	1 = under 20,000 (28.6) 2 = 20-100,000 (13.3) 3 = over 100,000 incl. suburbs (57.2) 4 = abroad (0.9)
	10	Region of Current Home	1 = Northeast, except New York City area (33.0) 2 = midwest (24.9) 3 = South (14.3) 4 = West (10.8) 5 = New York City area (15.0) 0 = abroad (1.9)
	38	Female Suffrage Status of Current State	0 = none, or abroad (29.6) 1 = partial vote (59.6) 2 = full suffrage (10.8)
Career	13	Highest Level of Education	1 = schools, tutors (36.4) 2 = some college (19.6) 3 = college degrees (21.2) 4 = postgraduate (22.8)
Development	14	Ever Attend Private School or Have Tutor?	1 = yes (78.6) 0 = no (21.4)
	15	Any Technical Training (excl. liberal arts college)?	1 = yes (36.9) 0 = no (63.1)
	16–17	Predominant Life Career (not necessarily current status) and Secondary Life Career	10 = profession 20 = education 30 = arts 40 = society or club

11 = business or farming (1.9−1.6)
12 = salaried journalists (1.8−1.1)
13 = government or social work; home economics
     (3.4−3.6)
14 = church, missionary (1.9−1.4)
15 = medicine (6.4−1.6)
16 = scientist or researcher (not elsewhere classified)
     (1.8−2.5)
17 = agitator or lawyer (3.3−1.9)

21 = public school teacher, excl. principal (2.7−4.8)
22 = private school teacher or administrator (4.1−2.3)
23 = college teacher (must have faculty status)
     (5.3−2.6)
24 = college administrator (1.5−0.3)
25 = librarian (1.9−0.5)
26 = administrator, public school system, incl. principal
     (1.4−0.6)

31 = performing arts (1.8−0.6)
32 = art education (not elsewhere classified) (1.5−1.4)
33 = lecturer, critic (not elsewhere classified) (0.5−1.5)
34 = writers and authors (except salaried journalists)
     (8.5−7.7)
35 = painting, sculpture, photography (2.6−0.5)
36 = art, music executive or organizer (0.4−0.7)
37 = illustrator, decorator, designer, architect (1.1−0.7)
38 = composer (0.2−1.0)

41 = society woman (Upper class) (32.7−12.4)
42 = club woman (Middle class) (13.3−3.3)

	17	Secondary Career	Same code as number 16, 0 = none (44.9)
	18	Educational Experience (teacher, school board, advisor)	
			1 = yes (42.7) 0 = no (57.3)
	19	Business Experience (salaried, private practice, or owner)	
			1 = yes (13.2) 0 = no (86.8)
	31	Ever Published Anything?	
			1 = yes (37.7) 0 = no (62.3)
	33	Active as Lecturer? (incl. college professors and ministers)	
			1 = yes (23.9) 0 = no (76.1)
	34	Member professional or National Organization?	
			1 = yes (29.6) 0 = no (70.4)
	35	National Recognition or Importance in any Field?	
			1 = yes (35.7) 0 = (64.3)
	40	Historical Recognition (listed in James, ed., *Notable American Women*, 1971)	
			1 = yes (3.9) 0 = no (96.1)
Values and Beliefs	22	Religion	1 = high status Portestant−Episcopalian, Presbyterian Congregational, Quaker, or Unitarian (54.7) 2 = other Protestant (13.7) 3 = Catholic or Jewish (3.0) 4 = agnostic, socialist, offbeat (2.3) 0 = no mention (26.4)
	24	Partisanship	1 = Republican (5.8) 2 = Democrat (4.0) 3 = Progressive, Progressive Republican, Socialist, Prohibitionist, Independent (8.4) 0 = no mention (81.8)
	39	Attitude Toward Suffrage	
			1 = active supporter (23.8) 2 = favors (28.3)

		3 = favors with any qualification (1.3) 4 = no mention (37.2) 5 = opposes (8.0) 6 = actively opposes (1.5)
Activities and Interests	20	Humanitarian Interest (e.g., YWCA, charity, philanthropy, hospitals, juveniles, etc.)
		1 = yes (62.3) 0 = no (37.3)
	21	Temperance Work? 1 = yes (6.0) 0 = no (94.0)
	23	Religious Activism 1 = member (42.2) 2 = activist (30.4) 0 = non-member (27.4)
	25	Interest in Current Events, Politics, Economics, or Sociology?
		1 = yes (54.6) 0 = no (45.4)
	27	Genealogical, Patriotic Interest?
		1 = yes (25.1) 0 = no (74.9)
	28	Member Sorority or Alumni Group?
		1 = yes (28.2) 0 = no (71.8)
	29	Community Art, Music, Theater, Museum Interest?
		1 = yes (29.1) 0 = no (70.9)
	30	Literary Interest? 1 = yes, esp. clubs (27.9) 2 = yes, writer (22.5) 0 = no (49.6)
	32	Travel or Foreign Study?
		1 = yes (25.3) 0 = no (74.7)
	36	Recreation 1 = sedentary (16.5) 2 = athletic, vigorous (12.4) 3 = both (4.8) 0 = no mention (66.3)
	37	Outdoor Enthusiast? 1 = yes (26.4) 0 = no (73.6)
	26	Membership in Any Woman's Club?
		0 = nonmember (22.9) 1 = member (28.4) 2 = leader (48.7)

APPENDIX B

SAMPLE CROSSTABULATIONS

The sample crosstabulations on the following pages illustrate the important relationships among a variety of variables. When these relationships were tested through a series of controls, the most important being age and region of birth, the basic patterns as described in the text emerged.

Table 3. Crosstabulation of Career Type and Religious Activism

Count Row% Column % Total %	Nonmember	Member	Activist	Row Total
Professions	54	92	71	217
	24.9	42.4	32.7	24.7
	22.4	24.8	26.6	
	6.1	10.5	8.1	
Education	49	95	49	193
	25.4	49.2	25.4	22.0
	20.3	25.6	18.4	
	5.6	10.8	5.6	
Arts	84	58	47	189
	44.4	30.7	24.9	21.5
	34.9	15.6	17.6	
	9.6	6.6	5.3	
Noncareer	54	126	100	280
	19.3	45.0	35.7	31.9
	22.4	34.0	37.5	
	6.1	14.3	11.4	
Column	241	371	267	879
	27.4	42.2	30.4	100.0

Chi Square = 42.73485 with 6 degrees of freedom
Significance = 0.0000   Contingency Coefficient = 0.21746

Table 4. Crosstabulation of Career Type and
Humanitarian Interest

Count Row % Column % Total %	Negative Interest	Positive Interest	Row Total
Professions	36 16.6 10.9 4.1	181 83.4 33.0 20.6	217 24.7
Education	96 49.7 29.1 10.9	97 50.3 17.7 11.0	193 22.0
Arts	94 49.7 28.5 10.7	95 50.3 17.3 10.8	189 21.5
Noncareer	104 37.3 31.5 11.8	175 62.7 31.9 19.9	279 31.8
Column Total	330 37.6	548 62.4	878 100.0

Chi Square $=$ 64.83751 with 3 degrees of freedom
Significance $=$ 0.0000   Contingency Coefficient $=$ 0.26244

Table 5. Crosstabulation of Career Type and Reform Interest

Count
Row %

Column %	Negative Interest	Positive Interest	Row Total
Total %			
Professions	62	155	217
	28.6	71.4	24.7
	15.5	32.3	
	7.1	17.6	
Education	109	84	193
	56.5	43.5	22.0
	27.3	17.5	
	12.4	9.6	
Arts	96	93	189
	50.8	49.2	21.5
	24.1	19.4	
	10.9	10.6	
Noncareer	132	148	280
	47.1	52.9	31.9
	33.1	30.8	
	15.0	16.8	
Column Total	399	480	879
	45.4	54.6	100.0

Chi Square = 36.90657 with 3 degrees of freedom
Significance = 0.0000   Contingency Coefficient = 0.20074

Table 6. Crosstabulation of Career Type and Suffrage Opinion

Count Row % Column % Total %	Favor	No Mention	Against	Row Total
Professions	149	60	6	215
	69.3	27.9	2.8	24.6
	31.8	18.5	7.2	
	17.0	6.9	0.7	
Education	102	78	13	193
	52.8	40.4	6.7	22.1
	21.8	24.1	15.7	
	11.7	8.9	1.5	
Arts	85	84	18	187
	45.5	44.9	9.6	21.4
	18.2	25.9	21.7	
	9.7	9.6	2.1	
Noncareer	132	102	46	280
	47.1	36.4	16.4	32.0
	28.2	31.5	55.4	
	15.1	11.7	5.3	
Column Total	468	324	83	875
	53.5	37.0	9.5	100.0

Chi Square = 48.96310   with 6 degrees of freedom
Significance = 0.0000   Contingency Coefficient = 0.23020

Table 7. Crosstabulation of Career Type and Woman's Club Interest

Count Row % Column % Total %	No Interest	Member	Leader	Row Total
Professions	46 21.2 22.9 5.2	48 22.1 19.2 5.5	123 56.7 28.7 14.0	217 24.7
Education	57 29.5 28.4 6.5	56 29.0 22.4 6.4	80 41.5 18.7 9.1	193 22.0
Arts	56 29.9 27.9 6.4	59 31.6 23.6 6.7	74 39.2 17.3 8.4	189 21.5
Noncareer	42 15.0 20.9 4.8	87 31.1 34.8 9.9	151 53.9 35.3 17.2	280 31.9
Column Total	201 22.9	250 28.4	428 48.7	879 100.0

Chi Square = 29.66991 with 6 degrees of freedom
Significance = 0.0000   Contingency Coefficient = 0.18070

Table 8. Crosstabulation of Humanitarian Interest
and Reform Interest

Count Row % Column % Total %	Negative Reform Interest	Positive Reform Interest	Row Total
Negative Humanitarian Interest	261 79.1 65.6 29.7	69 20.9 14.4 7.9	330 37.6
Positive Humanitarian Interest	137 25.0 34.4 15.6	411 75.0 85.6 46.8	548 62.4
Column Total	398 45.3	480 54.7	878 100.0

Corrected Chi Square = 240.99387 with 1 degree of freedom
Significance = 0.0000   Phi = 0.52627
Contingency Coefficient = 0.46572

Table 9. Crosstabulation of Woman's Club Interest and Reform Interest

Count Row % Column % Total %	Negative Reform Interest	Positive Reform Interest	Row Total
No Interest	147 73.1 36.8 16.7	54 26.9 11.3 6.1	201 22.9
Woman's Club Member	139 55.6 34.8 15.8	111 44.4 23.1 12.6	250 28.4
Woman's Club Leader	113 26.4 28.3 12.9	315 73.6 65.6 35.8	428 48.7
Column Total	399 45.4	480 54.6	879 100.0

Chi Square = 135.18604 with 2 degrees of freedom
Significance = 0.0000   Contingency Coefficient = 0.36510

Table 10. Crosstabulation of Humanitarian Interest
and Suffrage Opinion

Count Row % Column % Total %	Favor	No Mention	Against	Row Total
Negative	125	170	35	330
Humanitarian	37.9	51.5	10.6	37.7
Interest	26.7	52.3	42.7	
	14.3	19.4	4.0	
Positive	344	155	47	546
Humanitarian	63.0	28.4	8.6	62.3
Interest	73.3	47.7	57.3	
	39.3	17.7	5.4	
Column Total	469	325	82	876
	53.5	37.1	9.4	100.0

Chi Square = 54.78104 with 2 degrees of freedom
Significance = 0.0000   Contingency Coefficient = 0.24260

Table 11. Crosstabulation of Reform Interest
and Suffrage Opinion

Count Row % Column % Total %	Favor	No Mention	Against	Row Total
Negative	133	219	45	397
Reform	33.5	55.2	11.3	45.3
Interest	28.4	67.4	54.2	
	15.2	25.0	5.1	
Positive	336	106	38	480
Reform	70.0	22.1	7.9	54.7
Interest	71.6	32.6	45.8	
	38.3	12.1	4.3	
Column Total	469	325	83	877
	53.5	37.1	9.5	100.0

Chi Square = 120.97365 with 2 degrees of freedom
Significance = 0.0000   Contingency Coefficient = 0.34817

Table 12. Crosstabulation of Woman's Club Interest
and Suffrage Opinion

Count Row % Column % Total %	Favor	No Mention	Against	Row Total
No Interest	55 27.4 11.7 6.3	130 64.7 40.0 14.8	16 8.0 19.3 1.8	201 22.9
Woman's Club Member	132 53.0 28.1 15.1	90 36.1 27.7 10.3	27 10.8 32.5 3.1	249 28.4
Woman's Club Leader	282 66.0 60.1 32.2	105 24.6 32.3 12.0	40 9.4 48.2 4.6	427 48.7
Column Total	469 53.5	325 37.1	83 9.5	877 100.0

Chi Square = 98.57257 with 4 degrees of freedom
Significance = 0.0000   Contingency Coefficient = 0.31787

INDEX